FAR FROM ANY COAST

ALSO BY C. W. GUSEWELLE

A Paris Notebook
An Africa Notebook
Quick as Shadows Passing: C. W. Gusewelle's
    Book of Cats, Dogs and Children

FAR FROM ANY COAST

Pieces of America's Heartland

C. W. GUSEWELLE

University of Missouri Press
Columbia

TO BILL BLEIFUSS

Copyright © 1989 by
The Curators of the University of Missouri
University of Missouri Press, Columbia, Missouri 65211
Printed and bound in the United States of America

Library of Congress Cataloging-in-Publication Data

Gusewelle, C. W. (Charles W.)
   Far from any coast : pieces of America's heartland / C. W. Gusewelle.
      p.   cm.
   ISBN 0-8262-0728-6 (alk. paper)
   ISBN 0-8262-0720-0 (pbk.)
   I. Title.
PS3557.U833F37   1989
814'.54—dc19   89-4727
                                                                          CIP

∞™ This paper meets the minimum requirements of
the American National Standard for Permanence of Paper
for Printed Library Materials, z39.48, 1984.

ACKNOWLEDGMENTS

The essays collected here were written over the last twenty years—a fair piece of time. And time is savage. Many of the people alive in these pages are dead now. Even some features of the landscapes will have changed. But no attempt has been made to take account of these predations and losses. For one of the satisfactions of writing is to stop time, to fix in place the moments as they were, so that they may be lived again and the voices heard, as near and as alive as they ever were, across the mute interval of careless years.

The essays in this collection originally appeared in the publications listed below:

"Moonrise to Mourning: Echoes of the Race," from *Audience*, May–June 1972; "A Continuity of Place and Blood," from *American Heritage*, December 1977; "Notes from Inner Space," from *Audience*, September–October 1972; "Memories of a Country Neighborhood," from *Missouri Life*, March–April 1981; "Before the Mountain Fell," from *Audience*, January–February 1973; "Strangers on a Train," Copyright by the author; "The Promise of Elysian," from *Blair & Ketchum's Country Journal*, September 1982; "The Fragility of Skepticism," from *Star Magazine*, February 5, 1984; "Truth and the Careless Ear," from *Harrowsmith*, March–April 1987; "The Broken Twig," from *Blair & Ketchum's Country Journal*, June 1984; "Bringing in the Sheaves," from *Blair & Ketchum's Country Journal*, August 1985; "The Egg," from *Star Magazine*, April 7, 1985; "The Leave-Taking," from *Star Magazine*, September 20, 1987; "An End of Loving the Land," from *The Missouri Review*, vol. 10, no. 1, 1987; "Retreat," from *Country Journal*, June 1988.

Photographs other than those by the author are the work of the following:

Norman Ackerman, pp. 120, 128
Wes Lyle, pp. 25, 32, 36, 234
Jim Richardson, pp. 133, 135, 140, 142
Rick Solberg, pp. 154, 156, 159

CONTENTS

I

HOME GROUND

1 MOONRISE TO MOURNING

Echoes of the Race

*He lived on a hill over the steep valley of Spring Creek and raised his family there
and kept dogs. Hounds, rather—foxhounds, of the Walker breed. More than three
thousand nights of his life (and likely nearer four thousand) he passed standing
with his back to fires in lonely places, listening to the hounds' doomed cry of
pursuit across distant ridges, running with them in his mind. And watched the
ground fog roll up like a sickness in the low places; was still there until the fire was
a white ash and dawn released him to go back up on the hill and resume his contest
with the stony earth.*

*Always for a hound, and sometimes for a man, the race is short. But to have had
a desperate passion and followed it to the end of strength, to die unafraid, to be
remembered—surely there is more than regret in that.*

*A woman, a wife, notices small things. That last year, when Ad Holt went out
in the night with his hounds, he had begun wearing his good hat, his good shoes.
Because already he knew what the others didn't. In the time left he would never
wear them out.*

I

Seldom is the fox caught. And never is he *meant* to be. So it is not truly a
blood sport; there is innocence in it. The point is essential, and to understand it you should be acquainted with that country.

There is a morning bus east from Springfield, Missouri—was twenty-
five years ago, at least, and must still be—across the last edge of patchy
upland, through Cody and Rogersville to the village of Fordland. And
unimportant points beyond—St. Louis, perhaps, or Cairo (Kay-row), Illinois.

From Fordland, the far edge of it, a country road leads south a mile and
some to its first leftward branching. Ahead and below, the waves of broken land run off to blueness under a haze of wood smoke. To Arkansas
these hills go, and halfway down that state, full of bugs and snakes and
fires in season, and empty dark. And they could be forbidding except that
now, with spring's advance, they are washed a luminous green. The dogwood is out, the redbud just finishing.

3

Beside that road is a fence, posts leaning, wires grown into trees. It is the last divide. He who crosses that on foot is committed.

And if the canteen rattles empty on the pack in the heat of an improvident noon, never mind. There's a town ahead. A place of decent people. Its name is Tigris, mother of civilizations, but it died unremembered years ago. The door of the John Allen Store, General Mdse., is nailed shut and further guarded by wicked canes of blackberry that have forced the rotting porch boards and grown up to make a thicket on a stage. Just across is the livery stable, broken by a tree and dragged down by wild grape. Garage & Welding—dead too, fastened with a rusted padlock. The tomato cannery, of galvanized sheeting, chimes impassively under the blows of clenched fists. On the hill behind are the remains of a dwelling, home of the master of Tigris overlooking his fief, consumed on a winter night by some accident with the flue. A mansion it was, judging by the size of the footings. Hugely the offending furnace looms, embarrassed to have survived.

From there the way lies still south and east to Ava, a town, not a woman. A living town. And then down into the valley of Hunter Creek, fed by a torrent of blue water rising eleven million gallons a day out of a hillside of collapsed caves. And south along Hunter to its meeting with Bryant Creek, misnamed because it is really a river, tumbling through bouldered chutes between dark pools where legendary bass prowl and where a calf, misstepping onto false ice on a blowy winter evening, might not be seen again until it floats.

The map says that the Bryant perishes not many miles beyond here, swallowed by a mammoth impoundment that curls its turbid arm northward from the next state. That may be fact, but one is not obliged to see it. Instead, where the river bends around a sandy flat below the abandoned Upper Brixey School, leave it and go back north along a lesser stream. It will bring you out on the Ava road, near a place where wild azaleas bloom in their season. And also near a little one-room store where the school bus stops and will carry you into town for the asking.

You will have come seventy miles on foot and taken a week to do it. Seventy miles in three counties—a distance won in a hundred stumblings over loose stones down impossible ravines, a thousand rakings in wild rose brambles, an infinity of twig lashes across the face.

You will have slept on the cold earth beside fires in the ruins of logging hamlets where the road forgot to go. Will have been clung over by ticks and bitten by spiders. Will have come to terms with darkness and the sudden near rush of winged things traversing it, and risen to the homely perfume of wild onion shoots crushed where you laid your blankets.

Passing down a streambed just at daybreak—and you are a shambling horror now, moldy, gone all to crusted filth with stubble beard and tangled hair—you will hear a voice come down from a clearing on the slope above. It is a woman alone beside a cabin, out in the first light to hang a washing done by hand before dawn. Her husband is nowhere to be seen—gone to field or to a neighbor's. Holding a pillowcase half-raised to the line, she calls again. Incredible words: "Have you had breakfast?"

It is a wholly different way of thinking. Life simply is too spare, too real, to be spent preoccupied with those confused, dread-longing city reveries of being raped or retired. Not, "What have you come to steal?" Not, "What right, what damned right do you have to march down my clean valley and across my morning, trailing your smell behind you like smoke?" No. *Have you had breakfast?*

Or you will chance upon a man with cows in a meadow under the cliffs of one of Bryant's bends. In an hour you'll know his life—where he went to find a fortune, why he came back, the names of his wife, his cows, his dogs. He'll even take you to the place where, as a boy, he sat alone and dreamed of being other places. It's a pool of clear water rising straight up out of the earth between the roots of a tree and spilling over to the river. He'll lie facedown, shirt wet, to drink from it and eat the peppery watercress, glad that he failed and came home; you're glad for him.

In the fastness of Shingle Hollow farther down Bryant there is a settlement of Trappist monks, twenty-some of them it was then, called there by their vocation, which is, in the name of God, to dredge sand out of that bend of the river and manufacture cement building blocks. Theirs is the silent order, so they are generous with everything but talk. The abbot may, however, speak—and does, at earnest length, of what a rake he'd been, of the temptations of the flesh and of the pleasures men forsake for the simplicity of bread and milk and making cement blocks. (Years later a restaurant keeper in the town will tell you how those pleasures claimed him back. "Got married." Eyes squinty with rejoicing. "Took another man's wife is what he did.") At eight o'clock their last prayer song rises among the hills. At a quarter past three they are awake again, truck lights bouncing through the trees down to the river and across to do God's work.

Of all the brothers' disciplines—silence, labor, and the forfeit of worldly goods—the serving of guests must be the most exquisite. A youngish monk comes with a tray of bacon and two eggs scrambled, buttered toast, wine jelly, coffee black. He says nothing. For the rest of his days such breakfasts will be forbidden him by solemn contract with the Almighty. He sits on a stool nearby, sideways to seem uninterested. But when a crumb of bacon falls from bearded mouth to floor, his eyes go to it with naked lovingness. Guilt fills the room.

Or finally, one late afternoon, you'll pass a little plowed hillside so poor that the stones seem almost to be a crop deliberately sown, the origin of the term *rock farm*. The sky has gone curdy gray, spilling wind. It has been seven weeks since a decent rain. Above, on the hill, an old man—bent, straw-hatted—flings out an arm in patient quarter-circles as he steps, spreading fertilizer from a bucket like a benediction on his ruined land. Later, much later, you will remember that the shower passed him by.

This, then, is Ad Holt's country. Hard, decent country—open and fair to any man, no matter how he talks or looks.

But a country, also, acquainted with disappointment. Where some men stay for want of hoping . . . and others come home from what they meant to be. Where towns die and dreams with them. Where a soul's salvation is near, but fleet afoot. Where the rain never quite comes in time.

And where the fox is seldom caught. *Mustn't* be. Or there'd be no fox to chase.

II

The years, the seasons turn. It is full dark now on a night in late fall at a place they call The Mailbox. This junction of two lanes has been a meeting place for men and dogs for longer than some in the present company have been alive. The layerings of buried fires tell of much habitation. And they are carrying wood again, pulling it from a flood drift against a culvert.

The hounds have been let out of the trucks and cast down across a bottom meadow of rank grass toward the creek and the ridge beyond. "I hear them," someone announces—a command to silence. But it is only the high *cheeping* of a pup engaged in a bit of furtive rabbiting.

"That's not any dog of mine," says Louis Huff. "Mine'll not open unless it's a fox."

The argument is as old as the game.

"Some people *claim* theirs won't," Howard Holt tells him. "But I say a foxhound'll run anything. Now mine—hell, mine'll run a deer. An armadillo. And if it's real close they'll even run a Volkswagen."

Ad Holt's house is up there in the dark on the hill behind them. Howard is a younger brother. Louis was a neighbor and a friend of many nights

Night at The Mailbox

who, for a long time afterward, built his fires at other places than The Mailbox. Kerosene is poured and a match struck. The *cheeping* from the bottom comes nearer and Howard takes a sudden step apart. "You better quit foolin' with those rabbits!" he roars into the night. The known seriousness of the offense smites the creature silent.

There are eight men now, men and boys, with others coming. And twenty-three dogs already on the ground, ranging along a mile of valley, across Spring Creek and up toward a long glade still called the Peach Orchard for what it used to be. The fire leaps up through the dry wood and kinship surrounds it, of blood, of marriage, of all the fires these men have shared before.

There is Don Graham, husband of Louis's daughter—a large, lean man, quiet-spoken, with a dignity of a force almost to frighten anyone without it. And Larry, his son. There is Lige Degase, oldest of them all, past retiring but not past making his bed on the damp ground in the shank of autumn; and Wayne, his nephew, not yet twenty, already committed to the hounds; and Randall Delp, his grandson, just turning sixteen, whose first dogs, two Walker pups, are still too young to run. And Raymond Hampton, stepson of Ad Holt, raised there in the house on the hill, married now, with children of his own.

One of them measures—doesn't really measure—coffee into a blackened pot and fills it with water and puts its side directly to the flames.

"Usually they'll find a fox here," Don Graham says. "Gray fox, anyway." The fox is an individual, known by his neighborhood and the race he runs. And as Graham has put it, you couldn't hire a man to kill one. "There used to be one over by my place," he remembers now. "He'd come out on the side of the hill in plain daylight and bark. We ran that fox five or six years, didn't we? Kind of a blue, smutty-colored fox."

It is the red fox that is most favored—for his boldness, his greater strength and the grand circles he will make to the edge of hearing and beyond, and for his unwillingness to *tree*, which can mean in fact to climb or go to ground. But on a night when it already has been most of an hour with no race at all, men get less choosy about the color of their foxes.

The coffee boils and is poured, searing, full of grounds. Ears to the silent dark, the men draw against the certain insurance of their memories of other races, other nights, and of the dogs that they have kept and sometimes worshiped and, in the end, either sold or lost or, rarely, had to destroy.

The Walker foxhound stands some twenty-three to twenty-eight inches from ground to shoulder. Once in a very great while an inch more. Except occasionally in his marking, little can be detected in him of the original English stock—those blocky, curried squires of dogdom that will bellow ahead of horses along a trail laid by a scented rag and are trained to come to the note of a golden horn.

The Walker has gone all to leg and ribcage and driving shoulders. He is a pure athlete, and he is a little bit insane. He does not give a damn for a horn. Or even for the lights of the flying automobile that would interfere with his business on some night road. Or even, much, for men—except that they, in the doubtful wisdom of Creation, have been given ownership of all food and maybe (to a hound's mind) of all foxes as well, which is the only reason for ever coming home at all.

So he is not lovely in any conventional usage, discounting his eyes—which are both fierce and melancholy, seeing beyond you to what he was born to be and do. No, a great hound's beauty is an inner thing. It is that indefinable vision that torments him, sets the one fragile scent supreme above all others and drives him belling through the blackness into fences and through bramble thickets, a hundred miles or more in a night. And after he has eaten and slept a day, it is the thing that wakes him, swollen-eyed and miserable, walking delicately on his bleeding pads, and sends him out to run again.

This is the beauty that hound men seek. And having found it, in their own dog or another's, they will cherish it and breed back to the line, hoping that the courage and the lunacy of that first obsessed creature will be repeated in all his generations. And in the end, this thing that makes him grand is the thing that also destroys him. At two years he will be sleek and prime; at four he will be old, scarred, perhaps three-legged from hanging in a fence. At six he will be finished. His life is distilled and refined until the short piece that is left to him is a consummate essence. The choice is to burn hotly or burn long, and somewhere in antiquity the foxhound decided—as some men do—that it would be hotly.

That being the established covenant, a man casts his hounds quickly, without sentiment or regret, though each time may be the last.

Two of Don Graham's have been out a week—stolen, perhaps, and sold away to run the Arkansas fox or the Mississippi fox. But more likely dead in a fence or beside a road. And there are other perils. The strychnine bait set out sometimes for a lamb-killing coyote. Or, occasionally, the outlander who buys a piece of this country that the hounds owned before him. And who then, for reasons of his own, decides to make his proprietorship absolute. A "No Trespass" sign will stop no running hound. A shotgun will. But a man who kills another's dog in these hills had better know what he's inviting.

"I've had one hound shot," Graham is recalling now. "Just one. It was found on a fellow's place. And I went over there and called him out."

Called him out. This large, quiet man coming slowly, deliberately up across a frozen yard.

"Turned out afterward there was a grudge between these two fellows in Ozark County. And one'd shot my dog and planted him on the other's place. Thinking I'd burn him out or kill his cattle. So I had to go back and apologize to that first man," Graham says. "Because I was in the wrong. He hadn't shot my dog." *And the second man? What of that second man?*

Another pot of coffee is set brewing in the fire. Once, briefly, the dogs opened on an old track and then as quickly lost it. Or else it was a young gray whose nerve failed him and who went to cover in the ledged hillside below the Peach Orchard. Two of Louis's hounds still are chained, and he leaves now in the truck to release them farther up Spring Creek, nearer his home place.

A chill has come down, but the fire and the stories warm the circle. Someone is telling of the time one of them went bodily under a heap of bulldozed timber after a live coyote. "Oh, God, such a yellin' and a thrashin'. Why, it reminded me of that fella climbed up a tree to shake a big coon out and the two of 'em got into it up there. And he yells down, 'Shoot him out! Shoot him out!' An' the fella on the ground says, 'Can't shoot up there. I might hit you.' An' he yells down to him, 'Well, by God, one of us has *got* to have relief!' "

Sometimes the tale has nothing to do with hunting of any sort.

Clearing of throat. "Uh, why—y'see, an old boy come over here . . . across the water . . . from a foreign country. An' he come over here an' stayed a while an' went back. Had a buddy over there that wanted to come over here. An' he said, 'Ahhh, I don't know.' Said, 'Over there in America they eat dog.' 'Naw,' other fella said. 'They don't eat dog.' Said, 'Oh yes they do.' So this old boy he was gonna come with him. And they got over here—why there's this hot dog stand out there an' he says, 'I'll prove it to you right now.' So they went out to that hot dog stand, you know, an' both of 'em got a sandwich. An' that old boy—one who come over last—he ra-a-aised the bread of his'n up . . . *Shut it up right quick* an' he said, 'What part did you get?' "

Laughter slowly rising, then pealing down the valley.

"He knowed what part *he* had!"

Hill faces: foxhound, fox hunter

Don Graham at the fire, listening, remembering

Louis Huff comes back in his pickup. All of the hounds are loose now except two of Raymond Hampton's—new dogs, one of them a solemn giant of a beast for which he paid a hundred and one dollars and which, because the hound is new to this country, he is reluctant yet to cast. Huff slams the truck door and comes to the fire.

"Didn't I hear dogs down that way?" someone asks him.

"House dogs," he answers. And the way he says it tells plainly that the difference between house dogs and running hounds is the difference between sparrows and eagles. "I don't know, boys. Maybe we're not going to have any race," Huff says. But unbelieving, unbelieved.

They call it a *race*, not a chase. Because it isn't the hounds against the fox. It is one man's hound against another man's, or against the memory of greater hounds, or even against some abstract, impossible standard of strength and endurance and clarity of voice. With the result declared publicly, inarguably, on the night. It's for that reason men race the fox together—or most of them do.

"But not Granville Prock," someone is saying. "Old Granville was kind of funny about it. A lot of times he'd go out by his self with just a lantern, no fire or nothing. And he'd pick himself a place and sit down and wrap up in his coat, that lantern under it, and just sit there until daylight come."

They agree it was so.

"He might ask you to go with him. But he didn't much care for another fellow taking dogs. The idea, you see, was that he'd rather you listened to his."

"That's how he was, all right," someone else says. "But he hunted a lot of foxes, Granville did."

"And he kept good foxhounds."

After eleven, another truck arrives. It is Rosco Ehrhardt, from down near Squires. Someone else brought his dogs—his Spot and the one called Crip, a good-running hound despite a hip that never healed correctly after an encounter with a car. Ehrhardt has been at Ava High School's football game in Mountain Grove, which the Ava team, the best in memory, lost fifty-something to six.

"It was closer'n it sounds," Rosco says.

"Was there a fight?" There has been bad blood lately between the towns. Something about a girl, or girls.

"No, but you never saw so many deputies. They had the law everywhere."

Louis Huff stands abruptly and turns from them, his back to the light.

"There it is," he says.

Raymond's hounds rise whining on their ropes.

"Shhhhh!" someone commands them.

"Now that's a fox sure," Huff says. All the men are standing now, the country and its fences and the lay of the roads as clear as an aerial photograph in their minds.

From very far away, the sound of it is beginning.

III

A later day, old Granville Prock, sunk in the despised embrace of his upholstered chair, the yellow sun of autumn noon falling through a window on the robe across his nearly useless legs, will confess the truth of what they've said.

"The trouble," he will say, "is that if I'd ever go hear a man's dog run, and if he outrun me, I'd have to have that dog one way or the other. Why, I had enough dogs that I could hunt every night if I wanted to, run six or seven at a time and rest 'em three or four nights."

Depending on how you multiply, that comes to either twenty-four or thirty-five foxhounds.

"I kept my dogs good, too. I'd go down to where somebody was butchering and fill up the back end of a truck with entrails, then I'd go down to the pen with a pitchfork and throw some of those in and, oh, they done good. Now two dogs I had was *outstanding*—and there's not but about one outstanding dog in every fifteen or twenty. You can't train one. It's got to be bred. Remember once being out with a fellow—preacher he was—and he said, 'I've got a pair of dogs and they're outstanding.' And I said to him, 'What you've got is pretty good dogs. Pretty good dog, he can run in anybody's pack. But, Mister, you don't know what it takes to make a hound *outstanding*.'

"Anyhow, these two of mine was named Little Sid and Old Jerry. Sid, he could have run away with a plow the first five or six hours—then Jerry'd come in. Well, one night I was with Eldon Loftus down by Romance. His dog ran away from mine at the start. And ran away from mine in the middle. And ran away from mine at the end. Now, you know, that'll make a man think. Rip was that dog's name.

"Wasn't too long after that I was walking with Eldon in town, on the square, and I said to him, 'What'll you take for that Rip dog?' And he said, 'Oh, I guess I'd take twenty-five dollars.' That was years and years ago. Well, it just happened we were walking past the bank and I reached out and grabbed the door with one hand and Eldon with the other and pulled him inside and bought that dog off him right there."

Prock's pale eyes will glitter with remembered triumph as he dries his mouth with a linen handkerchief. Then a later memory will dull them again.

"He was as good a dog as ever walked, Rip was. But he got caught in a man's steel trap—stayed fourteen days and nights and the whole foot came off. Isn't that about what always happens when you get a dog that's pretty special? Some fellows don't mind the three-legged ones. But me, I haven't found a hound on four legs yet that was fast enough quite to suit me."

Granville Prock was sheriff of the county in the 1940s and '50s, raised a family of eight children by buying and trading livestock, and is pleased to say that he never worked a day of his seventy-two years at a regular job. All his nights were his own. But it will soon be three years since a stroke put him in his chair. And when his wife sometimes says that she spent a marriage playing "second fiddle" to his dogs, he denies it and adds—objectively, without self-pity—"Anyway, I live *right here* now."

At last, more than a little skeptical, Prock will turn his eye on the gadget which (it's claimed) holds an echo of all those lost nights.

"Turn it on, then," he will command. "It's been a long time since I heard a foxhound bark."

The tape spools will turn. And faintly at first, a sweep of dark meadow and the Peach Orchard between, their voices will reach to him from the high ground.

"Yes!" he will cry. A boy's smile.

Then nearer.

"Whose dog is that one?" Incredulous that anyone who'd been there shouldn't know.

And finally, as they vault the last ridge and their tumult breaks full down over him: "There—*that* one! That fine, clear-mouthed one . . ."

IV

". . . Yours, Don? Or is it Larry's?"

"That's Larry's pup—his Likker pup," Graham says.

Hands clasped behind them, backs to the light, they are awash in the sound of it. Mounting, mounting, receding. Gone. Too quickly—so that expecting and remembering are confused. Louis comes in from his solitary station behind the trucks.

"Those dogs I let out last have started one too," he tells them. "And, say! I believe that's the hardest thing a man ever done—listen to two fox races at once. Needs four ears."

Lard is making little smoky explosions in the bottom of two black iron skillets the size, nearly, of dishpans. There are potatoes frying in one. And in the other succulent wafers of sliced meat. Veal, call it. Or else don't ask what season the deer died. Loaf bread, and doughnuts warm from being set near the coals. And more coffee.

Lige Degase retires to the ditch for the customary purpose.

"Hssst," someone says, and the chewing stops.

"Somebody out there."

They listen together.

"Way out by the road, ain't it? Somebody parked."

The chewing resumes; halts again. The men crane their necks to look beyond the trucks.

"What's out there, Lige?"

"Somebody's havin' a fit or something," he informs them.

Whaaagh, heee-agh-agh-agh-agh, harree-agh-agh . . .

No laugh like that ever passed sane lips. The men look at each other in the stillness.

"God damn, it's a-comin' closer!"

Lige Degase returns to the group. Someone tries half-heartedly to start a story. But the sound bursts out again—this time right among them.

"What the hell you got in your pocket?" one of them asks Lige. It is a little sounding box, no bigger than an orange, which he winds by pulling a cord. They laugh with it, suddenly relieved.

. . . Heee-agh-agh . . .

"He's gonna get down, ain't he?"

"By God, he's really gettin' with it!"

Someone speaks of the device's probable usefulness in getting talkative maiden ladies off party telephone lines. More laughter, slower now.

The cold in the valley has begun to bite. Fog from the stream has billowed up to the base of the fence below the lane, receded once, and now is rolling up again. Louis Huff brings a sleeping bag from the car and unrolls it on the ground—spreads it, but doesn't use it. The two foxes still are running, and though the sound is more sensed than really heard, Louis honors it by standing.

"One of those just might be the old red one," he says. "If the two bunches ever gets together we'll really hear something."

Larry Graham, wrapped in a tarpaulin, lies snoring softly on the ground against his father. It is three hours, now, until dawn. "Better turn Don or Larry one over," Lige says. "One of them's drawing air." The talk around the fire has declined into occasional coughs, groans, and slow clearings of throats.

It may be wondered why foxhunters do not suffer affliction for their sleeplessness, their beddings on frozen earth, the collisions of their softer parts with stones and knobby logs. The answer, of course, is that they do. The thing that drives them can no more be explained by logical folk than the terrible genius of a short-lived hound can be understood by the tethered ones who yap and protest his magnificent passage. They want no pity—and deserve none.

"You know," says Raymond Hampton finally, "I can stay up the whole night and work the next day just as easy. But then that *next* day . . ."

"Listen, any time my dogs is ready to go huntin' I'll go," Howard Holt tells him. "Because you ever stop to think—one of these times you're not goin' to wake up that second morning anyway. And if you didn't go hunting . . . well, you just missed it, that's all."

Somewhere on the upland beyond the Peach Orchard the two races are converging, the sound beginning to come clearer. All but the nearest stars have gone out.

"This hour of morning," says Rosco Ehrhardt, "a hound's got the foolishness out of him. When he barks he really smells that thang."

"If you got to work why'nt you get on home," Graham tells him. "I'll pick up any your dogs that come in."

Sometimes a man will leave just his coat. And a hound, if it's hunting in unknown country, will return and lie on the familiar smell until the man comes back.

"Oh, I stayed this long. Just as well stay 'till light. I can't leave an' that old Crip out doin' what he's a-doin'." Ehrhardt sighs. "If he can do that, the least I can do is sit here an' listen."

The dogs have joined now, as Huff believed they might—the few having gone to the sound of the many. They are just behind the ridge, and coming.

"I think they're going to catch it this time," he says. It is a figure of speech.

There is a point at intermediate distance where the voices of the dogs come perfectly clear and separate—Okie distinct from Polly, Crip from the Likker pup, Pluto from He'll-Do or Jeep. And so with them all. That's where a dog's measure is taken.

Now, though, as the men stand wordlessly—some just awake and stiff from lying—the fox leads down the steep hill face, driving for the water or for some place among the ledges that only old foxes know. And suddenly the cry that fills the valley is not only nearer but wholly different—a cry not of many things but of one, not of hounds racing but of *the race of hounds* become a single creature. Uttered in the terrible astonishment and rapture of having encountered, in that dark place, both the meaning and the end of being.

And when it is gone, the night has never been so empty.

Different people live now in the house on the hill over Spring Creek. Good people—who have told Matel Holt, Ad's widow, that she is welcome to spend a day with them there, two days, a week. She hasn't though. "It would just bring back a lot of old heartaches. The loneliness, you know—it never goes."

Below, where the lanes meet, boys still go to sit in the night with men, waiting to be men themselves. Then being men, kept company by boys of their own. The layerings of their dead fires get deeper—will until one day the world is fenced entire with woven wire, or the bulldozers have made a desert, or the fox is gone.

Cancer kills as cruelly as any fence.

"It hurt awful bad to see him that way," Don Graham says. "It got so a man had to just drive himself to go up that hill." They remember that Ad Holt sold two of his dogs to a man from Mississippi and lay there, wasted in his bed, with a hundred-dollar bill in each hand and told them, "See here, now? If a man keeps good dogs they'll be worth some money."

And at the very last, when he was beyond the doctor's or anyone else's help, they just turned his dogs loose to run and opened the windows of the house. That's what he wanted them to do.

2 A CONTINUITY OF PLACE AND BLOOD

Sometime in the sleep of every year, between the browning of the oaks and the first greening of the spring wild grasses, that country flamed.

The rainless days would laze on in powdery file. The thin earth of hillside clearings turned to the plow would pale from brown to gray, and then begin to ride up on the wind. There was beauty in such days—a sense of reach and distance. But the rattle of dry leaves in doorway woodlots just at evening was terrible to hear, and anyone who neighbored with the timber did well, before retiring, to mark which quarter the wind blew from, and how strongly, and what it smelled of.

For when the fire burst finally up out of the creek bottoms and across the ridges, it came with a suddenness never quite remembered. Driving everything before it—deer, blind-flying birds, pigs gone feral in the greenbrier thickets, sometimes the people themselves. Raging barn-high up the dark flanks of the hills, turning rank meadows into white-hot lakes.

Men did not stop such a fire. And in absolute, admitted truth, they did not care to stop it. The fire, they said, killed ticks, made pasture. All across that country, long after the burning, could be found the remains of tortoises that the fire had overtaken on their way to somewhere. The olive, outer skin of the shells had peeled down to chalk-white empty helmets, wonderfully complicated in their jointing, that fell away in clicking segments when they were touched with the toe of a shoe. It was sad to find them so, pointing not away from the direction the fire had come, as might be thought, but toward their forgotten destinations.

Spring rains flushed off the ash, and the topsoil with it, into streams running milky gray out of their banks. The first fine grass came, then birdfoot violets. The healing seemed unfailing, the nearest thing to a miracle that could be claimed in those raw hills. But it was never complete. Always the ground was a little poorer, the game a little scarcer.

It is proper for lowland rivers to meander. But the streams of the Ozark highlands bend and recurve upon themselves in a way that upland rivers are not supposed to do.

Some 320 million years ago, the seas that once covered much of this continent's interior receded, leaving behind their heavy sedimentation of

sandstone, shale, dolomite, and limestone, leaving also a network of estu-
arial rivers that wound tepidly through the emergent fern forests, sheltering the amphibians and watering the newer things that crept.

Over the next 100 million years the humid forest flourished in the luxuriance of growth and the slow, slow burn of decay. Then, for reasons and
by processes unexplained, an uplifting occurred. This event happened
over perhaps thirty thousand years. When it had ended, a dome more
than fifty thousand square miles in area—as large as England—had been
raised in the interior of the North American continent. The uplift, which
we now call the Ozarks, included roughly the southern half of the present
state of Missouri, the northern one-third of Arkansas, and smaller adja-
cent parts of Oklahoma, Kansas, and Illinois. It was bounded on the east
by the Mississippi River and on the west by the beginning vastness of the
central plains.

The tidal streams that traversed it were now highland streams, but captive still in the wandering channels they had long ago begun cutting down
through the leavings of the sea. This carving of the dome continued until,
in the succeeding 190 million years, the streambeds have become a maze
of convoluted valleys, many of them hundreds of feet deep.

I have traveled more than a few of those valleys, on foot and by water.
One spring some years ago a friend and I had come down a steep, narrow
stream near the center of the highlands and drawn our canoe out on a
gravel bar to make evening camp. The river muttered past over its stony
bed—a river from which, that magical day, the two of us had caught and
released seventy-six smallmouth bass.

Directly across from our bar was a towering limestone bluff, shelved
and layered, a good deal of the geologic history of the region written on its
face. The writing was in a language we couldn't read, but still we were
moved to speak of what patience it must have taken that little stream to
wear its valley down.

It is satisfying to know now, at least in shorthand, why it is that Ozark
rivers meander. And why, in the water-carved declivities of the highlands,
a careful looker can find sharks' teeth and the fossils of trilobites and sea
clams and chain coral, so far in time and elevation from the primal sea.

A dozen miles upstream from the Missouri town of Osceola on the
Osage River, in the northwestern Ozark borderlands, there is a series of
cave shelters extending several hundred feet along a narrow footpath
under the overhanging lip of the bluff.

Nearly thirty years ago I passed a winter in a woods cabin in that neighborhood and got to know an older man, part Indian, who remembered his grandmother telling of the natives' removal. The story (or legend) was that the chief of that group above the river stayed behind with his daughter when their kinsmen were taken off to Oklahoma, and that the two of them fasted to death in protest of the loss of their wilderness home.

Pothunters long ago dug up and carried off anything of worth from the flour-fine, never-rained-on dust of those shelter floors. But the evidence of two thousand years or more of habitation is not so easily erased. Scrambled by careless shovels, to be sure—but not obliterated.

A profusion of chert flakes tells where a man sat pressing a deer antler against the edge of his stone blank, shaping a projectile point. A bowl-sized depression worn to perfect symmetry and smoothness on the top of a boulder beside a shelter entrance evokes the imagined sound of stone pestle falling, falling, in the stolid rhythm of a life.

It was a band of the Osage that used this particular bluff, or at any rate used it last. It is no wonder that they found it appealing. The dry shelters afforded comfort. The river gave nourishment and transport. The level floodplain on its far side was fertile for planting. The setting gave protection.

With the slope falling away so sharply as to forbid frontal attack, with the path along the bluff too narrow in most places for more than two men abreast, and with fine promontories on the upper rim from which lookouts might hoot warning, the location was beautifully defensible against any enemy except passing time.

The Osage were the last of the Ozarks' dominant native peoples, and there is no knowing with any certainty how long man occupied the highlands before them.

Clovis projectile points, fashioned some twenty-five to thirty thousand years after the crossing of the Bering land bridge from Asia by the first small migration of Paleo-Indians, have been found in the Ozarks, though not in association with any datable materials—bones, the ashes of a primitive hearth. Were they in fact dropped there by casual hunters? Or were they perhaps traded for as curiosities or ceremonial objects millennia later? We do not know. But we do know that by the end of the prehistoric period, the Osage people had come to occupy the greater part of the region. Their area of heaviest settlement was along the river in Missouri that bears their name, though they dwelt and ranged freely through the interior and western Ozarks, resisting the pressure of the Caddo people from the south and the Illinois and Quapaw from the east and southeast. Wrapped in the fastness of their hills, self-sufficient,

Cave shelter on the bluff of the Osage River

provincial, suspicious of contact from without, the Osage clung to their woodland ways.

One recent fall morning I walked a small crop field in the central Ozarks with a sixth-generation hill man who, since boyhood, has been fascinated by the beautiful stone tools left buried in the ground by the people who preceded his forebears to that valley.

Shredded stalk litter covered the earth and made any artifacts hard to see. We had given up and turned back toward the truck when a glint of chert in the harvested corn row caught my eye. It was a piece of a corner-notched woodland point, possibly as old as three thousand years or as new as three hundred. And not a foot away from that in the row, where the plow had stirred them out of time, were two settler potsherds. We rubbed the point and sherds clean, and straightened to survey the place.

From the evidence in our hands it had been the site first of an Indian camp or village and then of a pioneer cabin. It was surrounded by tillable land, yet on a distinct prominence far enough from the stream to be safe from any sudden rise of water.

It was plain to see why men over the centuries had wanted to live exactly there. But in that common wanting there had been unredeemable loss for some.

"I begin my tour where other travellers have ended theirs . . ." noted Henry R. Schoolcraft, ethnologist and explorer, in the first entry—Thursday, November 5, 1818—of the journal of his Ozarks expedition. Schoolcraft had a flair for self-dramatization, if not for exactitude.

In truth, Schoolcraft and his companion on the journey were lamentable, though plucky, tenderfeet. They struck off from the mining settlement of Potosi, the westernmost Ozark outpost of any consequence, full of the spirit of adventure but ill-provisioned and carrying guns unsuitable for the region's game.

A fair share of the time they were lost, wandering along and across rivers they called by the wrong names. They sprained their ankles and exhausted their shot and prodded their packhorse into a stream over his depth, wetting their remaining powder. And at the end of these exertions, having clawed through enough greenbrier and topped enough steep ridges to conclude that Thomas Jefferson's purchase for three cents an acre had been "dear at the price," Schoolcraft and friend arrived at the confluence of the White River and North Fork in Arkansas—to find that quite a vigorous, if still widely dispersed, vanguard of habitation had preceded them there.

American farmer-frontiersmen had entered the land in the eighteenth century, and their numbers grew after the 1803 purchase of the Louisiana Territory. Theirs were the isolated valley cabins Schoolcraft stumbled upon during his trek. Ambition, restless romanticism, and the pressure of expanding population were propelling Americans west. The two decades from the mid-1820s to the mid-1840s were the main period of initial Ozark settlement.

The natives of the highlands soon gave way before the thrust of white occupation. The Osage surrendered claim to most of their lands by treaty in 1825, and during that same period, a few years either side of 1830, the region's other tribes also were being relocated. Finally, the Cherokee crossed the highlands on their "Trail of Tears" from the Southeast in the winter of 1838–1839. Some strayed from that sad march and were assimilated into the hill population. But by 1840, at the latest, the Ozarks had been emptied of all but scattered handfuls of their original inhabitants—and these, too, were gone by 1875.

Just as the interior of the region had forbidden heavy Indian occupation, so it would support only a thin salting of white settlers, and to travel the area even now is to understand why. Civilization moved principally by water, and many of the rivers of the Ozarks were only seasonally, if ever, navigable. Generous valleys were rare, and tillable land in the narrow stream bottoms limited. Steep hillsides were densely timbered, often shallowly underlain by rock. Through the rest of the nineteenth century the main body of western settlement would push through and around the highlands. In relative numbers, it would leave the Ozarks but lightly touched.

The Indian trails, usually following uplands and ridgetops, became wagon roads, the lines of early white commerce. Later these would become military routes and much after that, in some cases, macadam motor roads or even Interstate highways.

Commercial water transport was feasible only on the major rivers of the northern, eastern, and southern Ozark borders—the Missouri, Mississippi, and Arkansas. Economic and cultural isolation prevailed over much of the interior. The creek-bottom farmers coaxed a subsistence from their cultivated plots and from lean hogs, ear-notched and loosed to root for survival in the forest.

In the 1850s, the first railroad lines came probing into the country from the east, drawn by the rich lead mines of the northeastern Ozarks and by the early timber exploitation. That civilizing intrusion was interrupted, however, by the outbreak of the Civil War. The major battles in the

Early Ozark barn, detail

Ozarks—at Wilson's Creek and Pilot Knob in Missouri and Pea Ridge in Arkansas—left the Union in nominal control but neither side in physical occupation of the region.

The armies concluded their set-piece engagements and moved on to fight elsewhere, abandoning the hills and their people to the predations of the Southern sympathizers called bushwhackers. In the regime of terror that ensued, great areas of the Ozarks were unpeopled and quickly returned to wilderness, the residents fleeing for sanctuary to the nearest fortified towns.

Not all the Ozarkers deserted their stream bottoms and hollows. Many stayed to defend their holdings, and many of those were murdered for their trouble. Today's painful memory of the Civil War—passed down in the oral tradition of family history—is not of identification as Yank or Reb, but rather of a long, lonely ordeal of capricious, purposeless, and un-asked-for pain.

The forest, when first man saw it, was an oak and hickory climax, with the native shortleaf pine interspersed in pockets—sometimes very large ones—on the favorable south and southwest slopes. As late as 1880, except for cabin building and the occasional cleared field, much of the highlands' interior had never felt a blade.

The look of such a hardwood forest can only be imagined now. The great leaf crowns interlaced above in a canopy that blocked the sun, retarding undergrowth. The forest floor was spongy with the duff of all the rotting leaf-falls from time immemorial. Elk, bear, turkey, and smaller game harbored there in profusion. I know of just one place remaining where such trees grow as must have then. It is on a narrow shelf beside one of the major Ozark streams, and why loggers bypassed the spot so long ago cannot be said, unless perhaps even then they were humbled by the majesty they saw.

The trees in that grove are white oaks, as grand as the pillars of any cathedral—so large that it would take four or five long-armed men to-gether to reach around one; forty feet to the first branch; each tree con-taining enough sawable lumber to build several good-sized houses. Some-day, when the largest of those oaks dies and is felled to prevent its damaging the others, I would very much like to be there and count the rings to know how many hundred springs ago it burst its acorn and became a switch.

The big timber companies of the East, having cut out the best of the white pine in the northern lake states, turned their eye on the interior highlands. And with the Civil War's end, the railroads took up their unfinished task of driving a network of commerce into the region. In the brief timber boom that was to follow, from about 1880 to 1920, the physical character of the Ozarks would be changed for generations and, at least arguably, forever.

The pine was cut first. Then the hardwoods for flooring, bridge timbers, and crossties. An expert tie-hacker, working freelance in the woods and choosing oaks just large enough to be properly squared by scoring and broad-axing, could produce twenty ties a day and get for them maybe a nickel apiece. The art survived into the early 1950s.

In Arkansas there was a brief turn-of-the-century run on native cedar to feed the pencil industry. And over the region in general, a modern cut from the 1930s onward of surviving oaks for whisky-barrel staves. Finally, the mature "trash" trees bypassed previously were found usable for today's low-value pallet lumber.

The overriding catastrophe, however, had been the early, systematic destruction of the prevailing oak-hickory forest. Removal of the mature overstory opened the woodland floor to sunlight. Stump sprouts and the emergence of less-desirable oak species turned the cut-over country into a jungle of what the natives termed *redbrush*, often practically impassable on foot.

To deal with the brush growth manually was impossible. Thus came into general use the practice of immense burnings-off and the annual march of wildfires across most of the Ozark highlands. There had been burning in the hills before the white man's coming. Indian hunters no doubt left careless campfires behind. Burning may have played some part in primitive agriculture. But never had fire ruled the Ozarks on such a ruinous scale.

The inferno might rise in any month between frost and green-up time, but, for some unexplained reason, Easter Sunday was especially favored. Families would go home from the sermon to dinner, then the men would take to the woods. Many of the fire sets were what were known as "string jobs." The technique could be as simple as walking crosswind through the hills, striking and dropping wooden matches in the leaves every several steps, or as exotic as dragging a lighted kerosene-soaked burlap bag behind a horse or even tying it to a wild creature.

The brush went, and with it the leaf mulch. Spring rains beat the barren land, carrying the ash away and the thin soil with it, washing the hills to naked beds of chert, then washing the gravel down, too, to fill the streams. I once heard an Ozarker describe the eroded slopes of his farm as "so worthless the only way you could grow a crop would be to tie two rocks together around a seed." The man was a factual reporter.

Their fertility gone, the unproductive fields were abandoned and, where any soil at all was left, went back to woodland, largely to blackjack oak—unsightly, given to rot, and without commercial value, but extremely fire tolerant.

The transformation had been as comprehensive as it had been swift. In less than a man's lifetime, the greater part of the Ozark forests had gone from stands of pristine timber of beauty and great worth to an annually charred scrub country, barely capable of supporting life.

A number of characteristics recur in descriptions of the world's developing countries, used both to define and to account for their backwardness: geographic isolation from the mainstream of commerce and culture; substandard means of communication and transport; a large proportion of the population engaged in subsistence agriculture; few resources, with the exploitation of those surrendered to outside interests; a paucity of political integration and hence of political power; and poverty by such objective measures as rates of illiteracy and of infant mortality.

In some degree, each of the above can be invoked to describe and explain the Ozark highlands. The population of the region increased substantially during the turn-of-the-century boom years as the railroads' expansion began drawing the Ozarks into the national economy. Lead and zinc mining continued to be—and remain to this day—an economic blessing to parts of the region.

But one of the principal resources, replenishable, if at all, only over the course of a century or more, had been the hardwood forest. When it was gone, and the timber companies gone with it, the people left behind—like those of the moribund Appalachian coalfields three decades ago—were a people the burgeoning nation had forgotten.

When I wintered in the Ozarks, burning still was widely tolerated, even tacitly approved, in areas not protected by the National Forest Service or the state forestry fire protection districts. And I came to know some of the incendiarists of that neighborhood by name and reputation and several by sight.

One of them I met firsthand.

For most of a week that late winter the night skies had shown sullenly red from the direction of the Osage River bottoms several miles to the southeast. A neighbor in that direction had lost his barn, with a combine harvester in it. In the mornings, the roof of my cabin was dusted with fine white ash. Then the wind shifted to north and west, and the long front of the fire turned back upon itself and burned nearly out.

The next day I went out with my beagles in the unburned scrub timber to shoot a rabbit for the pot and was standing against a tree, waiting for the little hounds to bring supper to the gun, when I first heard and then saw the man coming toward me through the woods, pouring gasoline from a glass jug as he walked. When finally he noticed me he stopped face-on, his expression a turbulent mixture of astonishment, defiance, and panting exultation. He was one of those I recognized, though we had never spoken and didn't then. It occurred to me to be glad to be armed, but he made no threat—just turned and went quickly back the way he had come, toward the beaten pickup truck that no doubt waited on some overgrown timber trail.

Much as you might hate his errand, it is possible to understand that man. He was in his thirties, one of a class the Ozark people call "branchwater folks"—meaning too poor or too shiftless to dig a well. He squatted with his many kin in a ruined house in a failed hamlet in the river bottom near a sulfur spring. His people had been early residents of the area, though they were landless and penniless now. All his life had been spent being affected by others. By the people who had ruined the country and the new ones who had come to own it. By the game agents who told him when and what he might catch or shoot. By the farmers in whose broken shacks he was permitted to lodge.

There is no human being so wretched that he will not seek some means of denying his powerlessness. The blackening of a thousand acres of forest is a spectacular assertion of one's ability to affect others. That very night, in the privacy of darkness, a match was struck and that piece of woodland burned.

An acre of Ozark land worth three cents in 1803 and twenty-five cents in 1900 could be bought for as little as a dollar in 1930 and for twenty dollars or less as late as the 1950s. Much of it changed hands on courthouse steps, auctioned to satisfy the unpaid taxes.

Two world wars called young men out of the hills, and many of them, after tasting the amenities of a different way of life, did not return. In areas where profitable agriculture was possible, mechanization brought about the consolidation of farms into larger units, sending people off the land and into small towns nearby. Then many of those towns withered in their turn, victims of the pull of jobs and services in such larger centers as Fort Smith and Harrison in Arkansas, Springfield and West Plains in Missouri.

The log cabins of the creek-bottom settlers were rotting back to earth. And now, throughout the region, a profusion of barns on marginal ridge farms leaned broken-spined against the sky, and unpainted board houses, weathered gray as polished slate, stood open to the work of vandals and time. As they had during the Civil War, although for different reasons, great areas of the hill country were again being emptied of people. This was no regional phenomenon, of course. It was part of the national rural-to-urban demographic trend, although more striking because of the already low density of population in the hills.

Meanwhile, other benchmark changes were occurring. First outside private capital, then the U.S. Army Corps of Engineers, set about damming the Ozarks' major waterways. Bagnell Dam, completed in 1931 by Union Electric Light and Power Company of Missouri, backed up the Osage to create the Lake of the Ozarks. One hundred and twenty-nine miles long, with a total shoreline of thirteen hundred miles, the impoundment at the time was the largest artificial lake in the world.

The impact of these reservoirs has been mixed. They brought construction money, and later tourist money, into the region. They also drowned tillable valley acres, swallowed communities, and displaced thousands of Ozarkers from lands on which, in many cases, generations of their ancestors had lived. The expansion of state and national forests took more acres out of private ownership, and fire prevention efforts put professional foresters in direct—and occasionally violent—confrontation with the prevailing fire culture.

The most scenic of the Ozarks' remaining free-flowing streams are within a few hours' drive of the major Missouri and Arkansas cities, and floating those fast rivers by canoe or johnboat has long been a joy for the city-bound and a source of modest income for local outfitters. When the choicest float streams were threatened by still more projected dams, conservation groups generated a successful move at the federal level to preserve them unchanged as National Scenic Rivers. In the course of this protection, more private property was taken to prevent damage to watersheds and forestall commercial exploitation.

In nearly every case, these publicly wrought changes in the Ozarks met resistance and left a residue of bitterness. It is a bit unsettling to be told by a river man, as my wife and I were some years ago, that we would do well to end our float at a different take-out point, since a landowner near the usual place had lately taken to shooting at canoeists. As no one had yet been hurt, it seemed likely the shots were only an innocent, if reckless, gesture of frustration. In the hill country, men usually hit what they truly aim at.

The fact is, Ozarkers are as rational as anyone else. A great many of them will admit privately that probably it is true the splendid rivers could not have been preserved except as a public trust; that a forest of real value is to be preferred to a scrub-oak brushland repeatedly swept by fire; that the reservoirs and the tourists have, indeed, been of economic importance to the region. But the issue is not logic. The real kernel of resentment, I suspect, is that in none of these matters were the views of Ozarkers themselves taken into much account. Again, as through all their history, decisions affecting the lives and lands of the hill folk were being made by people outside.

The larger towns, particularly those to which transportation routes, mining, recreation, or hospitable surrounding farmlands gave some special advantage, have thrived. But through much of the interior highlands there prevail today the conditions of what Dr. Robert Flanders, history professor at Southwest Missouri State University in Springfield, describes as a "semi-arrested frontier."

Isolation has left the hill people medically, educationally, legally, and economically disadvantaged. They suffer also from a generally low quality of public administration. The law of the town does not reach far into the countryside. Disputes can turn rather quickly to violence. Vigilantism and barn burning are a part of the culture.

During prohibition, my wife's father went into the hills occasionally to seek out and deliver paychecks to men who had worked as extra hands on state road projects. Not many miles out of town, other vehicles would begin falling in line behind his, all honking their horns. Soon he would find himself at the head of a blaring caravan that alerted backwoods distillers to the approach of this stranger in an unfamiliar car—a possible revenuer. There's a story of a visitor to the Ozarks during that period who was curious to see a whisky still in operation and, after some inquiry, found a lad willing to guide him for a quarter, cash in advance. The man wanted to pay on return. "But," the boy explained, "*you ain't comin' back.*"

The intent here, however, is not to reinforce the stereotype of Ozark people as lawless, depraved, stammering, shambling figures of comedy. Most of them are none of these things. They are proud, capable, independent, suspicious (with historical good reason). They also are loyal, warm, even tender, to anyone decent enough to offer uncritical friendship in return.

With the reversal in very recent years of the American rural-to-urban population drift, the region entered on a period of dramatic change

Afternoon on a clear, quick stream

whose economic consequences already have been great, but whose effect on highlands culture could be catastrophic.

The availability of land, lower cost of living, and the recreational appeal of Ozark woods and waters have attracted a tide of newcomers from the outer margins of the region and beyond. Some of these have been younger families, wanting to sink roots away from the press and problems of the cities. More have been older, retired couples—not uncommonly Ozark natives returning after spending their working lives elsewhere. It is necessary to wonder whether the best features of the highlands' people and their values can survive this modern onslaught of tourists and immigrants, any more than the early forest survived the savaging by an exploitative timber industry.

In Harrison, Arkansas, some years ago, I met a thoughtful and sensitive man named Dr. G. Allen Robinson, then still an active physician in his eighties, who practiced medicine thirty-three years in New York before returning to his native hills. Forebears on both sides of his family came to the highlands from Alabama and Tennessee in the first half of the last century. In 1832 or 1833, his maternal great-grandfather, Peter Beller—miller, merchant, farmer—settled on a stream near a cascade that took its name, Marble Falls, from a formation of red rock that the tumbling waters had polished.

Dr. Robinson lived on an acreage at the outskirts of Harrison, in a home designed for him by another Arkansas native, architect Edward Durell Stone, and built of hand-squared timbers from ruined barns and cabins, floored with cut sandstone from settler hearths and chimneys. He took me out from there, on a bitter winter day, to visit the Beller grave and then to see the place where old Peter had helped quarry from the hillside overlooking the falls a great marble block for the Arkansas stone in the Washington monument.

The falls still exist as a feature of the landscape, but outside entrepreneurs have "developed" the spot: a hillbilly village in the valley, amusement rides, a cable railway up to the ridge, a short ski run with artificial snow. Snacks, curios, a surfeit of demeaning cuteness. The mailing address of what used to be the Marble Falls neighborhood is changed now to *Dogpatch, U.S.A.*, celebrating the cartoon Yokums who have shaped a nation's view of Ozarkers. You may be sure that Al Capp is no hero in the hills.

This Road Crooked and Steep Next 20 Miles, the sign had said. Faithful to that promise, the macadam had left the ridgetop and curled down through a haze of gathering evening into that lonely, lovely section of the highlands in northwest Arkansas called the Boston Mountains.

Past a clearing where a hill woman was carrying the night's stovewood into her cabin. Past a gray clapboard church, baled hay showing in the arches of its glassless windows. Through the village of Plumlee, and past a stone building—another church, or perhaps a school, also windowless—a stolid mass against the last peach-pink wash of skyline. Finally another cautionary sign: *Hill, Use Gears. Three-Mile Grade.* Then down abruptly into the valley of the Buffalo River.

In what remains of the expired mining hamlet of Ponca, the lights were just going out in the general store. Beside the store was the Lost Valley Lodge, a large old house converted into primitive apartments, to which for many years people have been coming to leave the world behind. That had been six o'clock in the evening, an hour in the dark of the year when life is indrawn to its most basic perimeter of walls and fire, and a silence of almost palpable weight claims the hills.

Now it was nearly nine o'clock, and, a slave to city habit, I was still awake, making my rude supper on canned beans and a bottle of soda pop from the store. Suddenly I became aware of a noise, quite pronounced but wholly unaccountable—a crackling hiss, as of a woods fire burning fairly near, or possibly someone running a faucet in one of the upper apartments. It made a considerable racket in the room.

Outside no fires were burning. Inspection of the upstairs revealed that I was alone in the place and that all the taps were closed. Yet back in the room, the mystery sound still could be heard. It was several minutes before I discovered the source of that great noise which had asserted itself so distinctly in the quiet of the valley.

It was the sibilance of exploding microbubbles of gas in the bottle of soda beside my plate. Such is the stillness of the Ozark night.

Yet, merely to know that silence and the hills and waters, or even the lightless, mapless caverns underlying, is not to have made acquaintance with the quintessential Ozarks. For the region, in the end, is its people and their character and way of life.

And getting to understand those is an enterprise of years.

Just past the town of Ponca in the valley of the Buffalo, where the pavement ends and the road forks, the right fork leads to a place called Boxley. And there a fine lady named Orphea Duty waits with her table always set for twelve. Anyone indelicate enough to ask might learn that she is closing fast on eighty. Her house, its core of logs invisible under white wooden siding and several enlargements, is the same one she was raised in. Her father was postmaster of Boxley and she the postmistress after him, for thirty-seven years until the place lost its post office in the late 1950s.

When she was widowed, Orphy Duty determined that her grief would not shut out the world. She has her church affairs, of course. And also her Tupperware business that takes her to parties around the hills. And the television.

But still she keeps those twelve places always set at her table. Travelers passing along the gravel lane in front of her house, whether they know Orphy personally or only have heard of her, may stop to warm or cool, as the season requires, or just to rest. They will be presented a choice with their coffee of two or three kinds of pie and one or more of cake. Her visitors tell Orphy about their lives and the errands they are on and, in return, get as much of the history and the news of that area as their time will permit them to know. That is the hospitality of the highlands, although admittedly in rare degree.

Matters of kinship preoccupy. In another Ozark valley far to the northeast, Marjorie Bales Orchard—who is found at the cash register of the Bales AG Store on the main street of Eminence—says her project began with a mystery: Who was the mother of Shade (Shadrach) Orchard?

In 1816, two years before Henry Schoolcraft struck westward into wilderness, a Tennessee man named Thomas Boggs Chilton already was settled near the emptying of Hen Peck Creek into the Current River. From his cabin clearing issued many Chiltons to people Shannon County, and Shade Orchard's mother, most certainly, was one of them. Marjorie Orchard's inquiry into the matter grew into a family history of one thousand manuscript pages, set in type and printed at the newspaper office just up the street. The publisher of *The Current Wave* ("Shannon County First—The World Afterwards") is Thomas Leroy Chilton, who declares matter-of-factly, "There's few people in this town I'm not some way kin to."

"Say, didn't any of you Chiltons ever *leave* this place?" a friend demands to know.

"No," someone else says, "they just ran other people out"—a reference to some issue of past seriousness that time has softened into the stuff of ritual humor.

The fascination with genealogy is both diverting and essential. Children begin to be instructed very early about such matters, so that no

A highlands still life

daughter of those hills arrives at the age for courting without having graven in memory the essential details of her relatedness—to whom, and by what devious percentage.

That is the Ozarks' continuity of place and blood.

Isolation has bred also a sense of neighborhood and an unconquerable resourcefulness. Because much of the highlands' agriculture is so marginally productive, men make do with old machines, traded in the commerce of farm dispersal auctions—machines with the life already wrung out of them, that an Iowan twenty years ago would have sent to the ditch. Such equipment breaks often.

In one Ozark locality I know there is a man named Morris (actually it's Maurice, but people say Morris) Underwood, whose neighbors swear that if he ever moved away, or quit fixing things, farming for miles around would simply have to stop. They come towing their sick machines up the lane to his hill—a hill on which there have lived so many generations of Underwoods that, on the topographic maps, it is identified by the family name. Morris waits there, always smiling, not because he is glad for their misfortune but because he knows they are bringing him a new challenge.

He is a huge, powerful man with great blunt fingers that can move as delicately as a surgeon's. There are many kinds of genius in this world, and Morris Underwood has true genius in those hands. There is no other word for it. I have never seen him refer to any diagram or manual. He has no need of them. The way machines are put together and the way they function are mostly governed by a sort of lovely, uniform logic. Cylinders must fire in a certain order, and in an engine—any engine—certain things must happen to allow them to do that. If a shaft is stuck fast in place, there must somewhere be a key, a pin. Not sometimes but *always*. There are laws in mechanics as invariable as the laws of nature. Morris's mind and hands are in harmony with this logic.

Once I watched him repair a tractor with a penknife. And I was there another time when an ancient hay baler was brought to him in grave distress. Something was wrecked in its innards. It would neither take hay in the front end nor discharge finished bales from the back end. When commanded to do either, it shook and chattered and made pitiable groans.

Morris walked around it and came back to the side where he already had decided the focus of the problem lay. His anticipation was plain to see.

"I've never worked on one of these," he said, speculatively but without the least fear. "When I get done, I'll *know* something, won't I?" Then he took out his penknife and began probing under the grease for the pin that he knew, beyond any doubt, must be there somewhere.

When I get done, I'll know something. It struck me that he had just expressed about as well as can be done the creed of a useful life. To have a gift; to apply it joyfully; to welcome problems for what they can teach; to go boldly onto new ground so that, tomorrow, you will know something that you don't know today. Unpaid accounts with Morris get embarrassingly delinquent. He never presents a bill. And if a settling-up should eventually come, always he will accept too little. Genius, in those hills, seldom commands its fair reward.

There was an Ozark farm, owned now by city people, that had been untenanted fifteen years or more, the oak-post fences brought down by fire, the fields gone back to broomsedge and blackjack sprouts, the house unlived in. I once knew the place as a trespasser.

Raccoons denned under the foundation and wasps swarmed in the attic. A trumpet vine, thrusting a tendril under a crack of bedroom window, had made forced entry and found purchase in the plaster of a wall, thriving, flowering, carpeting the floor with leaves as seasons turned. Wind and rot and squirrels had opened a hole the size of a washtub first through roof, then through inner ceiling, letting in the rain. A few years more and the house itself would start to lean.

A man named John Lewis came there late one autumn, his health already broken, hard weather not many weeks away. He and his wife, Oma, stood inside together for long minutes, then came out, and she announced with a kind of crazy, proud defiance, "We've lived worse places." Through sickness and evil luck, theirs had been a succession of new beginnings. So now they set about making yet another home.

Oma was a strong and loving woman. Among other things, she could bake a mock apple pie whose soda-cracker filling was as succulent as any apple that ever ripened on the branch.

As a boy, John had schooled some, and as a young man soldiered when asked to. He had dug for house coal in those Osage hills in what is called a dog hole—a two-man mine so cramped and wet that he'd had to work a hand pump to keep from drowning at the low place in the crawlway. Wasted gaunt as the hounds he had loved to follow through the night woods, he arrived in his fifties with more than a country man's ordinary equipment of skills. He was a master carpenter, a fair farmer, a good mason. He could plumb a little, and wire a little. On days when his breath came freer, he could carry a chain saw into the timber and make more fence posts in a day than any well man I have known.

And with all of this he was an intellectual, in the honest meaning of that word. Sickness had led him to read much, first to pass time and then for pleasure. Ideas engaged him. He considered what he read. His own thoughts came out as finely turned as his carpentry, though always quietly, almost shyly spoken—for he seemed embarrassed sometimes by the richness of language he had come to command.

Well, in time the fields lay mown and slick as they ever had. The derelict house, new-painted and made sound, stood safe against the passing of more years. And John turned to Oma near the last and, calling her "Momma," said, "You know, we dug this place out of a jungle."

Like genius, greatness has many definitions. John Lewis was the kind of man and friend you are privileged to know once in a lifetime. He has gone now to lie beside his brothers in a country churchyard in the hills.

The Ozark highlands are changing, and *must* change. But it is not unreasonable to hope that, in the process, something of the character and values of the highlands might endure. For, in that country, enduring is a practiced art.

In May, several years ago, I went on foot to what I calculated then to be one of the Ozarks' remotest spots, far from any passable road. And in that wild valley I came upon a place where a settlement once had been, probably in the first decade of this century. The route of the narrow-gauge tramline could be seen, along which logs had been hauled to the mill.

The wildfires of a great many autumns and springs had done their work, and nothing remained of the houses that had been there—not one board or shingle. Yet the number of the dwellings and their location along the stream could be placed exactly. In each dooryard, some caring hand had made a planting. And stubbornly, through the ashes of all those burnings, the flowers had come to bloom again.

3 NOTES FROM INNER SPACE

They have come on a brittle winter afternoon—Roy and Jeannette with their frozen smiles—to see if this time they might make a union that no man will put asunder. Have come to the very place where Prince Buffalo, a Big Hills Osage, took to wife and may even have bedded sweet Irona, who was of the Little Hills faction.

Buffalo and his Irona have gone to dust, but the greatness of their love lives on under the careful stewardship of Eddie Miller, the manager of Bridal Cave. In the twenty-three years since the cave was opened to the public, five hundred sixty-six couples have said their vows there. The pictures of some of them are displayed on the walls of the souvenir shop on the bluff above the cave entrance.

"You'll be the five hundred sixty-seventh," Eddie Miller tells Jeannette and Roy. "It's a world record." And though the groom's grin is fixed, his eyes go bugging in absolute wonderment from face to face and finally to the shelves of gewgaws, looking anywhere to discover *Why me?*

"Yeah, but how many of them's still married?" one of the men, husband of Roy's niece, asks Eddie Miller.

"Listen here," Jeannette says, "if he thinks he's gonna divorce me he's outa his head."

The bride's father is wandering among the shelves.

"Hey, c'mere," he calls. "Lookit here." He is holding a box with a cellophane window and three corncobs inside. Two reds and a white.

In an Emergency, it says, *Break Glass. Directions: Use red cob first. Then use white cob to see if you need other red cob.*

"Gimme a dollar and I'll sing for you," Roy's nephew-in-law tells him.

The bugging eyes fix on him. "I'll give y'five dollars *not* to sing."

Eddie Miller is watching through the window.

"I guess the preacher hasn't forgot," he says, and the bride's face gets a sudden no-funny-business look. But Eddie meant it for a joke. "He'll be along pretty soon."

A car pulls into the gravel parking area, bearing customers—a boy in buckskin and a girl in saucer-sized pink sunglasses. They come into the heated building and give Eddie their dollar seventy-five apiece.

"When's the tour start?" the boy asks.

"Right after these folks get married," Eddie tells him. "You might as well see the wedding and start from there."

"Crazy," the boy says. He looks at the girl.

"Crazy," she agrees.

The groom's eyes lock on them. *Why me?* But they don't know, either. And wouldn't tell him if they did. Their eyes inspecting him are as cool as the coroner's at the window of a wrecked car.

"When, man?" the boy asks Eddie.

"Ten minutes."

Minds blown by it, they get soft drinks from the machine and wait for the nuptials.

Other kinds of love take people underground. Tom Aley loves the knowledge that can be gotten there, and so does his friend, Deb Walley. Except for that they are as unalike as any two men you will find.

Aley is thirty-three years old, with two university degrees in forestry and part of a doctorate in geography, a hydrologist by occupation, a six-foot, three-inch Californian with a scholar's beard.

Walley is fifty, a small, slope-shouldered man who has so constantly preferred the out-of-doors that the skin of his hands and face looks to have been rubbed with walnut juice. Ten grades of formal schooling have been followed by a million turnings over of rocks, a hundred thousand contemplations of still pools, cumulative years of reading scientific literature for the pleasure of it. And all that he has seen he has remembered, so that in the ways that count he is a learned man.

Their cave is Tumbling Creek Cave, also called the Ozark Underground Laboratory. Tom Aley is its owner. Deb Walley is its natural spirit. Together they are its intellect.

You cannot be married in Tumbling Creek Cave. Short of forcing its locked entrance, you cannot go inside at all unless the look of you and your reasons for being there satisfy one or the other of these two men. This day the visitors are two Explorer Scouts from a nearby town. As he usually does, Tom Aley is taking them first on a walk over the stony hills, explaining the relation of the world above to the one they will find below. At a place where the path passes by two dry streams running down to a leaf-littered depression in the earth, he stops. The boys stop with him, and Deb Walley behind.

Aley's eyes narrow, studying the two stony creases in the hillside. He is seeing, or thinks he is, the secret percolations of ground water through fissures in the soluble stone, the creation of new passages, the enlargement of his dark kingdom in the earth. As indeed he may be—though the time frame in which all this is happening is of interest only to gods.

"There's something going on here," Aley says. Whispers, almost, in a voice drawn thin with suspicion. He whirls on the sunken place, as if by turning quickly enough he might surprise great forces in motion. Behind him on the path, the boys look down at the common earth with new uneasiness and spread their feet a little wider, getting better purchase for the geologic tumult that Aley's tone suggests is imminent.

"Yes . . . there's something going on. I just can't quite figure out what."

And on then to a little pond, lying glassy-still under the winter sun. Lifeless, to the boys' eyes. A noxious puddle, scum-covered, rimmed with the hoofmarks of grazing cattle. Then Tom Aley crouches, his finger probes the muck. Something moves. Many things move.

Under the boys' eyes, the smallest flee the larger, and those the larger still.

"What is the difference," he asks them, "between the life cycle in the pond and that in the cave?" And he waits—will wait as long as he must for their imaginations to quicken. Finally, tentatively, one of them says, "The sun?"

To the teacher, nothing is more beautiful than the process of a mind's opening. *"The sun,"* Aley agrees. Again, the magic is in his manner—as formal as a man conferring medals. "And in the cave, what replaces the sun as the source of energy?"

More confidently now: "The bat?"

"The bat," Aley says. And they consider the delicate wonder of it. Until Deb Walley carries it forward.

"Oh, there's other food comes in—coons and other animals that carries in organic matter and deposits their *feekus.* But ninety percent of it, you might say, is the bats. They drops their guano. And fungus grows on it. And bacteria eats the fungus, and microscopic animals eats the bacteria, and mites eats those and so forth. And the same for the aquatic life—the amphipods and the isopods and the snails. The smaller always getting eat by the bigger."

They listen solemnly to Walley's evocation of that fierce world, whose violence all proceeds from the droppings of the winged mammal who is the sun.

"The salamander is the top dog in there," Tom Aley adds. "He's the top of the food chain. And we don't even know where he lays his eggs. Probably don't know the full extent of his dietary habits."

They pass on then through dead leaves between the winter-barren trees, the teacher leading, to fresh mysteries. To a teacup-sized hole in the hillside which, when blown into, gives back the breath in a steamy cloud—certain proof of some cavity there that one day perhaps Aley and Walley will open and explore. And to a place where a stream tumbling down its gravel bed vanishes among the stones. Aley has poured marking dye into that sink and found its traces in Tumbling Creek itself, inside the cave.

"Whatever goes down," he tells them now, "must come up." A law no less true than its commoner opposite. Fouled ground water drains into a hollow of the earth and, after passing under a hill, is drawn up still foul directly from a well or bursts forth as a spring, called pure from ignorance. Who, then, would lightly leave his nastiness on the land?

Not Tom Aley—or anyone who visits the laboratory's grounds. Above the cave entrance, on the hillside next to the headquarters cottage, there is an outbuilding of the customary architecture. But when the cover inside is lowered, that trips an electric switch that in turn sets off a blast of fan-driven flame in the basin below, and all matter there is incinerated to a fine disposable ash. When in use, the device rumbles and shudders impressively. Its trade name is the Destroilet Toilet, and it has sent more than one unwarned visitor bolting wall-eyed into the open.

Respect. That is what Tom Aley is teaching. For the water, because it supports life. For life, because it is so complex. For the salamander, because he is top dog. And after learning all this, quite gently, only then will they be prepared to go inside the cave. A cave is fragile, he tells them. A cave heals slowly.

They sit on the leaves on the ground. Except Deb Walley, who chooses a boulder. And he lies on that, his body shaping instantly to it, remembering everything he ever saw or ever heard. The winter sun silvers the stubble growth of his beard. His startlingly pale gray eyes look down on the others, remote and unblinking as a hawk's. But he is not looking at them at all. He is considering the question of where the salamander lays his eggs.

Charlie Watts once drove to Mexico, tied his rope to a boulder, and went over the edge a thousand ninety-eight feet in free descent into an inverted funnel in the earth called The Pit of the Swallows, the seven-sixteenths-inch line at midpoint spinning out to gossamer fineness and finally vanishing above him as well as below. And then he climbed out as he had gone in, because of course the alternative was to die at the bottom of that hole, which he did not intend to do.

So there is a third and most dangerous sort of love that leads to the underworld.

The hazard, though, as Watts will insist, is not in the cave or pit itself but in the manner in which it is approached. When he hung from that strand of nylon over the Mexican abyss, he knew its strength to the pound, its response to friction, its amount of stretch. And because he is an instructor of mathematics and a sworn enemy of error, he depended on it in utter confidence.

Some people go into the crevices of the earth to discover the limits of their fear or foolishness. More than a few of those do not come out. A man might return to his rope and find that, freed of his weight, it has contracted and hangs twenty feet above the floor. He is a dead man.

Food, water, proper clothing—those are nice to have. But in the spelaean world, there is one thing more essential, one absolute staff of life. And that is *light*. A man whose light has failed in a cave of any size or complexity can find a hospitable stone and compose himself. Or he can blunder off ledges and into blind passages until he is a howling, bleeding lunatic. It makes no difference either way. For unless someone knows where to look for him, he, too, is a dead man.

Charlie Watts's rules, the rules of any experienced caver, are quite simple. Never go into the earth alone. Three is the minimum party—one to stay with an injured person, another to go for help—and four is preferred. Always have a *safety*—someone on the outside who knows where you have gone and when you are due to return. Respect the limits of your skill and equipment. And always carry more than one source of light.

It is because of these rules, observed by inflexible habit, that he can stand now, with no qualms whatever, thirty-one years old, perfectly fit, ruddy with anticipation, and consider the dark aperture where a stream comes whispering out of the side of an Ozark hill. Beyond that modest hole, steel-gated by permission of the landowner to keep the destructive and the foolhardy out, lies the wild, wet monster called Carroll Cave. With its ten miles of mapped passages and its sixty-four unmapped side corridors, it will likely, when fully charted, be the largest known cave in the state that has more caves than any in the land.

With Watts is Bill Bingham, bearded forty-two-year-old truck-freight handler, who has considered skydiving and, with some regret, decided that he cannot spare the time from climbing mountains and exploring dark places. Also Bill Kling, twenty-six, systems analyst for a computer firm, a tall stick of a man who plans to retire to the self-sufficiency of an organic farm in his mid-forties. And Kling's wife, Valerie, twenty-two, whom he met in a cave and who is quite at home there or on a rope.

The four of them now, to the perfect dazzlement of the novice with them, put their aluminum canoe in the flowing stream. The carbide lamps on their hard hats spear the darkness ahead as they propel the canoe against the current, using handholds on the ceiling. But the roof drops lower. Keeps dropping, until just ahead the space between the stone above and the water below is perhaps fifteen inches. No more than that.

And now with awful casualness Charlie Watts does on purpose what, in the sunlit realm, happens only by accident. He steps overboard, the others following, and sinks the canoe.

The fifty-five-degree water of Carroll River clamps the body, pressing out all breath with a rush. And carrying the dead weight of their swamped boat between them like pallbearers, they move forward cautiously, the little yellow tongues of their lamps showing the way, toward the first of the low places they call the *neckbreakers*, beyond which, until 1957, no man had ever passed.

Four years ago Tom Aley carried in from the woods outside two dry sticks the thickness of your finger and laid them beside the narrow foot trail in his Tumbling Creek laboratory cave. A slow, gray mold covered them. Small white mushrooms rose from the mold. Bacteria covered the mushrooms. Now things can be seen to creep there, breeding, living— God knows, loving?—in the animate nimbus created by those two sticks.

The balance of cave life is that delicate. The hunger that relentless.

The treasure of Tumbling Creek Cave is the richness of life it contains. Eight species of bats, of which the most numerous is *Myotis grisescens*, the little gray bat, in his colony of one hundred thousand. Three species of salamanders, including the Ozark blind. One frog species; two of fish. Crayfish, spiders, millipedes, beetles, crickets, and other things—fourteen vertebrates and forty-two invertebrates in all—some of them nearly too small to see, but each invested with the awesome dignity of *being*.

Because of this, Aley and Deb Walley have built their trail through only one-fifth of the total cave, carrying the fifty-pound bags of portland in on their backs and patting the cement carefully into the damp cave earth. The remaining four-fifths has been left in its natural state, and will be as long as Aley has anything to say about it. What he did with those sticks was deliberate. But consider the violence, over the years, of a thousand careless feet, each carrying in one unnoticed leaf, each one of those surrounded then by pyramiding civilizations of ravening things, prospering and multiplying in the slow burn of time—only to perish utterly when the leaf, with its false promise, is gone.

From the standpoint of numbers, it would be a numbing carnage.

Water dripping from the cave ceiling strikes a stone, gathers in a pool the size of a cupped hand, then flows in a rivulet no larger than a soda straw down a foot or two of gentle slope. Across a convenient place for walking. A man might miss seeing it altogether in the limited light of his cap lamp. But to the lesser beasts that hunt its shoals and rapids, that trickle is a raging Amazon. They have ordered their lives to it, committed themselves beyond all options. The passing man stumbles, puts down a hand to catch himself, destroys the pool, changes a river's course. Wipes his hand on his trouser. Passes on.

Genocide.

Or two other men pass along a gallery beneath a maternal roost of gray bats. They are careful men, meticulous about where they place their feet. Decent men. "We've missed the turn to the East Passage," one of them says.

"So we have," says the other. "Pity." And they turn back.

Pity, indeed! For at the sound of the first syllable resonating in that buried chamber—by the very fact of the men's *presence* there—startled batlings lost their clutch on maternal fur, maternal teat. Silently they fell, silently were borne away by the water of the stream below. Not many of them. A hundred, three hundred.

Tom Aley shudders just with imagining it.

Being top dog, the salamander goes anywhere it pleases him to go. For some reason unknown to Aley or anyone else, it pleases several of them to stay on a certain ten-foot stretch of wall above the stream in one part of the cave. Never any other wall. *That* wall. Usually between five and eight of them. And by some further mystery, also currently unanswerable, these wall salamanders are a slightly different hue of brownish pink, more translucent than their fellows of the floor region.

There are nine this day, a fine display. Deb Walley is down beside the stream, his pale eyes searching them out, missing none of them.

"In his juvenile form," Aley is telling the Explorer Scouts, "the Ozark blind salamander has functional eyes. But as he passes into adulthood, the eyes atrophy and a sort of skin grows over them. That happens whether he's raised in darkness or in light." For boys and salamanders, there is only a little time to be young. Aley lets them think on it, hoping they will decipher the metaphor for themselves. Then he rises off his heels.

"Let's go see the stromatoliths."

And you would follow him whether you cared to see them or not. He teaches that well. Deb Walley, though, lingers behind. He is still down at the wall beside the clear stream, playing his light across the moist stone, looking for that tenth one.

The Reverend Calvin Moore of the Linn Creek Methodist Church is seventy-four years old and semiretired, a regal little man in a black suit and black hat. And no matter that he has answered dozens of these calls from the cave, it always embarrasses him a little. Always will.

"*Heh,* well—" He follows after Eddie Miller and the two customers and the wedding party down the outside steps from the souvenir shop to the cave entrance on the lower face of the bluff.

"—that is, I'd rather marry them in a church. *Heh!*"

The state's largest lake lies just fifty feet below, stirred to a glittering chop by the cold wind. There is a floating dock anchored there for anyone who might choose to visit the cave by boat.

"But if they want to be married in a cave—" the Reverend Mr. Moore says weakly. Really explodes it, then: "*HEH!* I'll marry 'em there." And he goes after the others, past the petrified turtle formation that, according to Eddie Miller, was featured in "Ripley's Believe It Or Not."

The cave is nicely kept, with trash containers to receive the torn film wrappers and the spent Instamatic flashcubes. The lights play on the onyx fluting of the natural pipe-organ formation and on the dripstone hump that forms the natural altar in the Bridal Chapel itself. In spring and summer, the bumper seasons, a piped-in recording of Wagner's Wedding March would fill the place, but just now, Eddie explains with real regret, the equipment isn't set up.

So, what does the mother of the bride think of all this?

"I don't know," she says honestly. "It's only the second time I ever seen him."

Not the groom. The *cave.*

Oh, *that.* She thinks that is all right.

"Well, I don't care what kind of husband he makes," says the bride's oldest daughter. "As long as he makes a good grandfather." She is a practical girl, with three little ones of her own at home.

Without the aid of Wagner, then, the principals and the Reverend Mr. Moore take their places before the giant organ.

Through mud to the knees, and under vaulted domes no carbide beam can touch, Watts and his party have progressed three miles upstream from a sunless shore where they beached the canoe. Sometimes wading. Sometimes striding on bare gravel. Then across a rock bridge over an area of roof collapse, and back to mud again. Once, on a stony sidehill, the novice's foot felt forward and came down firmly—on nothing. And during that oh-so-long instant of pitching off into the outer blackness, the other foot—the anchored one—kept bravely contriving all manner of little tricks and adjustments. Until finally the brain, wonderful computer, sent up the card that said, "Oh, damn. Forget it," and turned to considering consequences. But there had been nothing worse than water below, to the neck.

And now they are sitting in a long chamber, recharging their cap lamps, a stub candle wedged between two rocks more for the company than for the light.

"You'll have seen about half the mapped cave," Charlie Watts says. "Seeing the rest of it gets to be a physical factor—strength, time. You almost have to camp."

"And *that's* something," says Bingham, his beard satanic in the candlelight.

"Fan-*tastic*," Bill Kling agrees. It is his favorite word.

"You crawl in your bag and get warm and sleep a few hours," Bingham says. "And then you've got to crawl out and pull on the same wet clothes and go on."

"Fan-*tastic*!"

Their frosty breath-clouds wreathe them as they sit, chilling with inactivity. Fantastic that must truly be, and more than that.

"But there are little fish back there in the pools in the lower cave—" Kling begins.

"Blind fish," Bingham says. "With nerve masks."

"—and if you stay in one place, no matter how long you watch one, he doesn't move. But if you step in the pool he'll dart away. I guess maybe food is so scarce that he has to remain motionless, conserving his energy because it's so long between meals."

"Or he could be staying still to pick up the vibrations in his pool," Bingham suggests. "Of a water flea, say."

"Maybe. But when he darts away like that, you think of how much energy you've caused him to expend. And you wonder just how much of his life span you've cost by stepping in his pool."

"On the other hand," Bingham says, "you may have carried in some food that he can use. It might balance out."

"Might," Kling concedes, but doubtfully. Anyway, it is theoretical and cannot be resolved. But careful cavers are sensitive, at least, to what lives around them.

Charlie Watts stands. "We'll go on to the waterfall," he says, and leads up again through a breakdown area to where the Carroll River disappears into the rock-strewn floor. Then down a short pitch into the Thunder River section of the cave, a separate stream system altogether. The cascade can be heard ahead now, growling mightily somewhere down the passage. And then seen, from above—standing on the lip. Bingham turns the beam of his waterproof lantern down onto the pool, ledged and shallow at its rim and dropping off to blackness where the force of the water, arching farther out during high flow, has carved it deeper.

The distance from upper stream to pool is not great. Fifteen feet, perhaps twenty, through a little descent passage and then straight down. They lower themselves quickly by rope, its use second nature to them all. Except the novice. To him, in the half-light and the noise of the fall, it is as formidable as the Eiger's north face under a blizzard.

"Two wraps around your right arm," Bingham counsels from the bottom. "Now pass the rope around your back, and take a double wrap around your left arm. Good. Now, let go of your handhold and lean out against the rope. *Lean out.*"

It is a trifling thing, which only seems much at the moment.

"Give yourself slack," Bingham says, "and walk down that wall."

A little thing, and yet a man might want to stand longer just that way— feet against the rock, body tilting crazily away. That is the exhilaration that people go into wild caves or onto the sides of mountains to find. Not the sensation of danger but of beautiful, absolute control.

The animals of the Pleistocene left their bones in Tumbling Creek Cave—the peccary and the jaguar. The locations have been recorded and the bones themselves removed for study. Another, larger creature prowled there, too, writing his signature in clawed pawprints as wide as two hands together where he slipped in the wet clay. Those are preserved forever under a thin layer of flowstone.

Biologists come there to do their bat studies. Deb Walley likes the bats, too. Especially on a summer evening, just at deep dusk, when he sits sometimes just outside the bat entrance, different from man's entrance.

"You can sort of hear them first," he says, "coming up from way far away. And then they come out all at once." A hundred thousand of them, sometimes more.

"A bat eats half his body weight in insects every night," Tom Aley says. "For the whole colony, that's about a half-ton of insects."

But the pride of Tumbling Creek is a snail. First Aley must service his instruments, kept there on contract from a university in Illinois to measure the drip rate of stalactites, correlating that with rainfall gauges on the surface. One day, Aley hopes, his laboratory may support itself entirely by contracts for such serious research. Meantime, he allows the occasional supervised tour. And now he takes his visitors in search of *Antrobia culveri*. An altogether new genus. Never described except here in Tumbling Creek.

He kneels on the bank, where the flow is wide and smooth over shallow bottom. Deb Walley kneels too, flashlight in one hand, his open pocket-knife in the other. In Deb's hand, the knife blade is an instrument of consummate delicacy. A surgeon's scalpel would be primitive beside it. Shining in the light, the point explores the water. A white isopod creeping slowly, carefully, with undoubted intelligence across a submerged pebble is unmolested. The knife passes it by. Then Deb Walley lowers his wrist a fraction and the vaunted snail, *Antrobia culveri* himself, comes up perched safely on the flat of the blade.

He is the size, roughly, of a grain of medium-coarse sand.

"Only here," Aley says. "In this one stream in this one cave."

So, there on the knife blade, this living sand grain reposes in its singularity.

"He's on the Missouri list of rare and endangered invertebrates," Aley says.

And in spite of itself, a voice challenges: "But does it matter?"

Does it *matter*?

Aley turns to see if just possibly, somehow, his ears have deceived him. But he knows they have not. And his face is long with the terrible sadness and pity of a man who has just heard the vanguard of the barbarian horde crest the nearest hill and start down upon the city.

The adventurers are clear of the second neckbreaker now, and back in the canoe. The smell of wood smoke comes in to them, telling of the world. They go toward it, and toward the light. And finally to the fire itself where they strip off their wet clothes—the novice with much shivering complaint, the others deliberately. Charlie Watts most slowly of all, knowing he will soon be dry and warm and prolonging the sweet expectation of it.

Then they go to a smaller cave nearby, called Perkins Cave, high on a hillside and dry for sleeping in.

Other campers' gasoline lanterns are there already, and sacks of food and blanket rolls arranged on the floor, though not the owners of all this paraphernalia. No matter, though. The large inner room could easily sleep thirty. A solitary little pip bat, thumb-sized *Pipistrellus subflavus*, drowses in a high corner. He has seen them come and go.

The newcomers choose spots of their own, and Valerie Kling heats a pot of her homemade vegetable stew on a portable stove, following that with her homemade doughnuts. The food warms them, contents them. Valerie's husband's dream of living off the land seems somehow more plausible now.

The original occupants return. They are five, four young men and the girlfriend of one of them. But they stay only briefly, to roll the sleeping bags and collect their gear, all in a sort of blur—an ordered frenzy. They are young, and life is everlasting, and they have decided to rush off into the night and sleep in some man's barn and hunt his fields the next day for artifacts.

One of the five is a heavy, round-faced, black-bearded fellow whom Valerie and Bill Kling call Pooh, or, alternately, Org. They were with him once on a Mexican pit descent when, out of drinking water, he resorted to a pool in which the locals were known to dispose of their dead livestock. It was covered with an airy gray foam, an inch thick, as Valerie remembers it. He pushed the foam aside and slaked his considerable thirst, and then stopped intermittently to retch the whole eight hundred miles from the mouth of the pit to middle Missouri. They may have mentioned other things about him; even his real name. But surely that is fame enough for any man.

"Peace, Pooh," Bill Kling calls after him as they go. "Have fun."

"Oh YEAH!" comes the answer, as if astonished that the issue of his having fun could possibly be in doubt.

The warmth of their own sleeping bags wraps them. They are on the edge of sleep, when into their room from the other direction, from the mile of cave behind, comes yet another party. Bedrooms are not always private places. Four boys, these are, ages twenty or so. They stop to make cave talk with the people lying in the lantern light. One of them is telling what they saw back there—what Charlie Watts has seen a score of times or more, has even taken groups of youngsters to visit. As caves go, Perkins is not extraordinary.

"What have you been in?" the boy asks Charlie.

"Carroll."

"*Carroll!*" He speaks it like the name of a saint. "Man, would I like to get inside that one some time. You aren't the fellows that have the key?"

"That's right," Charlie says.

"Well, sometime . . ." the boy begins, naked covetousness in his eyes. He presents his credentials in words—the caves he has been in, the names of cavers he knows, his whole repertoire of terminology.

In his sleeping bag, his back against a boulder, Charlie Watts is looking up at them. Looking at the bare, unprotected heads of two of them. At the absence of any emergency kits on their belts. Looking, most of all, at the one carbide lamp and one flashlight shared by them all.

"Sure," Charlie says. "Maybe sometime."

But in an uncertain world, one thing may be relied upon past any doubt. That hand shaking Charlie's will never, ever, ever hold the key to the monster called Carroll Cave.

"Dearly beloved," the Reverend Calvin Moore tells them, his little testament open on his palm.

And one can imagine what that place must have seemed to the ones who saw it first—whether Buffalo and Irona or the less graceful race that preceded them on this earth. The beauty of it must have nearly struck them blind. And the beauty lives still. No number of flashcubes in the hanging trash baskets or cigarette filters in the Mirror Lake can spoil entirely the marvels that time and flowing water have wrought.

The groom's ring sticks at the knuckle. Jeannette has had it made good and snug. She means for it to stay on.

Poor Roy is stumbling over his vows, too. Choking a little. Because he knows that he may be doing this in a peculiar place, before curious company, but that by God it's sure enough the *real thing* in the view of the law.

"Let us pray," says the Reverend Mr. Moore.

The long-haired girl has her eyes closed behind the pink saucer glasses, and she and the boy in buckskin are moving their lips with the others. They go through the receiving line, too. It is the only polite thing to do.

And then, with Eddie Miller leading, they go on and take the tour.

4 MEMORIES OF A COUNTRY NEIGHBORHOOD

The land is not a museum; its people are not museum pieces. Live long enough, and all the roads you used to walk will pass through country never seen before.

—Brademus Gray

Whenever an idea begins percolating about which I am still uncertain, and when nothing found in a book suffices quite to clarify the point, I often listen to hear what Brademus Gray might say on the matter.

Gray is an authority on nothing, but opinionated about everything. And he turns a nice phrase.

(I should confess straight off that he is only a fiction—a character made up once for another purpose. But afterward he refused perversely to be still, and we have since been in intermittent communication on a variety of subjects.)

Recently I was considering the subject of change—in particular the change that in a bit less than three decades has overtaken a certain country neighborhood of my acquaintance. As I sat to write, memories came back, a confusion of them. Mostly of things gone and people gone.

Then Gray spoke up, to argue that regret was not only useless but beside the point. *The past always seems very sweet,* he said. *But was it really so sweet for those who lived it? Look again, more closely, and be fair.* He is strong-willed and often abrasive. But I have never found that his being only an invention in any way lessened the value of his advice.

So I have drawn on a sheet of paper a map of that neighborhood, taking care to make it as exact as memory will allow. About time I must be less orderly. Seen from a distance, the stream of years seems to move in either direction with equal ease. Things unknown become known, then are forgotten, then perhaps are remembered again. Better to forget time altogether.

The place will remain unnamed here on the chance that, left to your imagination, it may come to resemble some place you know.

The westernmost feature on this map is a house atop a cold hill. There, on a winter evening, an old man sits dreaming in his chair—wife gone, children gone, the house empty so long that no images ever come to haunt. (At least he never speaks of loneliness.)

It has snowed. And now the old man starts half up from his chair, vacant-faced and freshly alarmed by the celestial WHANG of the burdened tin roof two stories above, reversing its rusty warp as it must have done every night of new snow in sixty years. On the wooden porch, his dogs shoulder and growl at the noise, the hair frozen rough along their backs.

The man gets up from his chair and moves from window to window, looking to the violets he keeps there on the sills. His white hair reflects against a cold, dark pane. He jabs his blunt farmer's thumb into the earth of the pots to see if they want watering—a custodial act, as matter-of-fact and unloving as the short, terrible arc he swings with a double-bitted ax to split a log chunk to kindling.

Near the house, but just outside the circle of the yard light, is his barn. One cow lives there; the cow's calf; three cats to chase the mice.

On a facing hill across a little fold of land is the ruin of a stone dwelling in which, a long time before, two girls grew up—sisters, with hair the color of honey in the comb. Only the old man remembers them, and in his mind they have never aged. They are girls still. After him there will be no one to remember.

In the spring lightning of another year, the man's barn will burn. He will build a small shed of found boards, so low he has to duck below its roof's edge as he drives his ancient tractor in. Going in, the engine will die or the brake fail. The tractor will roll backward and he will give a short cry. And someone will find him there, pinned and broken between steering wheel and eave, dead a day, his dogs growling at the neighbors who arrive.

The cats will leave first, to live in someone else's barn, and the dogs will skulk away unclaimed into the world. His lane will grow up in saplings and become impassable. His violets will go to powder in their pots on the sills of a house filled with bales of hay. His name will go unspoken.

But none of this quite yet.

Cresting the hills by the house where the old man dreams a few cold seasons longer in his chair, the lane passes down through a large wood, then bends across an iron bridge and wanders northeastward—passing out of night and winter on the way—to join a larger road where sits a store.

The store is on the map's north edge.

You know this place. Outside is a gas pump. Inside, one long, high room with shelves from floor to rafters. At the front, a wooden counter. Toward the rear, a tall stove around which, even when the stove is not lighted, men sit by habit to publish the daily journal of spoken news.

The storekeeper is a young man. He has a wife and small children. His life has order, and he knows clearly his direction. Some customers he *carries*. That is, he keeps their tickets in a metal box, clipped together, against the promise of payment to come. But only some. From other customers he wants to see the cash. His mistakes of trust are few. By day he pumps gas, fetches things off the high shelves with a long-handled hook, and counts out change. By night he totals up his receipts and his receivables.

His satisfaction is complete. But it will be brief. The young wife soon will be in her grave. Shortly after that the stove will burn the store. His shelves of goods, his ledgers—everything will go to ashes. Nothing will stand on that corner again.

However, he does not know that now. And, passing on the road at some hour when the store is locked, you might find a light on and notice him behind the counter, examining the clipped-together bundles of tickets as he takes them from the metal box, perfecting his accounts.

The neighborhood lies in a skewed triangle, the base resting approximately along a river. The old man's house on the hill establishes one bottom corner. The doomed store its apex. And at the third corner, by strange coincidence—or maybe not so strange, since the final choices are always only two: fire or rot—is another store waiting to be burned.

The general scene is the same: a lethal stove, empty bottle crates with men sitting, the merchandise banked up and receding into shadow. But this is a larger establishment, and appended to its rear is a high-roofed room—a dance hall once (women still alive remember the music to which their feet were trod on there). That room a place of storage now, with a wheel-less carriage in it, and iron beds, broken mirrors, machines whose use is no longer known, other artifacts.

All this presided over by a different, rougher kind of man than was met in that other store. Immense, black-haired, and sometimes watery of eye. Sometimes unable to stand. Who hides his whisky bottles in the fabulous confusion of the storage room to save them from his wife. But does not bother to hide the empty ones, which are of no further use.

He is, by his claim, half-blooded Indian of the tribe that used this area first. So he is custodian of those kinsmen's memory, but also of the history of the town—notwithstanding it has ceased to be a town.

Three hotels were there, a bank, an ice-cream parlor, a club for sports-
men anchored on the brow of an overlooking ridge, houses, streets, a
fishing camp beside the river. Gone, all of them, to one or the other of
those two old friends, fire or rot.

"The biggest town between Kansas City and Springfield," he says, smelling
powerfully of what he's drunk, and rolls out the old plat on the glass top of
the long counter. The paper is faded, broken at the edges from too much
fingering.

On the drawing the streets are clean and geometric. But, on the ground,
they are only shallow depressions hardly visible in the tangled forest that
has swallowed them. Not a dozen houses left, and not half of those—the
ones on higher ground—truly lived in. In winter the low river flows black-
green under fissures in its ice. Then in the spring rains it comes boiling up,
ocher-colored and full of flotsam, and pools where the town was, lapping
at the very porch of the store itself. Between these floodings the lower
houses receive the casual tenancy of certain people and their pigs, often-
times together.

Under the paper on the glass counter, under the glass itself, are wonderful implements fashioned by Indian hands. Bird points and lance tips and
grooved stone maul heads polished fine.

"I know where the old ones sleep," he says, leaning close across the plat of
the town. He is in a kind of transport of whisky and dreaming. *"Places
where jewelry and pots and stuff lay right on top of the ground."*

His heart is unsound. But he has a horse well broken to the gun and he
rides behind two dogs to find quail in places where his legs refuse to take
him. That much remains. That and a grandson who is still a round-faced
boy. The boy will grow almost into a man, then will overturn a car and lie
crushed, an invalid. The store will burn. The two bird dogs kenneled
under its floor will burn with it. And the man, almost as if by mystic
volition, will go to his bed and there cause himself not to waken.

All this still is some few years ahead, though. He cannot possibly know
any of it. For, if a man had any such presentiments as those, what would
there be to do but dream and drink?

"I could take you to those burying places," he says. Draws back, then.

"Except I won't." And falls into a dark and sullen silence that forbids
prying. Then presently goes off alone into the storage room on some
necessary errand.

You know the corners now. The dimensions of the neighborhood are
arbitrary, established by the length of a comfortable walk. The greatest
distance from any part of it to any other, even from its northmost tip all the

way to the river on the south, must be approximately five straight-line miles. Certainly not more than six. No one can say authoritatively. No one has ever gone that straight-line way.

The interior of the triangle also contains points of interest.

Against the face of a sandstone outcrop, beside a crystal rivulet with lilies massing at its edge, several large, dark openings can be seen all in a row. Some man of unremembered name is said to have spent a fortune (how much was called a fortune then?) causing those passages to be cut into the stone. He had in mind to operate an underground amusement park. A railroad would link his caverns. There would be saloons and so forth. But his fortune was not sufficient. The passages were partly dug. Some dances actually were held in them. Then the money was gone, and after that the man was gone. And after that, farmers found the caves were useful for storing potatoes through the winter.

Some men keep cattle. Others swine and fowl. But one man, a man of the neighborhood, keeps a herd of automobile carcasses. It fills him with satisfaction to see them grazing window-deep down the russet incline of his brushy pasture.

No one knows where the cars come from. They are never seen arriving. They just appear there, their numbers increasing at a measured rate, raising the possibility that his herd, like those of other breeds, may calve in season.

Naturally, his house will burn—an event which you have gathered by now is unremarkable. He will get a trailer with a telephone. Lightning will strike the telephone and burn both the instrument and the table on which it sits. The phone company will suggest that what he needs is a wall model. The next time the lightning will burn not only the wall but the trailer as well. After that he will manage without a phone.

But even after these reverses, he will look out the trailer window—as he looks now from the window of his house—down across his pasture at his herd grazing in the bushes. He counts their number and finds none has strayed. Neighbors speak of them as his *inventory*. They will not sicken and die. They multiply without assistance. In any relevant human frame of time they are immortal. Beyond that, they are alone among the things he owns in their imperviousness to fire.

He has heard of cars with telephones in them and can hardly imagine the recklessness of that.

To the left beyond his pasture is another, owned by someone else. Or owned by no one, for it is grown up entirely in broomsedge and wild rose. No fence contains it; there is no one to build or keep a fence.

The house behind the pasture is empty. In a grove of dark cedars can be found a dozen headstones, chipped round but bearing no inscriptions—the dead nameless and unvisited, their memories gone cold. And the mystery is why *this* house has *not* burned.

Hunters have sheltered there, waiting out storms, setting blazes atop a piece of tin laid directly on the wooden floor. Wildfires have borne down upon it . . . then parted to flow around, like current around a stone, or have been turned back by changing wind or quenched by a sudden shower. The barn has burned, and the dry pastures a score of times. But not the house. It is waiting for a man and woman who will come to live there, the man to die there. It is as if the house were guarded in some powerful fashion by this service yet to give.

It will be ten years before those people arrive. The place is untenanted. But that fact is unknown to the young man who just now can be spied warily approaching the boundary fence at the line of trees behind the pasture. That one is The Pup—known so by the people of the neighborhood, who think him comical and possibly a little crazy.

He lives in a cabin on that side of the fence, and goes each month or so on foot to one or the other of the stores for his provisions. Whiskers cover his face and he speaks strangely. He has allowed the winter to come upon him without a stack of wood outside his porch—cuts wood each day, living from hand to stove, the way the poorest savage would. He has been asked what, exactly, he is doing there, and he replies, "*I write.*"

The postman can vouch for that. Envelopes go out from the mailbox. The same number of them quickly return to the mailbox—those going and those coming all written in the same hand. The fellow is engaged, at a minimum, in a queer correspondence.

The people of the neighborhood are not strangers to writing. They write their wills. Sometimes they write letters. But they have never heard of a job of writing that could not be finished. "*I am revising the Bible,*" he finally tells one of them. The heresy of his enterprise offends them, but otherwise they are satisfied with the explanation. It confirms that he is mad.

He has many times looked down across the pasture at the house, believing it occupied. He is thinking now that he would like to have a rabbit for dinner. Rabbits surely would live in the tall grass around the house or the plum thicket behind it. But he is timid in the matter of trespass. He would expect the barking of dogs, then a shouted warning. Then possibly a gunshot. His eye rests fondly on the thicket where he knows the fat rabbit is.

The Pup, vain about his little stack of stove wood

But he disappears again into the shadow of the wood's edge and goes hungry back toward his cabin, wondering what amazing word the mail might have brought.

Directly across the gravel road from The Pup's lane is a timbered swale, on the near edge of which stands—or nearly stands—the wreckage of a settler hut, clambered over and obscured and dragged partly down by a luxuriance of wild grape, the stem of the vine as great around as a mason jar.

From far down the road, from out of autumn's silence, a trailer appears. A small, wood-sided trailer of a homemade sort, in the tow of an ancient car. Car and trailer stop beside the road, on a level place of sand and shale. The next day they still are there, the trailer disconnected. The man has chopped away the vine and gathered brush to build a fire that he stands beside, his breath pluming up frosty in the early light.

The wreckage of the hut has been laid clear.

"From Oklahoma," the man says in answer to a question. *"We mean to stay."* This last as if expecting argument.

He is nearly seventy, a knobby, wizened little fice of a man, drawn fine by hard luck. And yet he has bought that piece of land. At ten dollars an acre, anyone can buy the land. His wife is ten years older and has worn out three husbands before him—a fact he mentions with wonder and respect. They are newly wed.

"You'll hep me clean the well," he says next. *"Top's all fell in. Got all kinda c'ruption down it. Snakes and bones. Maybe worse."* The Pup is game enough for snakes and bones. It's the *worse* he's leery of.

That is November, and the wind makes a sound like walking in the trees.

The wiry little man raises one partly fallen side of the hut. And then, by levering with poles and by the use of ropes drawn through pulleys attached to trees, manages somehow to winch the whole structure, shriek-ing, into square. A building again. Finds cast-off sheets of tin for patching the roof. Finds windows from other fallen houses elsewhere in the neigh-borhood. Winter will pass to the patient rapping of his hammer. Toward spring—near the time of moving from the trailer to the house he's made, however cramped and cobbled—his wife will take an illness. Some days she will walk bent sideways with pain. Other days she will not leave her bed.

"Colic," the little man will say. Then, later, *"An ulcer for sure."*

She has lived a long time and seen amazing things, and some days the bearded young man will cross the road from his cabin and sit in the trailer to hear a story she might tell. *"Oh, it's there to talk about,"* she will say. *"So much—no place—no startin'."* In the slitted light from the ventilator beside the trailer bunk, she is just a narrow silver tracing of forehead and nose and chin and folded hands and bent knees to the end of the mattress.

On a shelf nearby, her windup clock can be heard ticking, loud and quick.

"Please. I'd like to hear."

"So much," she will say again. *"No beinnnin'—no endin'."* Then her face will turn in the light and her hands begin to move, touching and going away and coming back to touch at the fingers, and into the distant, dry tiredness of her voice he will hear a music coming.

"Well, there's a sod house. You know Oklahoma, boy? A sod house to begin. And I remember an Indian boy—pretty, long face. And wagons a-goin' and the stream of ferns and the everlastin' spring comin' out under the big rock. There's a dress and there's child pain and there's a sickness and a fire and there's a wagon to Kansas. Oh, there's a red afternoon, burnin' in the flat places, and the bluestem over the wagon wheels and—oh, Lord!" Her voice bursting strong. *"So much!"*

In the stillness, then, the clock will tick, all her music spent or sadly changed.

"She's buried three before me," her husband will repeat, convinced of her durability. For her pain he brings her bottles of patent antacids, but when the sickness is cancer of the stomach these do not provide relief.

By May she will be gone. Soon after that he will reattach the trailer to the car and drive away to somewhere. Someone else will buy the land and quickly burn the hut and raise a new house in its place. These people's brief stopping here will be as something imagined.

But that is the ending. Now they are only beginning. *"You'll hep me clean the well,"* the man says—a statement, not a question.

Eighteen feet straight down the hand-dug hole, laid up with rocks around, the opening at the top appearing to The Pup no larger than a bright quarter—no, a dime. Eighteen feet on a knotted rope, the walls slippery with seeping water, bits of crumbled earth and pebbles raining off the upper edge, until finally he is waist-deep in what they haven't managed to draw out by bucket: the dead snakes, the bones, the *worse*.

"How is it?" the question echoes down.

"Pretty awful."

"Well, be keerful of the damps."

"What are the damps?"

"A kinda gas. Can't see 'em, but they kin kill you 'fore you know it."

"Jesus!" Suddenly working faster with the bucket. "How can you tell if they're here?"

"When you quit answerin' back."

A seldom-visited meadow declines through berry tangles to a branch. The branch bends southward toward the river, and at that bending, where the next hill starts to rise, a small cave can be seen. Long ago someone laid a half-wall of logs across its opening and used the cave to stable animals in.

Now, in season—that is, when tadpoles swim in the branch and the berry canes have begun to leaf; from then until the next hard weather—that is Curley Glissom's home. He lies on his straw bed and listens to quail whistling in the grass.

Across the stream and partway up the meadow sits a school bus, wheel-less, elevated on cement blocks. Why or how it came there, by whose agency, is unknown. But that is Curley Glissom's home in winter. He is clever with machines and has gotten the motor so it runs. On the coldest nights, he starts the bus and sits in the driver's seat and lets the heater blow.

He neither sows nor reaps. He wears found clothes, sets wire snares for game, borrows his gas from the cars of city hunters who dare to park too near. He needs little and wants nothing. He is in perfect harmony with all about him. And I imagine him to be happy.

I say *"imagine"* because he is not in a strict sense real. The *place* is real, as are all the other places and people I have described here. The rest is all true, with only two exceptions: Curley Glissom, like Brademus Gray, is an invention, but an invention of so many years ago that I almost believe in him myself.

I can't tell you precisely what he stands for. Resilience, possibly. Resourcefulness. Some cadence distantly remembered. A high tolerance for that acute sensation others might call discomfort, but which, by a slight turn of mind, can as easily be accepted as nothing more or less than the proof of being alive.

Real or not, when I walk into that meadow—or almost any other place in all that neighborhood where people have been and gone and left a stillness behind—I see him often and clearly.

That completes the map. Retrace the way and you will come again to where we started—to the house where, on that winter night, a man sprang awake from some dream and rose from his chair to see if his violets needed watering. The house still is there. But thirty years have passed, and of course the man, the violets, and the barn are gone. The lane is impassable now, so that you have to come at the house another way, across the open top of an adjoining hill.

From there, with the country spread out below, you can observe the larger pattern of change.

The bulldozers have been at work. The woodland has diminished. The farm fields have grown larger and more regular, and young men—grown taller and bolder than their fathers—drive across those fields on tractors whose cost was greater than the price of the farm.

The utilities have cast their net of wires. The roads have been widened and paved, though at this distance there would appear to be fewer reasons of interest to travel them. The neighborhood as I remember it, the one on the map we navigated by, was both more elaborate and richer in detail.

"But the pain!" Brademus Gray is whispering at my shoulder. *"Consider the pain, man. Because whether they put a name to it or not, that's what it was. Surely you wanted more for them than that!"*

And as usual, damn him, he is right.

II

EXPEDITIONS

5 BEFORE THE MOUNTAIN FELL

The time was early January. The hour, that numb, hollow-stomached one between night and morning. The temperature had fallen and what rattled now like birdshot against the windshield of the pickup truck was a mongrel wetness, neither sleet nor rain. The truck's headbeams—refracted, diffused—described the world as a transient spot of glazed blacktop road, five steps wide and narrower at the sudden bridges, broken under heavy wheels, heaved by frosts. The stream whose course the road traced could not be seen. Nor could the mountains. But those were sensed, always.

Five people were in the truck, going to meet a bus that would take them to the statehouse where, at noon, they were to see the governor of the Commonwealth of Kentucky. To them it was an errand of some importance.

A man with one eye. Another heavy-paunched, with legs crushed in an old mine accident, panting like a runner in the cold air. Those two riding behind, under a camper shell. In front, the heavy man's wife, another man, the oldest, whose left hand, burned in babyhood and bandaged tight by an unlettered mother, healed with the fingers grown to each other and to the palm itself—a defiant wad of a fist. And lastly the driver, a woman of forty-six who most mysteriously stopped aging in her thirties or possibly late twenties and may, in absolute fact, be getting younger, who is lovely, both actually and in ways presently to be discovered.

They are soldiers in an army. A curious army, as is evident, but an army nevertheless—not to be taken lightly either by the maximum leader of the Commonwealth or by the princes and sycophants in its lesser jurisdictions.

What follows concerns these people and their kinsmen and acquaintances, some of them from valleys across the mountain; also their communities—Lookout, Henry Clay, Hellier, Greenough, Allegheny—that neighbor in walking distance along a creek whose name is Marrowbone. Really, though, it is an account of political powerlessness and of consequent abuse—that which the people sometimes visit upon themselves and one another and on their land, but which more generally they suffer at the practiced hands of others.

In the end, it also testifies to the durability of decency and hope, two most amazing graces in these people. Not in all of them, but certainly in some.

So now, in a truck on a dark road, a part of the army was moving. The pickup's rear wheels slewed on the wet pavement at the turns, and the two men riding behind spread their hands palms-down on the cold metal to keep from being thrown. In front, the old man with the permanent fist was comforting himself, in a baritone gone reedy from his years and too many baby Roi Tans, with the words from an old Regular Baptist hymn. I am homesick now for heaven / For my mansions in the sky . . . *The windshield wiper swept the glass, revealing nothing. Edith Easterling—sometimes she is Tead Easterling and sometimes Johnny Bear—was impatient for salvation in nearer terms. She wore slacks and sturdy shoes. Her shoulders were bunched up inside her leather jacket as she fought the wheel. She was driving the truck like a man, driving it hard. There was a bus to catch, and she meant to be on it . . .*

I

The days in the valley are ordered by habit, as alike in most ways as shucky beans on a string. Before it is quite full light, Kermit Ratliff crawls from bed, his mending ankle stiff from sleeping, shakes the grate of the coal stove, and opens its draft. In a hundred other houses, night-banked stoves also are shaken. Plumes of brown smoke rise up and tremble in the dark breeze and ride away down the stream.

From the living room window Kermit sees a yellow light blink on three houses south and knows that his younger brother, Foster Ratliff, also is astir. He goes then to the kitchen, shakes the second stove and warms beside it, starts the coffee. Soon Vadney comes padding in in her blue robe and woolly slippers to make breakfast. Or sometimes, at Kermit's asking, Big Breakfast—a working man's morning meal that he no longer needs but craves in spite of that.

They eat in the stillness of the kitchen. The stove creaks. Across the railroad track, the galvanized colossus that is Lawrence Ratliff's general store shades from blue to silver in the growing light. Lawrence is first cousin to Kermit and Foster. The store's roof shelters also the U.S. Post Office, Lookout, Ky.

And now Foster can be seen coming from his house. He climbs the railroad embankment, crosses to the post office, unlocks the door, goes inside. He reappears with an American flag and puts the staff in its sprocket on the outer wall; goes inside again. A sudden cloud of saffron coal smoke belches from the post office chimney.

Kermit rinses his coffee cup and takes his coat and cane from beside the door. "I guess I'll see if there's any mail," he tells Vadney. It requires no response. Except Sundays, he will announce this—in these words and at this certain hour—every morning of his life. He goes carefully down the wooden porch steps and up across the tracks, eyes searching out little flat places, clear of pebbles, on which to place the foot that never stops hurting and never may.

Foster Ratliff's round face is as innocent as a boy's, but his hair has retreated to a silver wisp of a lock well back on his forehead. He has been postmaster since 1946, when he came home from the army. His father was postmaster before him for as long as anyone can remember.

Business is steady. There are money orders to be sold and recorded. There are the letters to and from the lost children of the Marrowbone who, on coming of age, went off to the factories of Cleveland and Chicago and Detroit City. There is the perpetual blizzard of paper, mostly form letters, between old miners and the government, old miners and their lawyers, lawyers and the government, the government and both lawyers and clients in duplicate. And there are the lesser gusts of tan envelopes, bearing the checks that result from all of this, that blow in with the mailbags and find their way back out again through the cage window.

Foster lives in his house across from the post office. His wife teaches school at Mullins some thirty miles away and lives with their children in her house there. On weekends Foster joins them. The arrangement makes for many silent hours. Two or three evenings a week he crosses to Kermit and Vadney's for supper, enjoying the talk but looking always away—at the floor, or wall, or something more distant than either.

If there is an error in his accounts he may need to go back again afterward, for Foster's books are stern masters. Sometimes he will mean to write one number but his hand, for no reason he can explain, will betray him and write another down instead. But there has never been a mistake he couldn't sooner or later find. Occasionally he will go to bed and it will come to him in a dream where the wrong number is, and he can go back in the morning and put his finger directly on it.

For twenty-five years, the faces outside Foster's cage window have been mostly the same ones. Although fewer. He cannot believe how quickly those years have gone.

Graying, aquiline, slightly stooped, Lawrence Ratliff waits in his aromatic cave. He waits, and they come—first to the post office and then the five steps to the door of his store. You would think it was obligatory.

The height of the shelves and the richness of their burden dominate all who enter. Magnificently the great hall recedes, almost to gloom. Tricycles perch in the dark upper reaches. Anything a general store might offer Lawrence Ratliff owns, and more. If it is not in sight it probably is in a

New morning, in the valley of the Marrowbone

back room. Food—tinned, bottled, and cellophaned. Clothes, plain and fancy. Hardware. Snuffs and chews in such variety and so handsomely packaged as almost to command a man to take up the habit.

The women patrol the long aisles with their lists and put what they select on the polished wooden counter. To be totaled, finally, and added to the account against the day when next the postmaster will put a tan envelope in the box. Lawrence takes only the most casual part in all of this. One or another of his ladies can do the waiting. He would rather hear the talk.

Midway back among the beetling shelves is a cleared space facing in upon a coal stove as tall as a man, with iron patches bolted against its sides. The men find places there, and their talk has a fitful morning cadence. In the waits between, bullets of clear or amber spit explode against the stove. The storekeeper sits with them, and listens. Behind his back, some of them will say that Lawrence Ratliff is a prying old man, a gossip. The charge is unjust. He does not pursue their secrets—they force them on him. All sides of every case are carried to that circle. Every damnation. Every possible defense. All schemes and counterschemes. The facts of an issue may be malleable but Lawrence Ratliff is constant, relishing a majestic neutrality.

They trade with him because they always have; because there is very little they need that he can't provide; because in the course of a year he will tender as much on trust as some banks do for collateral. And because they remember families, their own families sometimes, who kept on eating when there would be no check coming—and when Lawrence Ratliff knew there wouldn't.

These only happen to be Ratliffs, of whom by honest accounting—excluding children and the dead—no fewer than five hundred thirty may be found within two days by horse of this place, one day if the horse is exceptional. Enough that there is a hamlet called Ratliff farther down the Marrowbone.

And there are other sovereign names: Three hundred Bartleys. Thackers, three hundred seventy. Four hundred thirty Mullinses. Four hundred fifty Adkinses. Five hundred Tacketts. Colemans, six hundred of them. Justices, only ten fewer. And still others—Belcher, Childers, Compton, Damron, Keene, Maynard, Newsome, Slone—no less distinguished, only less prolific, that join them on the plaques of grimy monuments outside the county courthouse and on the pale stones in the numberless little hillside burying grounds.

Kermit Ratliff, disabled coal miner

Kermit's brother, Foster Ratliff, the postmaster of Lookout, Kentucky

Two of these cemeteries look down now on Kermit Ratliff as he makes his careful way from his cousin's store back to his house—one on each round shoulder of the hollow known as Poor Bottom, where it widens to empty its branch into the larger creek. A watery sun has crept over the hills that wall the valley, striking the grave markers luminous—the brightest objects on the landscape, brighter even than the postmaster's American flag.

In this country, the ones not yet dead are watched over always by the ones who are. The burying is done on high ground because, philosophically, it is nearer to salvation, and because, practically, it is safer from sudden flood. But there are worse things in the mountains these days than floods to molest the dead.

From the edge of Lookout, the broken skeleton of an old coal tipple can be seen spilling down the hill face behind the hamlet of Henry Clay. In the late thirties, more than a thousand men a day went under the mountain in the Henry Clay mine. As lately as thirty-seven years ago, there still were five hundred. Then one Tuesday in 1952, at the window where they received their wages in company scrip, not money, and in the little house where they drew their headlamps before going to the pit, those five hundred found a notice posted: *After Friday,* it said, *there will be no more work at this mine.* In 1960, three winding miles up the Marrowbone at the larger camp of Allegheny, a like notice appeared in the Blue Diamond mine.

The mine rats came out, lean as knives and so big the people could hardly believe they were rats. And with those moments of stricken disbelief, the modern history of this segment of the valley began.

Those who could, fled. Those who could not, waited. Sallie Jo Mooner still waits, and the single coal grate that heats her rented half of a clapboard camp house in Allegheny is a feeble thing against this raw morning.

Sallie Jo's childbearing has left her large—there were seven in twelve years, the youngest now six. And her troubles have left her plaintive and teary-eyed. At the start of this cold day, those troubles are several and specific. Her oldest boy, the eighteen-year-old, has just gone off to look for factory work in Chicago. The dangers waiting for him there terrify Sallie Jo. She has no food for the six still at home. To draw food stamps worth one hundred sixty-two dollars she needs ninety-six dollars in real money. An unimaginable sum. And even if she had that, she has no way to get the twenty-five miles to the county seat, Pikeville, where the stamps are issued.

Finally, her daughter Cassie is sick. The girl is fifteen, favoring her mother and inclined to her heaviness, but flattered by youth, with caramel brown hair. Already dressed, she bends cramping on the end of the bed, as near as possible to the warmth of the open grate. Probably it is only the flu. It might be appendicitis.

That is Sallie Jo Mooner's day.

At midpoint on the Marrowbone between Allegheny and Lookout is the other of the principal hollows, besides Poor Bottom, opening on the upper valley. Bowling Fork is its name.

For the Bartleys of Bowling Fork the daylight has not yet arrived—won't until midafternoon. In darkness they mounted a stony truck trail—Elmer Bartley, four sons, a nephew, and three others unrelated—and warmed briefly beside a coal stove in a shed. Then, except for the father, they started their cold machines and drove three-fifths of a mile down a gentle hill under the mountain.

The Bartleys are coal miners, by choice or because the alternatives, if there are alternatives, are not apparent. The fact, in either case, is that they enjoy—swear that they enjoy—their calling. It is a man's place under there. The talk is earthy, the company pleasant. True that the sweet after-smell of exploded dynamite can give a headache no aspirin will touch. And that the rock dust, floating solid white in the beams of their cap lamps when a drill is running, collects in their lungs, killing them just a little every day. But when you are still in your teens and twenties, conse-quences seem impossibly remote.

Six years the Bartley mine has tunneled deeper into the hill. They are working in the Elkhorn Number 1 coal seam, whose thickness here varies from thirty inches to five and one-half feet. As small mines go, it has been a productive and safe one. The top is sound. There is no gas. The coal is clean of rock.

Marvin Bartley, at twenty-eight the oldest of the sons and partner with his father, is the foreman underground. He is a tallish, lean, well-spoken man. And his talent for moving effortlessly in limited space is a gift not even he can explain. Head erect, body folded at the waist, hands clasped behind him like a skater, he can travel the mine the day long without tiring.

Thirty inches, understand, is lower slightly than the table at which you sit to eat. To see Marvin Bartley loping freely under a thirty-inch roof through a labyrinth of entries and galleries whose every turn is mapped in his mind is to apprehend a special sort of freedom and competence no man would easily give up. He will mine coal until breath fails or the mountain falls.

The four stood on the steps outside the bus station, which was locked at that hour, and waited for Edith to come back from parking the truck. The heavy man balanced on his ruined legs, blowing just from the effort of that. The rain still came, driving in under the little portico, and the people's breath jetted up white in the light from the door of the empty station. Edith returned then, and waited with them. A car pulled up. Two men got out and the driver went on.

"You two's all, Shine?" Edith asked.

"You see us. There's some more waiting in Allen, at the depot there."

The one called Shine was an immense, stately black man of fifty-six years who had brought his name and his soft accent from the coalfields of Alabama more than twenty years before. The other was white, two years older, puckish-faced, slight as a jockey, with a brown hat pulled down level across his eyes and a yellow feather in its band.

The hand of the clock inside on the station wall moved up toward the hour. And the army had grown now to seven.

II

She is in all ways a child of the mountains. She knows the hardship, the heartbreak, the violence there. She understands the greed and corruption of mountain politics. She is acquainted with the forces that have disfigured and would ultimately destroy the mountains themselves and those who dwell in them. What distinguishes Edith Easterling is the fierceness of her belief that she and people like her, acting on their own behalf, can somehow prevent this destruction. The evidence to date suggests that she is wrong.

The design of her life, not untypical: born a Coleman, the last of ten children; motherless at ten months; left high school after the second year; was married at nineteen to Jake Easterling, a man of thirty-one with five years of elementary schooling who went into the mines at fifteen, was crippled there at nineteen, but would load coal another twenty-nine years on that shattered, unbending knee; herself bore four children, three daughters and a son.

Those years slipped by, passive as dreams. Like the others of the valley, she rode with the cyclic collapses and revivals of the coal industry. She watched the courthouse jackals come up the Marrowbone on election day, their fists full of company money or union money, to buy the people's votes—votes that were freely for sale because the people did not much care which set of thieves ruled in Pikeville or in Frankfort.

She watched her man's health break like a mule's under impossible toil.

Edith Tead Johnny Bear Easterling, keeping dreams alive

Saw the valley's schoolchildren, those few who did stay on to graduate, come to the ceremony with their cardboard suitcases packed and bus tickets already in their pockets. Saw a once-powerful union turn craven and abandon its own. Watched strip mining begin its dismantlement of the landscape; heard the courts sanction it; watched the rivers turn first to acid sewers and then fill up with vagrant mountainsides.

When she was six, her stepmother sent her to school carrying a slip of paper with her name written on it. But she had always been only Tead or Johnny Bear, and when the teacher called Edith Coleman no one answered to the name. Today Tead Easterling knows who she is. And who she is mystifies and sometimes worries her children and her husband. Even, a little, her. Although they have all learned to live with it.

In the early 1960s, as periodically happens, the people of the Appalachian mountains were rediscovered by the federal government. Washington officeholders and their appointees ventured into the valleys and up the forgotten hollows. Legislation was passed. Funds were appropriated. Bands of young volunteers arrived, supported by the government or by their churches, armed with a general mandate to do good works. In years to follow, under various names and political sponsorship, the war on poverty in Appalachia would flicker on—and still does. But it is an ineffectual crusade. Poverty in the mountains is not the problem; it is a consequence of the problems. Much well-meant legislation missed the mark; much of the money it provided disappeared inside the county courthouses and was never seen again. Yet the exercise was not altogether without result. For if much that was promised was never received, something was received that wasn't promised—or even perhaps explicitly intended. The gift was an idea. An old idea, reborn and refined in the black South, whose power was irresistible and whose possibilities some of the mountain people began to grasp.

It was the simplest of theses: that the poor and the weak, behaving in concert, can make the guilty tremble. The degree to which certain other men despise and fear that notion was soon evident.

The symbol of the idea on Marrowbone creek is a squat thirty-by-fifty-foot cement-block building on the ledged bank of Poor Bottom just up from Edith and Jake Easterling's house. A hand-lettered sign beside the door identifies it as the Marrowbone Folk School.

In 1967, the problems seemed plain enough. The strip and auger miners had become the dominant political force in the county, perhaps in the state. At a rate the eye could measure daily, they were tearing the land apart, turning green mountains into a desolation of shattered stone and raw earth, uprooting the dead, sending glacial slides of ooze down upon the homes of anyone unlucky enough to live in the way. The timid courts and the captive politicians could not, or at least would not, prevent it.

But stripping was not the only affliction. Favoritism, cronyism, cynicism, nepotism, and every other nameable political vice infected government wherever it touched the people—law enforcement, welfare, school administration, county services. The United Mine Workers' union, once a mighty refuge, had become a flaccid thing, pocketing its royalties on stripped coal while the bulldozers made miners jobless.

It was all of a piece. And the exploiters were encouraged in their predations by the belief of many of the mountain people, learned and relearned through the generations, that it was pointless to hope for better. Anyone who sought to disabuse them of that idea became the enemy.

In 1967, the people of the Marrowbone tried to buy an unused school building on a hill outside Hellier for a meeting place. The owner, on quiet advice from the courthouse, changed his mind and refused to sell. The next day, the prosecuting attorney had three of the organizers arrested on charges of sedition. So the people built their own building, on that scrap of Easterling land up Poor Bottom. They raised two thousand dollars, and Edith, who was working, put her paychecks into the project. The band director from the high school at Elkhorn City, behind the mountain, helped with the work. It cost him his job.

When they opened the doors late that November, unlicensed cars rolled slowly past on the crumbling blacktop road up the hollow, turned, and came back again, noticing who entered. And the calls began. *Tonight's the big night*, soft voices would whisper on the telephone. So Edith and Jake Easterling bought insurance on the building. And she replied that, all right, damn them, if they dynamited it she would build it back.

As insurrections go, the one on the upper Marrowbone was mild enough. When someone had a complaint or a problem, the banked coal stove would be shaken and a meeting held. A hundred might come, or only ten. And in the slow, disjointed, independent fashion of mountain folk, they would consider the matter. There were weekly rummage sales of donated clothes—shoes for a quarter, dresses for a dime—so that the poorest of the children could go decently to school. There were books, so that the barely literate could improve that neglected skill. There were craft classes for the wives of jobless miners and the widows of dead ones. There was instruction for the people on the mechanics of obtaining from the leaden bureaucracy their rights as they understood them. There was a duplicating machine from which rolled an occasional newsletter, binding the valley together with items of interest about its own.

Such was the business the poor people were about.

There was another organization in the Marrowbone valley, or rather in Pikeville, from where the county was ruled. Its name was the Independent Coal Operators Association, and its money—the money from stripped coal—bought local politicians, bought favors from the capital, bought cooperation even from officials of the supine mine workers' union. The strip operators were not sure, exactly, what was going on inside that building up Poor Bottom Hollow. But an industry engaged in turning mountains into mud banks is well advised to fear the intentions of the people who live on those mountains. At very least, it was fair to guess the troublemakers at the Marrowbone Folk School were in some way hooked up with the Reds.

The president of Pikeville College had been indiscreet enough to let a group called Save the Land and the People hold meetings on college property to protest strip-mine destruction. Then the president's wife went up on Marrowbone to give sewing classes to the Godlesscommunist ladies at the Folk School. The college trustees had had enough. They ran a total on their endowments from prosperous strippers and concluded that the president had better resign. He did, and took a job fighting poverty for the federal government.

[Much later, with a fury he is at no pains to conceal, Dr. Thomas Johns will remember the events of those days—the verbal and physical punishment inflicted on his children. The obscene telephone calls, and the threatening ones: *Your wife better not go back up that hollow or she'll get run off the road.*

The fifth man in as many years to be thrust into the snakepit of the college's top job, he had found the institution enmeshed in a county patronage system. To break that, he put work contracts out for open bid and disregarded local political advice on faculty appointments. Black student enrollment was increased. Active recruiting was begun among youngsters of the poorer families, and funds were raised privately to assist them.

Where Dr. Johns sinned most grievously was in believing that the college should concern itself with the problems of the region. Because, ultimately, that concern would lead up hollows like Poor Bottom and to the issue of strip mining itself. In coal country, explosives are freely available and their use well understood. Toward the last of his two-year tenure, Dr.

Johns was taping the hood of his car at night so that he would know if anyone had been under it while his family slept.]

Finally there was the affair of the running water. County tax money had been appropriated for a system to serve the Marrowbone. But the people of the upper valley, led by that Easterling woman and her neighbor, Uncle Jim Hamilton, an upstart preacher man with a gravel voice and a shiny club for a hand, had come forth with a most impudent idea. They demanded a voice for the people of Marrowbone in the selection of water commissioners to operate the system.

Justice was swift. Edith Easterling and Jim Hamilton spent two days at the county courthouse, defending themselves against the Kentucky Un-American Activities Committee's assumption that public protest of any sort must be Communist-inspired. State law provided for such inquisitions. And no matter that the hearing droned on to no conclusion at all, KUAC and the county had the last word.

The water line would wait years to be built.

The station clock said five past seven. Then ten past. Tead Easterling had borrowed a dime from one of them and was talking long-distance to the person who paid for the charter.

"We're here," she said. "It's cold and raining and we're on the outside. And there isn't no bus."

Inside the station, a young man filled a coffee pot and set it brewing, peering curiously through the glass at the people on the wet steps. Then the pay phone rang back, the sound of it startling along the dark street. The others blew into their hands, waiting. She hung up.

"Says the bus was comin' out of Charleston," she told them, "and it ought to been here by now." The young man came and unlocked the station door and they went inside to the warmth.

Jake Easterling misses mining—misses it worse than anything except his wife when she is away.

He is a proud man, a man who in his working days regularly led the sheet in mines where there were several hundred loaders. They shoveled coal by the ton then, before machines and flat shift wages. A dollar fifty for each ton-and-one-half car. He could load twenty or twenty-five cars in a day and be out of the mine early. And on one day, a Saturday it was—he is seeing now every detail of the smoothness of the floor, the quality of the coal, the safeness of the roof, as clearly as an aging ball player remembers the color of sky and crowd and the name of the pitcher against whom he struck the winning hit—on that day he put thirty-six loaded cars on the track outside the mine, one hundred eight *thousand* pounds of coal. And then went out and stood looking down that string of cars and had to marvel himself at what one man with a shovel could do.

But on another day, on an afternoon when he had finished his turn, Jake Easterling got a queer feeling and the nails of his fingers turned blue. And the doctor told him he had mined his last car of coal.

This morning the coal trucks are coming loaded down the Poor Bottom road from the top of Caney Mountain, and he remembers how hard it was those first years, sitting by the lane, seeing that coal still coming out and knowing he wasn't any part of it. He tried once to go back, wasted down to one hundred forty-five pounds on his six-foot frame. "But I couldn't make the coal go in the car," he recalls, astonished by it even yet. "Couldn't *hit* it, y'see. I knew how to do it—what I wanted to do. But my body wouldn't do it." So they told him to go home.

With their daughters married away and their son, Jake Danny, in an auto mechanics' school at Paintsville, sixty miles north, the idle days get long. He puts on his wool plaid coat and limps across to the Folk School, the arthritis like a knife in his crippled knee, and tends the stove to keep the pipes from freezing. Pasteboard boxes full of shoes and wadded clothes for the next rummage sale are stacked about on chairs and on the floor. A coal truck comes past outside on the ribbon of asphalt, geared-down and braked to a cautious crawl under its twenty-ton burden.

Jake locks the building and turns behind the truck down Poor Bottom. To the post office first, then the store. And then across to Kermit and Vadney's. Vadney is his wife's older sister. Kermit is not there. One of the envelopes in his box that morning was from his lawyer, saying that further medical evidence was required for one or another of Kermit's disability claims. He has gone around the mountain to a doctor in Elkhorn City, and that will take the day. Jake goes back up the Poor Bottom road.

He moves deliberately, husbanding each half-drawn breath. Another truck rumbles down by him. The mist hangs like smoke against the high flank of Caney Mountain, where the coal is coming from. It pleases Jake Easterling to know that his son, who has never gone inside a mine or ever wanted to, will be something besides a miner. But for himself—in ways that don't come easily to words—he misses it. Terribly.

Sallie Jo Mooner is also at a doctor's—one in Pikeville. It turned out that Edith, in the night, though having business herself with the governor, had found someone to drive Sallie Jo and her sick girl. When the man appeared, he was carrying Edith's ninety-six-dollar check for the Mooners' food stamps.

On the winding ride down Marrowbone toward the highway—past Lookout and Rockhouse and Wolfpit and Regina, past the bootlegger's place and the Southland Bible Institute and Conley Tackett's store to the flowering of used car lots, coin laundries, and dairy bars that announced Pikeville ahead—Sallie Jo had tended her moist eyes with a handkerchief and cataloged her afflictions.

She was husbandless these five years now. Her man had taken up with a younger girl—a girl with no husband herself and nine children living and several others dead, all fathered by no one she could name. *"I just couldn't understand that, him a-layin' with her and knowin' what kind of woman she was. So I had to get rid of him."* (The girl, Cassie, riding behind, white with her own pain but hearing that, and, worse, hearing it without surprise.) Money was a problem, always a problem. The banished husband was supposed to pay a hundred twenty dollars a month child support, but he'd left the state and the money came only occasionally. Her rent had gone up. The outdoor toilet collapsed and she asked the landlord to fix it. He did, then raised the rent on her half of a house from twenty-five dollars to thirty.

"I've been worried terrible. My boy goin', 'an now her sick. Why, all the food I've eat this week wouldn't fill yer hand." Lonely in her barren house, with even her youngest now in school, she thinks sometimes she would like to have another baby for the company it would be. "But I don't guess I will," she had said. "I'll not get married again, so I guess I'm done havin'."

Edith Easterling is Sallie Jo's loving angel. It was Edith who gave her money so that there would be a Christmas dinner; who brought toys so the smaller ones would have something to open; whose own check lay safely inside Sallie Jo's imitation patent purse. The completeness of this dependence shames her. But she has a way of justifying it.

"Edith, now—" she had said. "Edith's got no worries. Her children's all done good an' she don't have to worry about much. Anyway, it gives her somethin' to do."

Now morning has passed into afternoon, and Sallie Jo, immense in her vicuna-colored pile coat, is still waiting with her daughter in the outer room of the doctor's upstairs office. They are thirty-fourth on the list of waiting patients, and they are lucky to have chairs. Some have to stand. A woman Sallie Jo knows inquires about Cassie, wondering if it mightn't be the girl is only wormy. That opens a field of discussion that is at once familiar and theoretical. Others join in. One worms her brood on a regular schedule. Another has heard that only a child who *drops* worms should get the treatment. But the one who began the discussion is a firm believer. She wormed one of hers thirty-five times, she says, and never did see a worm.

"Lawd, buddy," Sallie Jo tells them—tells the room—"when I wormed mine they came out of 'em in bunches big as fists. They was ate up with 'em." Helpless, Cassie blushes scarlet through her pallor.

The first woman moves to share the seat of her chair with her grandson. She also shares with him her Kool Filter King, from which he takes long, lung-satisfying pulls, exhaling through his nose. He is a sweet-faced towhead, two months past his seventh birthday. His mother catches him at it.

"Kirby," she shouts, "you put that down or I'll wear you out." He takes a last drag and passes it back to his grandmother. "Oh, he's terrible after 'em," the mother tells the others. "Them and cigars—he likes them little cigars best."

It will be past three o'clock before Cassie has her five-minute audience with the healer; another hour before she is admitted to the hospital, from which she will emerge on the third day, much improved in spite of having had no treatment or medicine of any sort. Mountain doctors are very busy, and the curative powers of youth and a warm bed are not to be discounted.

Heavy-lidded and angry, Kirby has retired to a corner of the room. He is striking book matches and dropping them in a spring-top ashtray. "Burn, buddy," he is whispering to the matches, but they always go out when he lets the lid snap closed.

The posters on the flaking station walls told them all the places they might go. The Golden Gate bridge against a flaming sunset. An Eskimo totem on a field of lichens. Disneyland rampant. The dome of the Capitol in Washington, bathed in a frosty blue light. But where they wanted to go was Frankfort. They waited and watched the morning come, hemmed around by a bewilderment of amenities. Jukebox, two pinball machines, a pay toilet with a dime slot on its outer door, an empty popcorn vendor, a candy bar machine with an aquarium bubbling on its top.

The outside phone rang again, and Edith went to answer. The goldfish made impatient turns against the slimy glass, waiting for the young man to come with their breakfast.

"We just as soon go on home," she told them then. "There's no bus comin'. Dispatcher in Ashland said he forgot."

"Forgot!" Shine snorted. The others snickered with him.

"Well, that's what money does," Edith said. "Pore people's always left on the corner, aren't they?" So the army withdrew, back down the wet street to where Edith had parked the truck. The heavy man stopped under an awning to get his breath, his wife beside him.

"When that bus got to be twenty minutes late," he told her, "I said to myself, 'Oh-oh. Look out!' "

Through the blue afternoon Kermit Ratliff has come home from the doctor's, carrying in his pocket a piece of paper with certain numbers and abbreviations written on it whose meaning he does not understand, but which, taken together with all the other papers he has collected, might serve to prove what his weakness and breathlessness already tell him.

Instead of turning now across the cement bridge over the Marrowbone into Lookout he drives straight on half a mile to Henry Clay, to the big brick building that used to house the offices of the Henry Clay Mining Company. The company has been gone nearly twenty years, but in the basement a light is burning.

There, under a weak fluorescent tube, A. M. "Happy" Taylor cuts the hair of men he knows and of the sons of those he used to know. His long face is pale from want of sun and somber as a funeral mask, and he is wearing as ragged a haircut himself as is likely ever to be seen on a man. Some of these heads he has been tending for thirty-five years, but his art has not become mechanical. He still approaches each one deliberately. There is a suggestion of uncertainty in his manner, even of awe, as if he had been commanded to carve a statue with a penknife. He gives the full dollar's worth.

A youth is in the chair now, flattop with ducktails. Happy Taylor circles the chair, considering what he is about to do. Kermit will be next, and after him two miners who have just come in. There are stacks of yellowed magazines, but no one reads. The sound of their breathing fills the silence, broken by the sudden little snarls of Happy's electric shears.

One of the miners thinks of something that has happened since he was last in. It happened while he was shoveling coal dust from under the belt conveyor in the mine where he works, around the mountain near Elkhorn City.

"I was throwin' that dust," he tells them, "and here this arm rolled up out'n it and, *lawd, man*—I felt the skin start crawling right down my back." The teller is Junior Scott, a neighbor of Kermit's just across the creek in Lookout. "I've seen men kilt," he confesses, "but I never seen nothin' shook me up that bad. I mean, when you feel that skin go to movin' and a-crawlin', then, buddy, *that's scared.*"

The point is considered. Happy Taylor works up lather in a shaving cup and brushes it over the boy's ears, up onto the ducktails. The slap of razor against strap is loud in the stillness. Turning on a nearer naked bulb for this fine work, he leans close, hesitates, draws back. He has developed hiccoughs. His shoulders jerk with them. The boy in the chair looks sideways to see if he is hearing what he thinks he is hearing.

"Beltline caught him," Junior Scott says, "an', buddy, it tore that arm clean off. I knowed who it was. Knowed that by the wristwatch. But what I didn't know was where the *rest of him* was. Turned out he'd clumb up on the beltline an' rode it on out."

The barber's seizure has passed and he leans in with the razor again.

"But you know," Junior says, "he took that awful good—good as anybody I ever seen. They said when he come out he just swung off the beltline and asked 'em, 'Any you boys see a fine arm come out with that coal?' "

What wonder, then, that after thirty-five years Happy Taylor has lost the power to smile?

Still in his black suit and hat, Uncle Jim Hamilton comes out of Lawrence Ratliff's general store and turns up Poor Bottom toward Edith's house. He marches small and straight, the sleeve with the club fist in it slapping against his trouser leg in agitation.

"I been to Lawrence's store," he tells Edith. "An' you know what Lawrence said? He tole me, 'Why, I knowed last night that bus of yours wasn't a-gonna run.' "

III

Adventurers tell, with whatever truth, of certain secret places where old elephants, most singular marvels of creation, gather to leave their bones in the African sun. In a manner less mysterious but no less unerring, the mountains of Appalachia are where the American motor car goes to die. Automobile carcasses, after the mountains themselves, are in fact the principal feature of the landscape.

Great gunmetal-gray Buicks, imposing as machines of war. The ubiquitous Chevies. Nashes with their naked rims aloft. A plague of thrown rods and shattered pistons and stripped gears has swept the land. And as in the Middle Ages after a scourge of pox or bubonic, it is pointless even to speak of burial when the dead are so numerous. In the summer, with the foliage out, some of the corpses are hidden. But when late autumn comes and the oaks and poplars drop their leaves, they are revealed again—lodged among the trees on the side slopes of the hollows, gleaming in the distance even on the high faces of wild gorges where, absent any road to push them down from or any conceivable means of carrying them up, they abide in wonder like that leopard frozen in the snows of Hemingway's mountain.

And there are other pollutants. Each day, on the winding stretch of blacktop from Lookout to the mouth of the Marrowbone, the ladies of the valley can be seen coming out with their baskets and sacks. They have finished their morning's cleaning. Inside, their houses are in order. They pause in the winter sun beside the road to visit, as ladies will. And then they cross over the blacktop and with the deftness of long habit fling the leavings of the last day down into the soupy waters of the creek where they flow among rusted car fenders, lodged tires, rotted mattresses, and discarded refrigerators.

Up the side hollows it still is possible to see the occasional outhouse, a sturdy edifice and well maintained, whose backside—where the seat holes are—is cantilevered directly out over the flowing branch.

Yet, all considered, the scale of these casual defilements—even the stricken and discarded cars—is small when measured against the land. And what men have fouled through habit, ignorance, or lack of public services, men can also, through law, recycling, and their own enterprise, eventually clean up.

Joe Coleman, who was one of Edith and Vadney's brothers, was no gilded saint. Vadney will tell you that.

"He could use his fists"—and this admiringly—"the best of any man I ever seen. I don't say that just because he was my own brother, either. Why, he would cut his hands all to pieces on a man's head. He was a fighter, Joe was. But yet, in another way, he was kind of a 'commodating sort of man."

In 1962, the Corps of Engineers arrived in the valley of the Levisa Fork, northeast of Lookout and the Marrowbone, to build a dam called Fishtrap. Its purpose was to control the damaging floods on streams whose watersheds had been scalped for timber and whose beds were choked by mountainsides dislodged by the strip miners. The contractor arrived with his own force of laborers. To the local mountain men—men of a region whose industry had died, who were agreeable to hard work but had no jobs or prospect of any—that seemed unjust.

Seventy-five or a hundred of them gathered one morning, Joe Coleman

Poor Bottom on a frozen day, choked with ice and worse

leading, and went up to the contractor's shack at the dam site to treat for jobs. Now Joe Coleman had once been to the penitentiary for biting a man's ear off, and a thing like that causes a fellow's reputation to precede him. When he walked into the shack, they were waiting with a gun. What transpired next was argued in the courts. The fact is that Joe Coleman was carried out dead.

It is unlikely the briefing officer mentioned that anecdote to Lyndon Johnson when he flew down in the autumn of 1968 to dedicate the dam. Neither, probably, did anyone ever bother to tell the late president what soon began happening to the reservoir itself, created at a cost of fifty-six million dollars of the public's money. What is happening to Fishtrap is the same thing that happened to the streams it was built to tame. It is filling up with mud bulldozed from the hills, at an astonishing rate.

In assembling the lands for Fishtrap, the government settled for control only of surface rights to the watershed. And the mining continued, under a set of controls that the government itself soon discovered to be shockingly inadequate. The price of that original parsimony is paid anew with each spell of heavy rain. Areas of new siltation are recorded, as they occur, on a map in the control house. A shaded portion tells where a silt bank replaced a thousand feet of one stream arm in the flood of 1970. And here—more shaded areas—are the acres lost in 1971. In the worst places, a single downpour has been known to bring a foot of mud cascading down off hills ripped open by dynamite and power shovel.

Now, at midday, a bitter north wind rakes down the lake and across the catwalk overlooking the water. Below, bulldozed and blast-shattered trees are rafted against the face of the dam, carried in by the week's rains. From time to time, the four reservoir employees go out in open motorboats to herd the worst of the flotsam to shore for burning. But it is an endless job. They are trying to clean an Augean stable with a toothbrush.

Vadney Ratliff once, shortly after it was opened, went up to the dam—to the place where they killed her brother—to see what it had all come to. There had been rains then, too. The rushing waters had scoured the trash-cluttered creeks—Becky Run, Simms Creek, Elkfoot Branch, Feds Creek, and the others—flowing down beside hill houses and through settlements to empty into the impoundment. She remembers above all the Clorox bottles. Nothing but blue plastic bleach bottles floating from the foot of the dam as far as the eye could reach. It was, she says, a sight on earth to behold.

Vadney is a woman of quiet humor and quiet loneliness. Her laughter bubbles easily, then subsides into long, pensive stillnesses. But even in repose she often smiles a small, secret smile. She knows there are things to be thankful for. Her home is hers. It is modern, with a bathroom Kermit built when they remodeled what had been an old camp house. Her washer and dryer are hers, too. They owe no one. She and the others like her along the valley—the thrifty, careful ones—have snatched for themselves a little piece of the dream. But it was gotten hard, and it is kept precariously.

The uncertainty was the cruelest thing. A miner's working life is short. His arm, or the rest of him, might come out with the coal on the conveyor. Or a slate rock bigger than a piano might let go soundlessly from the top. And his shift mates, after they had broken the rock away, would collect what they could of him with a shovel. A woman lived with the dread, above all else, of seeing a man from her husband's mine come alone down the road to her house. The most terrible messages arrived that way.

Kermit is napping now on the couch, as he does nearly every afternoon, his foot in its elastic stocking arranged carefully on a cushion. His arm, where it was shattered and then mended with steel pins, is blue with coal dust healed in under the scar. He is small and gray in sleep—so many of the miners are really slight men, for all the heavy muscling of their upper bodies.

Apart from his shortness of breath, those were his two hurts. The arm was the first. When that happened, Vadney and their older daughter, Phyllis, went up to Cleveland—the younger daughter, Don Reeda, was already married then—and found factory work until Kermit was well enough to mine again. Then they came back to the Marrowbone, to Lookout, and accumulated the things they have. When Kermit's ankle was broken, she knew that he would never work another shift in the mines.

Each week, for a little time yet, a fifty-seven-dollar unemployment check will come in the mail. It is possible that out of all the X-rays that have been taken and all of his shuttlings between doctors and lawyers and the post office, Kermit will be awarded state or federal compensation. But Vadney, being of a skeptical nature, does not dwell on those possibilities. She has learned not to worry—tries not to let herself, at least—about things she can do nothing about. The laws that compensate miners for their disability are among these things.

She can only be prudent with what she has. She is keeping her old wringer washer and its tubs in the shed behind the house. The automatic one that she bought when Kermit was mining still works fine. But she knows that if it wears out, with no check coming in, she will never own another.

Old miners remember. They remember the hurts and the maimings, the dead friends, the coal they loaded in bad light and stale air for twenty cents a ton before the union came. But as they talk, they almost forgive these things—just as they try to forgive the coughs that wrack them and the nights that they sleep sitting up to keep from suffocating with their crippled lungs.

Because what they remember more than all else, in the end, is the pride of having done it.

"That mine I was in," Jake Easterling is saying, "the ambulance came every day. And some days it came two or three times. Man would go by on a motor and say, 'So-and-so got his self killed a while ago'—a friend of yours. Hearing that would just about knock a fellow down. It sure would."

That's what he starts to tell. But then he recalls that the coal in a certain place came out clean and of a good size for shoveling, that there were plenty of cars. Remembers warming to the work—really *fanning* that coal, as he says. And that his name had led the sheet that half-month, and the next half, and the next.

And the same with Uncle Jim Hamilton, wreathed in cigar smoke and sunk into his chair in front of the open grate.

"Nobody knows," he says, "what this old man has went through with— not even my children. Many's the time I've run two hundred, three hundred feet through places so low you had to run stooped over—me a-runnin' for my life an' that mountain h'it a-comin' down." Once the mountain caught him, or part of it. A slate fall in the Henry Clay mine tore eight ribs loose from his backbone, broke four others in front, broke an ankle and his jaw.

"Biggest part of the time, though, I could tell when it was a-comin'. I'd tell 'em, on a Friday, say, 'Boys, better get yer 'quipment out and pull yer steel, for she'll be down by Monday sure.' An' they'd do it, too. They knowed I wasn't very often wrong. An' *load coal*—" He snatches up his shovel from beside the fire, showing how the heel of the handle had been cut away to make a yoke for his scarred fist.

"That's how I done it, with my cripple hand agin the handle like that. An', son, they wasn't nobody went under that hill could load any more coal than this ole man did."

Kermit Ratliff, too, risen from his nap on the couch, has driven up Marrowbone to Bowling Fork and the house of a friend with whom he was raised and mined coal. Delbert Bartley at fifty-five is two years younger than Kermit, but he might be seventy. A shock of unruly white hair rises above a face that does not mask his delight for company. He has been disabled two years now with black lung, exiled from the only work he knows. Delbert Bartley began mining in 1934, and remembers his wage to the dime. It was two dollars and eighty cents a day in that mine.

"I worked ten days to make twenty-eight dollars," he tells Kermit. "But that boy of mine, now, he makes twenty-eight dollars every day—and he hasn't been in the mines but about two years."

That boy is Estil Bartley, not yet twenty-one. He was born a twin to his sister, Destil. For a long time people just called them Boy Bartley and Girl Bartley. A good many still do.

Boy Bartley went off to Carolina out of high school and ran a loom in a textile mill. But when his father was turned out of the mines disabled, Boy Bartley came home to work for his Uncle Elmer in the little mine up Lick Branch below the house, driving an electric car that pulls the four-ton wagons up loaded from the face of the coal to the driftmouth.

He likes driving a *motor*, as the machine is called—likes driving almost anything. Its actual speed may be ten miles an hour, or less, even. But as he flies down the long incline into the heart of the mountain, ducking to clear the low places in the top, the walls flashing past in the side glow of his headlamp, there is a fabulous sense of motion.

Soon Boy will be leaving again, maybe back to Carolina, maybe some-place else. It is good, he thinks, to be away on your own. "But I'll miss the mines," he says softly, as he says everything. "I shore enough will, buddy."

Boy Bartley, on days when he is not driving his motor under the moun-tain, drives his truck or one of his two cars on top of the mountains. It passes the time until Monday, when he can go back up Lick Branch and haul coal again. This day it is his pickup truck, an older one but sound, its lug tires clawing and sliding up a gobby, half-frozen trail. There, on the very top, is a rolling grassy place called the Flatwoods, a natural park a mile or more long and a half-mile wide, threaded through with foot trails, where for as long as these mountains have been settled people have come to picnic and boys have brought girls for loving. On a hummock in a grove of pines there's a cemetery with a dozen stones. One of the graves is fresh, yellow earth crumbling and bright plastic flowers beaded wet.

Someday they will come to strip the Flatwoods for coal. There's said to be a fourteen-foot seam underlying all this. Boy Bartley gets down from the truck and kicks the earth with his shoe. Just kicks it, and the coal rolls up black in the wet grass ahead of his toe.

Uncle Jim Hamilton, with a shiny club for a hand and an angry heart

On a clear day there at the top, a map of the country unfolds below, but now mist clouds are lapping white against the side of the mountain, parting to slide around it, hiding the valleys. Boy Bartley turns the truck back down the way he came, stopping at an overlook below the lowest clouds.

"Lookit there," he says, and has to whistle to himself. "They're tearing that mountain *all to pieces.*"

The technique of it, the engineering prowess implied by a feat of such scale, the machinery itself—none of these is visible at that distance. Only the consequences. Boy Bartley has parked on the very lip of a dizzying ravine. Across a gaping reach of distance is the mountain he means. But it is not a mountain any longer; it is a mesa—its side remade in shelves and verticals, a step-pyramid with its top removed.

And down the side of that has come the mud, glacial in proportions. A flow of sterile muck not to be measured by the foot but by the quarter-section of frontage. So large that the gullies eroded in it are themselves considerable terrain features, carrying foul streams of a size almost to deserve naming.

Down reaches all that—eight hundred feet, a thousand—down to the bed of Sycamore Creek, which vanishes entirely under the slide and comes out the lower side as a snaking, ocher ribbon. Having ceased to be water and become some other substance, the stream would most certainly stop flowing if the valley were less steep. By gravity's persuasion it oozes on, toward its meeting with Elkhorn Creek, and thence, a bit diluted, to Russell Fork, and north on that to the Levisa Fork, mingling all the while with the ruins of other hillsides in torpid suspension.

Boy Bartley's eyes, pale and neutral, traverse the hideousness.

Indeed, there is a kind of magnificence about it. The grandeur of sheer size—of blitzed cathedrals, of killing grounds after the battle has passed on, of nuclear clouds over coral atolls. From the lip of that ravine it is possible to understand that a rusted automobile, or many, a mere Clorox bottle—or all of them made or to be made—are as nothing alongside a sundered mountain.

They are carelessness; this is a virtuosity. They deface what is. But this *changes* what is—creates new facts for eternity's contemplation. One stands humbled before it, hating what one sees and yet feeling somehow privileged to have been present in the very hour of cataclysm.

Boy Bartley whistles softly again, then climbs in and lets the truck roll on down in gear.

Home now from his visit, Kermit Ratliff is plagued by the ankle, which aches and itches at once. Having scratched it red, he is soaking it in a pan of salts on the kitchen floor. In the living room, the television is droning as it usually does, unheard, unwatched. A conservationist and a spokesman for the strip-mine industry are arguing their differences in technical terms—feet of overburden, degree of slope.

The law is satisfactory the spokesman says. In the past, some harm was done. But the technology of strip mining has changed. The age of reclamation has arrived. The land is safe.

The open face that stares out unwatched into the Ratliffs' living room, the brow so concerned, the eyes so wide and unblinking—surely that can only be the face of an honest man.

IV

When the hill people look at the town, they see a walled citadel of power and privilege. When the town looks back at the mountains, along the crooked streams and up those silent hollows, it sees dark mysteries of fecklessness and deliberate want. They are alien countries, bound together not by treaty or even by law but by coal, their common noun.

Wake on a still morning in a hotel room fronting on Main Street somewhere in coal country. Listen. And know that you will remember always the sound that is the first to announce the day. The sound of men coughing. Not the barky after-rattle of some winter complaint. A different sound. Measured, patient. Coughs uttered in careful anticipation of all the ones to follow, without relief or any expectation of it. The sound of ruined lungs trying to expel *themselves.*

The men are standing on the walk below the window in pairs and threes. And across, in front of the bank. And others farther down. Some with fingers gone or hands entirely; bent spines remembering the weight of slate rocks; and all their faces an unhealthy gray, with pallor under it, if that can be imagined. Their mouths move, but no sound of talking comes up to the window. Only the coughs. So used to it are they that their shoulders scarcely jerk.

A miner is coming directly from his shift to the bank, the dust still on his clothes and a check fluttering in his hand, his wife behind him with a child clamped by the wrist. They disappear inside, come out again. He is holding money now and they divide it, there on the sidewalk, counting from one to the other.

A pickup truck rattles past along the street, carrying a tombstone braced with timbers in its bed. They turn, all of them—the miner and his wife, the men talking in front of the stores—to see if they know the name on the stone.

Burying—the deliberate kind, as opposed to the accidental—is the certainest thing in a coal miner's life, and mining people try to send their men off properly. Some of them buy burial insurance. Others settle it in installments in advance. Brafford "Boot" Hall, operator of a Pikeville mortuary, does from a hundred thirty-five to a hundred fifty funerals in a year. The price can range from two hundred ninety-nine dollars to six thousand, but Hall feels duty bound to steer his clients to a plan that suits their means.

"Half or more of the men we get are miners or retired miners. I'd say two-thirds of them are pretty badly mutilated," Hall says. "That means a lot of plastic surgery. But we hardly ever close a casket. We keep 'em open, even if it does mean a little extra work."

Boot Hall is a tall, dignified man with silver hair, and he is proud of his town, his country.

"This Appalachia stuff!" he snorts. "There's been a lot of nonsense written. Oh, sure, like anywhere, we've got a certain number of people up those hollows who live in poverty. Who'd do it no matter what you give 'em. But, listen—"

Boot Hall leans near, himself touched by the wonder of it.

"—it's *inherited*," he says, whispers almost. "They pass it on, from mother and father to sons and daughters. And so forth. All the way down through that whole generation."

For many coal miners not yet ready, quite, for Boot Hall's services, the most important place in town is a low, glass-fronted building just up Second Street from the mortuary—the district office of the Social Security Administration. It is there that a miner files claim to federal disability payments for a crippling injury or applies for black-lung benefits.

The ailment known as black lung is unique to underground miners. Its proper name is coal workers' pneumoconiosis, and its effect, after years of breathing mine air freighted with coal dust, is to destroy the lungs' capacity to nourish the bloodstream with oxygen, leading often to acute pulmonary and cardiac failure. To perish from black lung is literally to suffocate to death.

In the first two years after passage of the 1969 Federal Coal Mine Health and Safety Act, some thirteen thousand claims for black lung disability were received by the Pikeville office, processed and transmitted to Bal-

timore for a decision by the Bureau of Disability Insurance. Two applicants were turned down for every one approved for benefits.

To the stricken man in the head of some distant hollow, turned out of the
mines for fainting too often, it is of limited interest that it was some face-
less committee in Baltimore that judged him sound. His application was
made to the office in Pikeville. And it is there, he believes, that his
enemies are to be found—allied, most probably, with the courthouse politicians. In fact, the thirty-two employees of the district Social Security
office all are federal civil servants, beyond the political reach of the courthouse or even the statehouse. And senior among them, on this particular
day, is Emory Reaser, the assistant district manager. Reaser is a big man,
prematurely graying at thirty-seven, who looks both athletic and stu-
dious—"A mountaineer from the sticks," he calls himself, "just like these
people are," married to a coal miner's daughter. The breathless sufferer
up the hollow, full of bitterness, would be astonished to meet Emory
Reaser and find that he is a decent man, a man to be trusted beyond any
doubt.

"As far as we're concerned here," he says, "they *all* qualify—every one
of them that applies. But no decisions are made at this office at any stage.
We only help them gather the information and the documents. And even
that isn't easy. You can't do business here like you can in a city. In a city, if
you had a question, you'd just pick up a phone and call. But a lot of our
people don't have phones. So you write to them, but maybe they can't
read the letter or else they don't understand what it means. And they lay it
aside and wait until the next time they come down from the hollow into
town.

"*Time,*" Reaser says. "It just takes time. Then, too, these people don't
trust government. If they did, our job would be a whole lot easier. They're
just leery of any government."

Part of the distrust stems from the very intricacy of the law itself. For
purposes of compensation, there are considered to be two stages of black
lung, simple and complicated, each with three subcategories of severity. If
the diagnosis by X-ray is of complicated pneumoconiosis, category C,
then somebody had better be paying up the burial policy and alerting Boot
Hall that his attendance will shortly be required. Any benefits due that
miner likely will be spent by his widow. Categories B and A of complicated black lung, descending in order of severity, also are compensatable
on the evidence of X-ray alone.

Simple pneumoconiosis—whether category one, two, or three—is
another matter. The precise formula for arriving at the final judgment,

balancing X-ray evidence against a mechanical breathing test, the latter correlated to size, weight, age, and other pertinent factors, is, by Emory Reaser's confession, beyond the capacity of even the educated layman to comprehend. That it confuses and angers men who left school for the coal pits at age fifteen should come as no small surprise to the government.

What the applicants do know is that there are some men drawing black-lung benefits who almost nightly follow coon dogs in wild races over dark ravines. That others, with as many as a dozen doctors testifying to their desperate complaint, reeling and choking as they walk, unable to speak a simple phrase without stopping to gasp for air, do not draw a dime. Because acquaintances in the mountains are lifetime ones and secrets hard to hide, they know of men who never set foot inside a mine portal and yet, by cunning or because of political connections, got on the black-lung rolls. They know others, many times denied while living, who were found on autopsy to have died of black lung's effects and whose widows were subsequently paid. The logic of that escapes them. And the justice.

Emory Reaser is aware that the gap of understanding between the office in Pikeville and the people of the hollows is wide. He knows that, in the minds of many, he is the enemy. And because he is a decent man, he is plainly troubled by that. He finds refuge in his certainty that the screening process is an accurate one. "The reason that these miners are being denied," he says, "is because, medically, they just don't qualify."

He does believe that—*must* believe it. Because even to suspect anything else would make the burden of his responsibilities insupportable.

Others are not similarly convinced, among them some of the coalfields' doctors.

"The fault," one of these declares flatly now, "is in the law." Fatigue can make a man arbitrary, and the doctor's weariness hangs on him like a coat.

Like Reaser, Dr. Paul LeRoy Odom is thirty-seven years old. His hair is receding over his forehead. His tie is loose at the collar. Paul Odom has a practice of fifteen thousand patients—mostly the very young and the very old—and yesterday one hundred thirty of those came through the office. He saw the last one at three o'clock in the morning, fell onto the bed for four hours, and was back at the clinic at eight. Briefly now, in late afternoon, the waiting room is empty.

"The black-lung law," he says, "places too much emphasis on the breathing test. A man can have forty years in the mines. He can be in the second category of black lung—can wheeze, smother, bring up sputum, not be able to walk across that street out there. But if he blows into the machine and does not demonstrate by that one test that he is totally disabled, then he doesn't qualify.

"An X-ray isn't a precise tool, either. If the man has worked underground, the chances are that what you see on that picture is black lung. But there's a subjective element in the diagnosis. And for a doctor who has lived with these people, who knows their medical problems—their shortness of breath, their smothering . . ."

He passes a hand across his eyes.

"The one sure way to prove that a man has black lung," he says finally, "is a biopsy of lung tissue after death. And that's not good enough. Not nearly good enough. More study needs to be done, better criteria developed."

Paul Odom read an advertisement in the *Journal of American Medicine* and visited the coalfields out of curiosity. That was seven years ago. What he found troubled his mind and made him stay.

Pikeville's Methodist Hospital is the principal medical service center for an area reaching a hundred miles in all directions, containing altogether about one-quarter million souls. On the hospital's staff—in a region of disfiguring mine accidents and chronic childhood illness—there is not one orthopedist or plastic surgeon, not one pediatrician. Doctors of any description are in short enough supply.

It is a crisis, Odom knows, that reaches beyond the coalfields. "These people are medically neglected," he says, "but so are the people in many of our rural areas. Rural America is becoming doctorless. And it's a tragedy that the medical schools, the AMA, and the powers that be have let this happen."

There is coughing in the outer room—a rasping, miner's cough. The doctor's respite has been brief. He forces himself up from his chair. For Paul Odom life has, in a sense, come full circle. He is the one advertising now, for a doctor to share his practice in the well-equipped clinic which, when he built it, was intended for two physicians. But the ads bring no response.

There are four patients, not one, in the waiting room. Three women, and a girl with a baby wrapped in a blanket, but no sign of the ailing miner. Then the baby coughs, and the huge man's sound of it fills the room. The receptionist leads the first of the ladies in.

There is a framed homily on the wall over the drinking fountain:

If a child lives with criticism,
 he learns to condemn.

If a child lives with hostility,
  he learns to fight.
If a child lives with ridicule,
  he learns to be shy.
If a child lives with shame,
  he learns to feel guilty.

There is no remedy suggested for children who live with all of these. The list moves on to happier possibilities. And the closing door silences the baby's enormous, resonant complaint.

Side by side on the lip of the bluff overlooking the town, the former hospital and the campus of Pikeville College, founded by the United Presbyterians in 1889, perch in cozy ecumenism. The brick hospital building stands empty since the removal of the institution a month before to new quarters on the opposite bank of the Levisa Fork. But the college is not really deserted. It is only wrapped now in the weekend slumber of small campuses everywhere.

Cut flowers in a china vase perfume the steam heat of a formal dormitory parlor. A clock ticks. There is no sound of habitation. Across a frozen lawn is the administration building, full of different smells—bookish and waxy. In some distant stillness, the click of a single typewriter asks accusingly where all the learners have gone.

Dr. Robert Cope, the president of the college, will be leaving shortly to tour the country, carrying the institution's message to moneyed friends. Some of what he is saying now, perhaps, is what he means to tell them.

"One of the distinctive features of our area is the character of our children. They are keenly competitive, resilient. They know what hard work is and they're not afraid of it. That's why I believe this area may be one of the last repositories of the qualities that made this a great country."

Cope is a small, vigorous man, his hair going salt-and-pepper at fifty-one—Wooster of Ohio, Ohio State University, the University of Madrid, Doctor of Philosophy. He wears a pale blue bulky turtleneck sweater; a houndstooth sportcoat hangs from the back of his chair. The college has eight hundred fifty students, most of them from the seven nearest coal counties of Kentucky and the Virginias.

"The three R's of the region used to be Readin', Ritin' and Route Twenty-three North," President Cope says, looking out over his gold-rimmed glasses. "But that's changing. More people are staying now, or coming back. And the opportunities are growing. We're putting emphasis on educating people for the jobs that are here."

All, however, is not pragmatism.

"If I had to describe our program succinctly, I'd say its objectives are to encourage an unquenchable desire not to be ordinary. And to *molest the mind*—to develop the imagination as well as the intelligence."

What President Cope does not add—cannot in mercy be expected to add—is that there are some rather precisely defined limits for this process of molestation. The boundaries are drawn by the men who hold real power in the community, who in some cases not only endow the college but also sit on its board. There was the time, for instance, that it came to the attention of these men that two students of the college had involved themselves in the activities of "those Communists" up on the Marrowbone. Robert Cope was still new, then, in the president's chair on the hill overlooking the town. But mindful, no doubt, of what had happened to his predecessor for offending the strip-mine interests, he drove out to visit the Easterling woman on Poor Bottom Hollow. Shortly after that, the students found it impossible to come.

In the administration building's silent hall, a bulletin board displays the names of the last semester's honor scholars. The list is headed by one Sik Tong Tam, but many of the names are the familiar ones—Ratliff, Tackett, Mullins, Justice.

Outside, the sun has revealed itself, without warmth, shining through a sudden shower of snow crystals blown on the cutting wind. From the building's porch, directly below, it almost seems, the town can be seen all of a piece. Nearest, the railroad track, a string of loaded coal cars moving slowly north. Then the business district, and the banks, bulging with their deposits. Then the municipal parking lot and the tan brick courthouse, discolored a neutral gray by coal dust, with its cream-yellow clock tower. And beyond all that, the river, running off to the far right, up toward where the Russell Fork joins, fed by the lesser creeks beyond.

To go from Pikeville College to the head of the Marrowbone, say, is an easy matter—forty-five minutes, no more, by car. But the trip in the other direction, for a child beginning in the hollows and coming down, can take longer than a lifetime. For that *is* alien country. And there are visions there to molest the mind beyond anything to be found in a textbook or a lecturer's notes.

Argus Mooner waits, head thrown back, Coke bottle upturned, a lank silhouette against the lighted doorway of the Allegheny store. Then comes down, the fire of his cigarette a fierce bead in the dusk, and folds himself into the car.

The radio whines a nasal plaint. *By-eee by-eee, Miss American pieeee* . . .

He is Sallie Jo Mooner's oldest boy still at home—bearing down on sixteen with pimples, red hair to his shoulders, bad teeth, pale angry eyes, and two dollars in his pocket. He works the radio dial in a blur of sound, then comes back to the same place, but at double the volume, and leans back satisfied, singing with it in perfect mimicry.

Drove my Chevy to the levee but the levee was drieee . . .

Down through Hellier, the tires tha-rumping through potholes and over the carcasses of dead cats. Past Henry Clay and Lookout. The mountains looming darkly at either hand, and other cars on the road ahead, brake lights flaring at the icy bends.

The law says that Millard High School is supposed to keep Argus Mooner until his next birthday. But some days he goes to Pikeville instead of to school. And some days he fights. The next time he's thrown out will be the fourth—and the last, they swear, birthday or no birthday. Getting Argus past sixteen is a trial of patience for all concerned.

Tonight, though, is the Millard homecoming. Yesterday there was a test in American history and Argus bet his hair against the teacher's two dollars that he would pass it. Did, too. Slipped in with a seventy. So tonight he has his hair and the money both. There's a dance after the game, and Argus means to stay for it. There'll be girls to look at. And there might be a fight.

The parking lot is crowded already. Inside, the band is playing.

James Ed Branham, the principal, himself a man from up on the Marrowbone, presides in the outer hall. He is proud of his school, built by the Corps of Engineers to replace the smaller ones drowned under Fishtrap's waters. Some of the seven hundred students are from down toward Pikeville, but many, like Argus, are children of the hollows. And young Mooner eases loosely past Branham now, in whose office he has had memorable moments, and on into the gymnasium where, almost unnoticed amid the stir of much greater expectations, the journeymen of the B team are finishing their work.

And then it commences. The cheerleaders in their newest uniforms. The all-girl color guard in its finest gold lamé. The deputy to the high sheriff propped against one end wall, pendulous stomach outthrust and a black-jack at his hip. Boy Bartley is there too, and names the deputy, shouting over the crowd noise. "He'll use that thing, buddy"—experienced testimony. "He'll break y'head."

The varsity comes on with a rush—miners' boys, some of them, trying to play their way down the creek and up onto college hill. Jerry and Ronnie Sparks, who just that afternoon were changing the clutch in a Chevrolet in their cold yard on the Marrowbone's bank behind Kermit Ratliff's house, are the starting guards. The band sets up a driving beat as the Millard Mustangs charge the backboard in their pregame drill, leaping, tipping, keeping the ball alive above the rim. Thirty-seven tips without a miss—a good omen. The enemies from Jenkins are theirs already.

At the half the nine girls come out in formal gowns, the spotlight following them this once in their lives, stately and slow on the arms of their escorts, who are the Mustangs themselves, some still sweaty from their labors.

For eight there are roses, for one a crown. Her escort, a benchwarmer, bends to confer the embarrassed, obligatory kiss, and she seizes him fiercely, exulting. Thus inspired he goes out and shoots fourteen points without missing and it is all over but the last minute running off the clock to a shrill

We gotcha beat, yeah, yeah!
We gotcha beat.
We gotcha beat, yeah, yeah!
We gotcha beat.

Then the parents are leaving—a smiling man with the pallor and gray hands of a coal miner, holding a long-stemmed rose, his princess down there somewhere on the darkening gymnasium floor with the others. Argus Mooner down there, too. The ones who eat free lunches and the ones who were nearly queen. The Millard Mustangs with their thirty-game basketball schedule and four books per student on their library shelves.

The most splendid of all was the band. It had no uniforms, but the trumpets rang with clarion boldness as trumpets are supposed to do. The snare drums rolled like a surf. The cymbals were mighty instruments in the hands of a boy so tiny he panted with the effort of clashing them. Down in front was the bandmistress, a pretty teacher with pride and love in her eyes.

You would have cried to hear them play "The Star-Spangled Banner."

V

For all that its turnings are a map in his head, there are places in the mine that even Marvin Bartley himself does not care to go alone. Old places— worked two years before, three years, longer. Where the timbers are mostly down. Where torn draperies of fungus, or pale loops of it like blanched intestine, hang from the decaying wooden roof bolt headers. Or where the headers are rotted away entirely, letting the top come down. Where the air is stale and close, and putrid waters gather in the low places, never to evaporate. Where sometimes the heaped slate from roof falls has left only space enough for a man to clamber over, his back against the stone top, and into the next foul stretch of passageway.

A man has no business in those old workings by himself. And when occasionally Marvin must go there unaccompanied he carries an extra light. Above all, he would not want his light to fail him.

Just the same, there are strange and wonderful things to be seen there. It sometimes happens that the whole slate layering of the top does not fall away clean from the sandstone above it but rather divides along an inner fault of the slate itself, some coming down and some staying up. A man turning the beam of his cap lamp up at such a place is looking, now, at something much older than the mine, older than humankind, older even than the mountain itself. He is seeing directly into the dark, steaming fetor of the Pennsylvanian slime, to the very time when coal was being made, when cockroaches the size of mice crept through the decay and dragonflies bigger than hawks wheeled over it.

Crouching, Marvin reaches up a hand to touch the roof—reaching, and seeming to know he does, across three hundred million years in time.

Some kind of fern it is, or what we would call a fern. But the whole impression of it as big as a window, the stalk branching and rebranching into a lacing of palmate fronds. In falling into the pool, or else in settling against the bottom, one of the palms broke, folded under, and creased that way. It is there in Marvin's light, an event more clearly provable than many that happened yesterday.

"And here—" he says, traversing to a tree, like a giant stalk of celery, deeply ribbed—a foot in diameter and running ten feet on a diagonal along the creamy gray of the slate. Its name, *Sigillaria*—fallen heavily, one imagines, in the wet silence. There is an uneasiness in that place, made worse by the dead air; a suffocation, as of looking up through water.

If such slabs as those could be gotten out entire . . .

"No way," Marvin says. "They come loose and fall. And they bust all to pieces. Once in a while you'll find a pretty chunk."

And moving with his fine, unexplainable grace, hands clasped behind him at the belt, he skates along under the uncountable ages, over a slate heap and back into the uncluttered passages and fresh, fan-driven air of the newer section where the men are working.

It is their habit, these dark mornings, to gather a little early in the low shed outside the mine entrance and squat talking around the coal stove until it is six-thirty, the time to go in. Being one of the youngest of them there, and also patient, Boy Bartley usually bears the greater brunt of their rough humor. The name itself—Boy—volunteers him for it. He smiles a shy, fixed grin, and his wide eyes roll white in the pitiless beams of their cap lamps.

This morning, though, he was reprieved. Junior Compton's wife had presented him a second child the day before. He distributed cigars that were either smoked on the spot, outside the mine, or put away in lunch buckets for later. And Fonso Smith delivered then a tedious, mock-serious lecture on how long Junior would be obliged to sleep chastely in another bed.

The cap lamps illuminated Junior Compton in his mortification.

There in the dark shed they had been undifferentiated except in manner of speech—all simply miners. But now, three thousand feet inside the mountain in the eternal sixty-degree weather at the face of the coal, they are men of specific and well-practiced skills. They have to be, to keep the loaded cars coming out.

If the Bartley mine, with nine men underground, fills nine twenty-ton coal trucks in the course of the day, the operation can be sustained. If a tenth truck is filled, that one is pure profit. Nine men, two hundred tons of coal. In that same day, a strip mine employing only four men and tearing at the mountain from outside with bulldozers and power shovels can send a hundred full trucks to the railroad loading ramp. Four men, *two thousand* tons of coal.

That is the competition the Bartleys have to meet.

They are working now in two parallel passages, or entries as they call them, fifty feet apart. With each fifty feet of forward progress they will cut a lateral passage between those, leaving a square block or pillar of coal supporting the mountain itself. Later, when they have driven as far inward as their air system or economical transport of the coal will allow, they will retreat from that section of the mine, taking the coal pillars as

Boy Bartley, driving his motor down the dark hill toward the mountain's heart

they go and letting the top come in behind them. The hill is a maze of these old workings, some pillared out, some not.

In the Bartley mine they are *"shooting it from the solid,"* as miners say—blowing the coal out of the face with charges of dynamite. It is midmorning now. At the end of one passage, they are loading coal from the first shot of the day. Down the long hill from the world comes Boy Bartley on his low electric motor—steering furiously, airborne from his iron seat at the worst rough places, ducking low roof. He backs his empty wagon directly under the scorpion tail of the Joy loader, which is run by his twenty-year-old cousin, Sandy Bartley. There is a sudden mighty clamor. In front, the Joy loader's steel claws make inward-gathering motions and the great machine advances into the heap of shattered coal, sweeping it onto its ramp maw and conveying it back to be dropped into the wagon, which Boy edges forward and backward to even the load.

Three minutes and it is done, a four-ton wagon loaded. Two men with shovels might have accomplished it in twenty. The Joy loader falls deafeningly silent and Boy Bartley, without a word, throws his motor in forward gear and starts back up the long hill on which, midway somewhere, he will pass another of his cousins—Dickey, who is nineteen, or Gurney, twenty-one—coming down empty.

In the other passage they are readying the next shot. Fonso Smith, with Junior Compton helping, is putting the last bolt in the roof. Rock dust hangs thick as white smoke in the beams from their cap lamps. And Fonso's lecture of early morning is being amplified.

"Two months, anyway," he is telling Junior. "Why, might even be three or four."

"Aw, come on now!" Junior protests. But there is no escape—no place to go.

Fonso brings a one-by-four-inch board down sharply in his ungloved hands on a projection of the bolting machine, splitting it just enough to slide under the bolt washer for a header.

"You may know a thing or two I don't about shootin' coal," he tells Junior, and tightens the bolt, fixing the slate roof up fast to the overlying stone. "But, honey, you can't tell me nothin' about pussy. *Because I come out of one."*

The others laugh and shake their heads ruefully at Fonso's indomitable and engaging coarseness.

Junior is the shooting man. They depend on him to lay that coal out nicely on the floor. Calculating the proper angle of each by eye, he drives ten holes into the face the full nine-foot length of the bit of his electric drill.

Then caps and wires the dynamite, handling it more casually than most men would handle sausages, knowing exactly what is correct to do and so relieved entirely of having to consider the consequences of doing what is not.

Tamps it in the holes, neither too gently nor too hard, seven sticks to the hole. And still with the same nonchalance they walk bent-over around a corner and through a plastic curtain to contain the fumes—around a corner only, taking their equipment and the dynamite cases with them. Junior Compton carrying his exploder box and unrolling the two wires behind him as he goes.

"I'm gonna shoot some coal," he calls out.

And from the other passage comes the reply, "Shoot it, then."

He attaches his two wires to the box, and precisely at that moment there is a low, distant-sounding bump. That is what some people say the charge sounds like going off nine feet deep in the face. Those people are deaf, maybe. Or else Junior Compton is uncommonly thorough about his work. In fact, what was just heard was only the rattle of an empty coal wagon passing over rough floor a half-mile out toward the driftmouth.

Because now Junior says, "Fire, fire," touching the red button in an offhand way. And in the sound of it—seventy sticks of dynamite in a closed place, the violence of driven wind and sense of the floor itself heaving, rippling, rising to meet the roof—there can be not the least doubt that this time he has done his job too well and the mountain itself is coming in.

It isn't, of course. It never does—or hasn't yet, at any rate. There is a click of pebbles falling in the stillness. They raise the plastic curtain and look in around the corner—only briefly, since breathing too many of those sweetish fumes could make a man's lungs go bad, and maybe his brain. But there the coal lies, well shattered as Junior meant it to be. And the Bartley mine is now nine feet deeper than it was a few seconds before.

Another motor goes rattling away up the passage, the youngest of the brothers bellowing the song of the day.

". . . whiskey and rye . . . Yeah, this'll be the day that I die . . . So bye bye, Miss . . ." And on out of hearing.

"Let's you and me eat my lunch," Marvin Bartley says. The men sit on the floor or on tool boxes, a little cooler than they might care to be, now that they're not working. In thirty minutes the air fan will have drawn the fumes from the face and Sandy Bartley can move his Joy loader there to clean up while they bolt and drill and shoot the room where he has just been working. Fonso is deviling Junior Compton again, but Junior, having finished his sandwich, is lying on the floor with his head on his arm, pretending sleep.

Marvin Bartley caps his vacuum bottle and closes his lunch bucket.

"You know," he says, reflectively—for he is a thoughtful man. "It seems like people don't know too much about coal miners. I guess they think we're only about half human and not quite bright to be here. Just dumb and pore. But those people have never been down here."

He talks with his head turned a fraction aside. It's a little consideration that miners practice to keep their cap light from shining in a man's eyes. Then consideration becomes unyielding habit, and you will notice that many miners outside the mine, or even retired from it for years, still do not quite face you as they speak.

"You get to liking it—to where you don't worry about yourself down here. It's not bad work for a man if he happens to care for it," Marvin Bartley says. "And I'd hate to leave it. I just can't think of anything I'd care as much to do."

He falls silent, then, and the only sound in the moist gloom is the sound of men breathing—young men whose lungs have not yet filled up. They are satisfied with their morning's effort. The coal has gone out well. And they are resting now, gathering themselves for the two hours that remain before they climb on the backs of the motors and ride up the hill toward a more hostile, less easily mastered place—that distant speck of brightness that widens to become the sunstruck outer world.

In only a day the season has turned from bitterest winter to nearly summer. It is welcome, even if it cannot last. From somewhere a January fly has materialized, fat and blue-bodied as August. The sun through the truck windshield makes her squint, lights her gold earring, burnishes her face to Indian tawniness.

Edith Tead Johnny Bear Easterling is about one of her unending errands—nursing the truck up the bouldered track of a nearby hollow to call on one of the unhappiest people of the Marrowbone. She ignored breakfast and forgot lunch, and now she is eating a banana, the peeling draped back around her fist, nipping off chunks of it with her perfect teeth as she drives.

Her people depend on her. For transport if they are sick. For money if they hunger. For encouragement when they are without hope. If they cannot find her at home, or if she has urgent business of her own that cannot be deferred, they are impatient, perplexed, a little angry even. *We needed you, but you was off someplace.* Edith Easterling is mother to them all, and a mother's day never ends.

"You know, Jake's an amazin' person," she thinks aloud now. "He really is. Once in a while he'll say, 'How about givin' me a little of yer time?' But that's about all. He knows I've got to do what I'm doin'." In the end, though, what does it all amount to? Sometimes that troubles her. Do her goings and comings count for anything, or is she only wearing away her life a day at a time, along with the truck's tires, in the aimlessness of her compassion?

"I think I just might run for public office," she says now. As if it were occurring to her for the first time; taking another bite of banana. "I could run for magistrate—fix the roads and try to clean up the creeks. *That's* important." But there is more to it than that. So much more. And she knows it, and falls silent, easing the truck on up the incredible track around the worst of the looming rocks and turning finally into a dirt yard beside a reeling log house.

It is the house of a woman named Tulsa Suttey, whose wretchedness, partly of her own making, is so comprehensive—so stunning in its range and elaboration—that it seems hardly relevant to note that there are fish in her well. But there are, four fat green sunfish lazing just under the water's dust-filmed surface.

Edith scatters the guinea fowl before her on the bare doorstep and goes inside. So porous is the structure at top and sides, lanced through with sunshafts and open in sprung places at the joints, that the distinction between outside and in is more a judgment than a fact. Tulsa Suttey is on the bed, face to the wall, in a sweater and tight Levi pants, light brown hair spilling on the rough covers. She turns then, and offers the courtesy of sitting up. The body of a woman of thirty is surmounted by a face that is older than anything—an ancient domed forehead frozen in the corrugations of a sob; pale flat eyes; a grin invented to forestall a blow.

She has borne nine daughters and four sons. Several of the girls married before their fifteenth year into calamities of their own. Several others of each gender are at home. Her husband left her and married another woman, and she herself has been living with a man—an abusive drunk who may bootleg a little but mainly takes her welfare money to keep himself in automobiles. Who abuses the daughters, too. Reviles them publicly. May even molest them. One daughter sits now looking at a snowy television screen.

"How've you been, Lucy?" Edith asks her.

"She ain't no different," Tulsa says. And the child, who may be seventeen, makes a shy smile but keeps her eyes on the television. "Doctor say there ain't nothin' for it."

The girl has a genetic abnormality that causes the skin not to form as it should. Great water blisters rise spontaneously on her body and burst, leaving fields of raw sores.

"I used to keep her skelp shaved an' you couldn't tell no way she wasn't a boy," Tulsa says. And the child makes a larger smile, learning to answer that way the humiliations she cannot prevent.

"Cain't comb it no way. She got a brush fer it."

There has been plaster on the ceiling once, but it is down. There is light through the tin roof above. On this hot day it is clammy cold inside, though a coal heater creaks with its exertions. The floor is a clutter of wadded papers and discarded clothes. What they breathe is not air but a cloying gas of rancid beer, spit, urine, spoiled food.

"Sometimes they come up inside her an' bust, an' if she bleeds they got to give her blood."

Child's wild helpless smile of alarm.

"How's Nita, then?" Edith asks Tulsa.

"She's got sick, Miz Easterlin'. She was gonna get married last Monday but I had to put her in the hospital."

"Married!"

Nita is fifteen—betrothed, it seems, to a man who came back to the hollow legless from Vietnam.

"I know, Miz Easterlin'. I'm a-gonna do my best to keep her from marryin' *that*. But you oughta see her. Picks it up outa its chair an' carries it around like a baby."

"She can't do it if you don't sign for her," Edith says.

"Oh, I'll fight it all I can. But it might make it worse." Tulsa considers her helplessness and shakes her head. "He drinks, too, Miz Easterlin'. Drinks awful. I tole her, you don't mind it now, but when you livin' with it an' then all day an' night the smell of it, an' its whisky breath—" She shudders. "I tole her, you'll quit lovin' it an' go to hatin' it an' lookin' for somebody else. That one of mine, he'll bring a friend of his sometimes. An' in a day an' a night maybe the two of em'll drink up to ten pints of whisky—that regular red whisky. There's nothin' I hate as much as drink."

Smiles then, sheepishly, at Edith, who has known her too long to be deceived by what she says.

"Now I'm not above it, you understand. I used to have a little drink myself. But now—Lord God, now all I want's to get away from it. Get the smell of it outa the house."

"Why don't you?" Edith says. "Get yourself a place to live away from this holler an' get away from him."

"Cause if he caught me he'd kill me. He's said that. Only way'd be to have somebody take him out an' get him good an' drunk an' us be gone when he come back."

Two other children come in from outside. The girl is a toddler with mumbling speech and a nose emptying rivers. The boy is of grade-school age.

"Hi, Tead Easterlin'," he says.

"*Miz* Easterlin'!" Tulsa chides him, and shakes her head at his boldness. Then, to Edith again, "They made me go in fer a hearin' today on account of Nita bein' out of school, an' Mister Branham tole me he was sorry he put me out over it, her bein' sick an' all. But I give 'em the doctor's note. They ought to knowed it from the note. Anyway . . . I seen Arch there."

Arch is the former husband.

"An' I tole him—I said if either one of us was to die, an' us in what we're in, why we'd split hell wide open. An' he said he knowed that. Said he was goin' to get rid of that thing he's layin' with. He tole me, said: 'Tulsa, there ain't but one woman in this world I love. I dream about you all the time. If I git rid of that thing will you let me come back?' He asked me that, Miz Easterlin'."

"Well, will you?"

The older girl is listening now, eyes going from face to face and her head making bright, hopeful little twitches.

"Not to marry. I don't need no man for that. I'm never goin' to marry no man again."

And Edith, not to her but to the girl now: "I bet you'd like the idea of your mother movin' to a different house—"

Nod.

"—an' gettin' gone from here—"

Nod.

"—an' of your daddy comin' back home to live with you all."

Fierce nod.

"Anyhow, I seed him there. Said to me afterward, 'Tulsa, honey, you got any money?' An I said, 'Ain't you got none? What's the matter, you hungry?' Said, 'Yeah, an' now I got to hitchhike back home or walk.' So I just pulled out *two dollars*"—her eyes shine at the mention of that sum—"an' give it to him an' tole him, 'Git on, then. Git on back to where yer goin'.'"

"Well, I'm sorry about Nita," Edith says. And it is more than a phrase. For the girl's eighth-grade graduation she had taken her into town and bought twenty-six dollars worth of clothes and had her hair fixed, and Edith remembers that she was the prettiest thing in her class.

"What I was wanting to do, when the weather got nice in the spring, was take three or four girls on a little drivin' trip. Over into Virginia, maybe."

"Oh, I wouldn't mind that none," Tulsa says. "Not her a-goin' with somebody reliable like you. If she ain't married, that is—an' lord knows, Miz Easterlin', I'll do what I *kin*. I always say travel broadens a person. Why, I believe a person learns more a-travelin' than they does in school. Take me, now. I only went to the third grade, but I learnt all the rest—readin', y'know, an' writin'—just goin' between here an' my sister's house. Readin' the signs on the road an' whatnot."

Edith stands to leave.

"You all've been keepin' warm, I guess."

And Tulsa nods. "Them hills back there's all full of old mines. Man that owns this land tole me, 'Tulsa, that house is yours as long as you live, an' you jus take all that coal outa there you want.' "

"You've heard the weather, then?"

"Huh-uh."

"They're sayin' it's goin' to snow by morning—"

"Lord."

"—an' turn off cold."

On the fluttering picture tube, Jack Nicklaus, a golden man, is stalking the first prize. He hunches over his ball, looks down a long sweep of perfect grass, waits, looks, looks again. The ball rolls for an eternity, curls, drops in. The golden man throws up his arms, richer by twenty-eight thousand dollars. The girl, Lucy, smiles for him.

"How cold?"

"They said five below."

"*Lord God.*" Wearily, with real distress.

But if you are a woman who crawls into the no-man's-land of an abandoned coal pit, watching the roof for cracks and setting a few timbers as you go, carrying your dynamite, and shoot the coal alone there and carry it down the short hill to the house in bags, house coal, against what the night could be, then you have cause to moan at such news.

Edith goes out into the hot afternoon, past the guineas scratching and the well with the sunfish in it, and drives back down the hollow, noticing now that the white lean-to on the road shoulder where the children wait for the school bus has been pushed over the edge and lies broken-sided in the filthy waters of the branch below.

And still, with evening coming, the false summer wraps them. Foster

Bridge over ruined waters: frail linkage between the hollows and the larger world

has crossed from the post office through pooling light and shadow, his accounts in order, and sits now at the table with a plate of chicken and dumplings before him and two pies at the side.

Edith is there, too, having meant only to look in but then smelling her sister's supper. For Vadney, who is a brilliant cook, the chief pleasure is to see people come hungry to their places and find contentment in what she has done. She presides benignly now at the side, smiling her little secret smile, fanning herself with a cardboard stick-handled Jesus fan from a Pikeville funeral home.

Kermit remarks again, as he did at the time, on there having been no mail for him that morning.

"Foster's not through readin' it yet," Edith says.

"Does Foster read it? What's he do, steam it open?"

"Naw," Edith says. "Foster, he just cuts it. Don't even bother to reseal 'em."

Foster's fork skips a beat against the plate.

"Ones I open I do."

"He can read through them envelopes," Vadney suggests.

"Can't neither."

"Poor Foster." Edith pushes back the remains of her pie. "All you get to read's the postcards."

"I do look at the pictures sometimes."

It is gentle talk, summer talk. Slow and fat like that August fly.

Now Edith is remembering the time that she and some of the other mountain people traveled to Washington to speak their minds to the gentlemen of Congress—thinking maybe they should try to go again sometime.

"It's good to do it," she says, and decides to eat the crust of the pie after all. "Let 'em know we're here."

"Uh," Foster says.

"Why, they wouldn't know you were alive, Foster, if they didn't have to send you your check."

"Shoot!" The low sun through the window behind him glows in the spun silver of his toplock. "They know more about me than I know about myself."

"Aw, now, Foster. You know the only time they see you's when they come down to buy your vote."

Kermit has gotten up and limped into the living room and gotten his French harp from a drawer. He taps it against his palm and plays the first, thin bars of a mountain song. "Wildwood Flower" is its name, a melody of aching loveliness, full of the lilt of sweet things remembered. But he stops abruptly and puts the instrument back in its box, not having the breath any more to play it as he thinks it ought to be played.

Foster is finished, too, now, and stands at the door in his billed cap, about to go. The sun has dropped behind the mountain but the breeze still comes down warmer than any breeze of January should rightly be. He feels it, and smells it. And is troubled by what he finds there.

"Come back, Foster," Vadney tells him, unnecessarily, and he nods.

"This is flood weather," he says. *"Washout* weather."

In failing light, in that corner of the Commonwealth, the army regrouped.

"They've not seen the end of us," said the heavy man, his breath a leafy rattle. "We'll go back down there to Frankfort and aggravate 'em to where they'll have to do something."

A yellow dog and a black one circled stiff-legged beside the road, and a coal truck rumbled off the mountain with the day's last load.

The club-fisted man, then: "We gonna let 'em know what kinda tore-up, hot-minded people they're a-dealin' with. Make 'em stop runnin' this muck off on us, ruinin' our wells—"

"Wreckin' our homes."

"—cause if they don't there's goin' to be highpower rifles pointin' down from these hills. That's where it's a-headin' to."

And the one with the milk eye glowing: "We was just seven this time. But one of these days we're goin' to have a thousand."

"Ef the coal operators or somebody don't stop the bus on us."

"I don't guess we can prove that. Knowin's one thing. Provin's another."

"Well, *you tell me* how come that bus didn't run."

So now, again, there is stillness. The mountains that rim the valley rise healed by darkness against the brittle stars. Stoves are banked with special care, for the temperature has dropped fifty degrees already. By morning it will stand at nearly ten below.

All the world—the trees, the houses, the very earth itself—creaks with the awful cold. Down where Poor Bottom comes whispering through a beard of ice to meet the Marrowbone, Kermit and Vadney Ratliff sleep the untroubled sleep of those who were provident.

Higher on the mountain, Tulsa Suttey sleeps the sleep of drugged hopelessness, fearing the night for what it is and the day for what it might bring.

And Johnny Bear Easterling? She doesn't sleep at all. A neighbor has a problem. So has the land. Someone needs to see the morning in.

6 STRANGERS ON A TRAIN

Central Kansas in summer. Treeless, nearly manless.

Grasshopper-headed oil well pumps nodding in the furnace of afternoon.

More distant—empty miles between—grain elevators, stark as tombstones, bearing the names of towns: Russell, Gorham, Victoria.

Past those. Past Hays and Ellis. The Interstate spinning out westward to a web. And then a point. That point supporting the swollen sun. The sun opening like a flower to receive the outbound pilgrims in their cars greasy with bug juice.

Wind a hundred degrees on the face. Parched lips shredding. Pupils contracted to points.

Ogallah! they shriek. *Wa Keeney!* Phonetics of torment. Also place names.

Has anyone ever done this and lived?

Main Street, Quinter, Kansas, runs south between low storefronts—Coast-to-Coast, Skogmo's—past the Hefners' frame house with wagon wheels on the lawn, then bends to meet a county road at the Q Motel-Cafe.

South of that, a clutch of gas stations.

The Dairy Queen, last water hole.

A flock of sheep grazing.

A farmstead cowering in the heat.

Then just the wind, come up all the way from Sonora with no tree or bush between to give it voice, announcing itself in the shell of the ear. Incline the head a bit and the wind will pass mutely on again, full of force but silent as a stone in flight.

There is a tentative, half-formed look about the land here. Uncompleted it seems to lie, awaiting some further act of creation. And now, in a sudden moment, the sun drops off that point of road out somewhere the other side of Denver, and blueness claims it all.

Very small against this twilit immensity the party of pilgrims has assembled. Fifty-four in all, counting wives and husbands and children.

117

A fashion model from Atlanta. A preacher from Wausau, Wisconsin. A doctor from Cape Cod. A real estate man from Columbia, Maryland. An architect from El Paso. An octogenarian lady adventurer from Cambridge, Massachusetts, who last year slept on a Himalayan mountaintop. Others.

For reasons that seemed perfectly sound when they wrote their checks for passage, they have come to ride across fifty-some miles of the Kansas prairie in covered wagons. Now that they actually are here, however, the enterprise baffles and depresses them.

Wooden bench seats from the circled wagons have been set in rows, like pews, facing an open fire. The people take their places on the seats and look straight ahead where the TV would be if there were one.

Those with children scold them assertively, thankful for something to do. The rest are silent. They are strangers. They would as soon remain strangers. They have begun to suspect that anyone who would let himself get involved in a thing like this must be a little bit quirky and maybe dangerous.

One of the party, it is learned—a man accompanied by four children and a son-in-law—has brought his family on eight of these rides. He is squat, bandy-legged, with tooled leather boots to the knees, bushy white sideburns, and a ten-gallon hat. The others inspect him sidelong, according him a hushed celebrity. A crew member ladles cocoa into paper cups from a kettle over the fire and the people drink it quickly, obediently, making no sound, look around scowling, and put the paper cups in their pockets. Another crew member uncases a guitar and proposes a group sing. Lips move grudgingly but no noise issues.

Then Ruth Hefner arrives in a stagecoach behind four white mules, in her flowered frontier dress and sunbonnet, and informs them breathlessly that they are having the time of their lives. She is a tiny, fierce, freckled woman incapable of doubt. And she refuses to see what those slack white faces and slitty eyes are trying to tell her.

"You're a wonderful-looking group of modern pioneers," she trills.

Someone coughs.

"Welcome to *a hundred years ago!*"

Gawd! They recoil in shuddering embarrassment.

A chill has come into the air.

They are waiting for someone to tell them where to go to the bathroom.

Full dark, now, and the travelers have retired to their wagons.

From the direction of the dying fire, music comes to them. A woman from one of the prairie towns is playing an autoharp and singing folk songs in a voice that chimes soft and clear. But they cannot be soothed by it. The floors of the wagons are hard. The wind has fallen and the dead air under the canvas tops is stifling.

At the moment of discomfort's shading into troubled dreams, they remember the Dairy Queen as a stately pleasure dome.

Something stirs. Something comes whooping from its wagon into the just-risen sun. It is the man with all the children, a fuzzy-sleepy-wild apparition of the dawn, mostly boots and hat and chewed cigar.

Straight across the circle he careens, with his look of violent purpose, and the others, watching under wagon flaps, look to their womenfolk and their valuables. But he is only going for breakfast.

They climb down, too, cramped, but finding the place less strange by daylight. And they have something in common, now—the kinship of survivors.

The wagon circle uncoils into a line, the horses stepping prettily in the traces, fresh from their spring's long pasturing.

In front, ahead of the stagecoach, is Foard Darnall, wagonmaster of the Hefner train, himself a rancher of substance. He is sixty-eight, lean to the point of caricature, skin as copper-colored as the horse he rides, voice between tenor and soprano, and he can make confetti of a paper cup at fifteen feet with his bullwhip.

Farther back, Art Bentley, eighty-nine, the scout. Played football for Kansas State in 1902. Demands, as a prerogative of age, to ride the most unruly horse in the string, a buckskin with the look of trouble in his eye. Art Bentley is a collector of guns, saver of Indian artifacts, finder of the teeth of sharks that prowled here when Kansas was a sea.

The wagon drivers are people of the neighborhood—farmers and men retired from town, and the wives or widows of them. People who walked dusty furrows behind horses fifty years ago, more or less, and like the sawing pull of leather in their hands. Younger crew people—horse handlers, hostesses, general helpers. Among them a Hefner son, David, a veteran of Vietnam. And his wife, Virginia, concierge of this rolling hotel. College students. High school students. One or two younger. A crew of thirty.

Already the sun is a thing to be feared. The wagon canvases give shade above and have been rolled up at the sides to let in the morning wind. Some of the pilgrims bounce on the wooden seats. Some go horseback. A

The wagons circled, the immensity of the prairie ahead

few choose to walk. Late rains have made the buffalo grass lush underfoot. Wildflowers speckle the prairie with pinks and golds. Art Bentley picks a sprig of my-lady's slipper and presents it to a girl on top of the stagecoach. Rosie, a pack burro with the U.S. Army brand—age thirty, at least, maybe forty, so old that half her face has faded white—sways blinking under the burden of a dazzled child.

The people are full of pancakes and eggs and boiled coffee and lean country bacon, and they have begun to think the venture might come to something after all. It is at least a possibility.

From a distance, this motley of beasts and pilgrims and machines might appear to be stationary. Presently, however, it can be seen to gain the horizon and pass over, down into the watershed of a stream called the Hackberry.

Much behind, nearly out of view, there comes an exile—a boy driving a pickup truck. Hitched to the pickup truck is a small building on wheels, with doors at front and back. Its name is The Green Palace. Downwind from it for several yards there is a faint essence of caustic chemicals. There is a shovel in the bed of the truck, and the boy knows what it's for. But his eyes betray a want of purpose.

Lunch on the Hackberry.

Horses unhitched but still in harness, tethered to wagon wheels, resting with one hind foot flexed.

The earth, the wind itself, are on fire. No stone may be touched.

A thicket of scrawny willows rises beside the streambed, and there the pilgrims lie, fingers sticky with chocolate cake icing, in shade that is mostly illusory. The sun seeks them out between the curled willow leaves. Ruth Hefner descends on them from the circle of wagons above, skirts swirling and a sheaf of papers in her hand. Reminders to herself.

"I hope you all have your raincoats," she chirps.

Heads turn slowly. They hear—but are not certain they have heard.

The dry leaves click and a cloud of chaffy dust mounts a wind devil into the cloudless, blue-silver plate of the sky.

"You've never been out in a prairie rain," she tells them. "We almost always get one."

Castle Rock, a turreted pinnacle of white shale, rises seventy-four feet directly from the grassy flats. The freezes and thaws are devouring it, but slowly. A crevice has grown downward between its two main towers, and one day the lesser part will lean out and fall.

A television personality once came to climb the rock. It was an event in the neighborhood. He went up a third of the way, hid in the crack a while, then came down and claimed to have gained the top. Art Bentley *has* done it, any number of times. Could do it now, he believes—a year short of ninety—but might need to take his time.

Around that, and up onto a narrow ridge where the fossil of an ocean fish is bedded in the soft stone, its vertebrae the size of walnuts. Someone pries the pieces loose and brings them to show, but they break to chalky dust in his hand.

The horses pulling hard now, lathered on their flanks, remembering the washy grasses of May and paying for their softness. Wanting water.

Here the pilgrims are on the Smoky Hill trail itself, the plains highway from Atchison, on the Missouri River, to the foot of the Rockies. Matted grass has reclaimed it, but the ruts are there—no mistaking them—wide grooves hammered down under an iron-rimmed passage of loneliness and ambition and unsleeping fright.

There is a little stir of excitement somewhere at the front. The caravan stops. And Foard Darnall dismounts, takes his plaited bullwhip from the saddle. Behind him it rises in slow uncoiling. Makes a floating circle on the air, so gently, with no suggestion of the exploding violence it intends.

Coolly in that last suspended moment, their two pairs of eyes empty of any passion, the man and the rattlesnake examine one another.

Head of a long valley falling off to night. The wagons safely circled and the beasts fed. The people feeding—ham steaks turned over a pit fire, sweet slabs of wheat bread from a farm woman's kitchen.

Heat lightning to the south.

Everywhere the dauntless, insistent voice of the little freckled woman weaving over them, giving it sense and importance. She knows that she can make these pilgrims care—believes that they have begun to.

A Hefner daughter, Barbara—straight, forthright Kansas girl—takes up her guitar beside the fire. *This land is your land,* she begins. A party of seven from Kansas City joined the train at supper, and it is their night of awkward newness. But the song rises. The others are singing. *From California to the New York Island . . .*

The sound of their voices no longer startles and embarrasses them. They think it might be nice to hear this standing out just beyond the circle, or even at greater distance.

The newcomers try, and find it is not so hard to do.

Behind drawn flaps, bedded on wagon bottoms that somehow seem softer now, the pilgrims cannot remember any other homes. They hear the coyotes begin; hear them steal closer. A few still are awake when, with a sucking sound against the canvas tops, a sudden breath of coolness comes pressing up the valley ahead of the rain.

It did not occur to Ruth Hefner, when her destiny revealed itself, to demand that it also be reasonable. Or that others share it.

Some of her Quinter neighbors believed the venture—Wagons Ho!, as she decided to call it—would invite ridicule on their town from city folks come out on weekends to view the rustics. Landowners had waking nightmares of gates left open and dry pastures set afire. Better, they thought, that it should fail. Quickly.

She argued. She cajoled. And in the first full season of operation she lost fifteen thousand dollars. Luckily, her rancher husband, Frank, is a patient man. So is their banker.

Ten years later, much has changed. The ranchers come out at night to trade stories by the fire, to talk a little history, to speak of the enduring pull of this empty land. And scores of others from Quinter and miles distant call themselves friends of the wagon train.

Last year the books balanced, the first time. Someday it could be a big business, which might spoil it. And possibly that is what Ruth Hefner fears. For sometimes spring letters come in from people who have heard of Wagons Ho! by word of mouth, or seen a paragraph in a travel magazine. And the letters go into the "Ruth Do" basket on the desk in what used to be the Hefner living room, there to be submerged until some process as mysterious as the tides, but less predictable, brings them forth again.

Thus her thoughts as she spins along the blackness of a gravel road are entirely of the people who are back there in the wagons *now*. Not those who might someday come.

And they are bending to it—they sang tonight.

A rain tomorrow will help. Invariably that draws them closer, though she cannot explain it.

The street of the town sleeps in darkness. Inside the house, she empties her dress pocket of pieces of paper with their urgent jottings. Provisions to be ordered. A man from Ohio has run out of film for his camera. The people from somewhere will be staying an extra day. Somebody in Washington has left word to return his call—something about the Japanese. But first she wants to telephone about an old iron rendering kettle for boiling corn on the cob.

The light in the house burns on. The "Ruth Do" basket screams its useless accusations.

Her vision is too personal to be shared.

In drizzle they wake, and eat, and pass down a five-mile slope of the Smoky Hill watershed to the river itself, and along that to a grove of cottonwoods, where they eat again, hearing the gentle patter of rain on plates of fried chicken.

Hair that came meticulously coiffed to Kansas lies now in plastered strings against wet foreheads. The doctor from Cape Cod, by habit thin-lipped and haughty (or shy), becomes expansive, voluble, lends a pair of dry shoes to a man from Kansas City.

Children cross the shallow river to hunt arrowheads. Never having found one before, and looking where none should be. No matter, though—they find one now, a beauty with only a little of the point gone. And a chunk of shale from the riverbed, crusted with mollusk fossils. One of the wagon drivers scratches it with a knife point and it gives out a sharp, petroleum reek.

Sky breaking in afternoon, a late show of sun. But the people are in jackets by the fire as the evening comes down.

On a hill behind, two teen-aged youths have gone adventuring and found wooden stakes numbered one through twelve driven at random in the prairie sod. They pull them up—have all of them except seven and eight, and are looking for those.

Over the hill and whooping down on the wagon circle come five Indians, crew members in warpaint and feathers. A bit of nonsense for the youngsters, who scatter before them like frightened quail.

Art Bentley lets fly a charge of black powder from his musket and then, as one dismounted savage strays too near, the old man rushes, drives a shoulder into him—K-State, remember, 1902—and carries him down. Lies there, too long, though, so that the people begin to think, *His hip! Oh, my, he's done a hip.* But he is only pinning his man. And later, still flushed with the excitement of it, he tells one of them he hated to drop that fine musket in the dirt. "But I saw that Injun coming and saw I could get him and it was a two-handed job."

Food to excess. And singing that begins unasked.

"Before it gets too dark," Ruth Hefner tells them, "some of you might want to take the nature walk. You'll see some plants that grow out here on the prairie. They're marked up on the hill."

The two pullers-up of numbered stakes trade looks of dumb horror. The father of one of them contemplates his shoe. But they are reprieved. An accordion has appeared from somewhere, and the wife of the El Paso architect can use it—with joy if not precision—and draws a crowd. There are no takers for the nature walk.

A man with a sheet-metal works in Cedar Rapids, Iowa, makes harmony in a fine, clear tenor.

Below the wagons, a windmill creaks and clicks beside a stock tank. Horses shoulder and nicker in the corral. Against the saffron dusk on the hilltop, a man and boy can be seen plodding hopelessly, carrying numbered stakes and looking for holes—any holes—to put them in.

". . . carried a hundred rounds for their muskets," Art Bentley, hawk-faced at the edge of the firelight, is telling someone. "And every man an extra flint."

They stay long, hating to let it end. And the wind, still smelling of rain, shakes their wagons as they sleep.

Last day for most of them.

Cloudless again, and searing.

They stop to look at a sod house, one of the last left standing, its roof in places open to the sky but the two-foot-thick earthen walls still sound.

They marvel at how long ago the land was claimed, how sturdy those were who claimed it. (Though to the old man riding with them it is nothing marvelous at all. As a boy he helped build this very house. Knew the people well.)

Later, because he thinks it might please the wagon riders, he flushes a jackrabbit from the high grass and drives it to them. Two others jump in front so he drives them all—wheeling at a flat run, leaning forward almost against the mane—and brings them across in front, as fine a show of horsemanship as anyone might like to see.

And when the mean-eyed buckskin decides not to be stopped, Art Bentley, unalarmed, just turns him to the river and lets him run himself out there, on sand bottom in water to the knees.

A distant, solitary tree marks the stopping place for lunch. Where they have always stopped. But something can be seen under it.

Foard Darnall rides forward to identify it; rides back in noticeable haste. The head of the train veers out in a majestic arc away from that tree. What is under it is a cow, several sunny days past its mortal seizure, the size now, roughly, of a Hudson Terraplane.

The pilgrims view it with cold dispassion. One becomes less finicky on the frontier. The wagons circle in the quartering wind and, at pains only not to look directly at the thing, the people give their whole attention to a hearty stew.

Finally, the river silvering below them on the left, and, on the right, Tooled-boots and his tribe of kin outriding like a brigand troupe, they come out onto another of those high flats.

And know, then, that it is over, because there are their cars brought around and waiting. Hate it, having preferred to press on to Denver just this way—the wagons swaying in a line, the children happy, The Green Palace never too far behind.

So that appetites which could not be fazed by carrion are dulled by parting. There are *abrazos*. There actually are tears.

Dug-up cacti and fossil clams and prize pebbles and captive box turtles are loaded into station wagons, which back and turn, raising dust.

The wind blows up from Sonora.

The few who are left wander aimless, abandoned, across the empty circle.

It comes at them across the reach of empty afternoon. Out of the sun, like the Zeros used to do.

A transcontinental motor coach, strayed far from asphalt, testing the footing as it comes, reeling on its springs. Four-eyed—headlights burning and, behind the tinted windshield, the driver's sun goggles.

Subsides with a whoosh of released air.

Opens its doors with a lesser hiss.

Emits, in a rush, twenty-two travel agents from Tokyo, Japan. Stetson hats. Levi's. One guitar. Many Nikon cameras.

They photograph the wagons. Themselves ensemble. Themselves eating. The driver beside his bus. The bus withdrawing. The bus on the horizon. The horizon afterward.

"Welcome to a hundred years ago!" Ruth Hefner tells them.

"You're just a wonderful-looking group of modern pioneers."

The Nikon shutters opening and shutting make an endless rustle, as of mice running through dry leaves.

They sit the benches uneasily, waiting.

They have seen the lights of Los Angeles, Las Vegas, and now the space and silence weigh intolerably.

Where is the action?

The lady with the autoharp comes out from town to sing for them. But the songs are delicate, the sound of the stroked strings lost on the wind. The newcomers have no patience for it.

Kiyoshi Yamamoto hits his guitar a ferocious whang.

Home, home on the lange, they sing. In English. Then in Japanese. More verses of it than have ever been heard in Kansas.

This duty done, they go early to their wagons. Their escort, a young man named Ed Shedlick from the U.S. Travel Service in Washington, lingers a little out by the fire, considering the cruel uncertainties of service to the flag.

The autoharp whispers sadly, telling that beginnings are always hard.

Pink dawn reflected on the underside of a woolly cloud.

A mile distant, silhouetted along the line where earth meets sky, a string of figures moves.

Too small to be buffalo, too upright to be wolves.

The string recurves upon itself, approaches, and the leader bursts in among the wagons, chest outthrust, nostrils flared. The gentlemen from Tokyo are keeping fit to win the world.

Outside the locked door of The Green Palace a man is waiting. Another joins him; then a third. It becomes a queue. Three minutes pass. Five. Nearly ten.

They clear their throats. They shuffle. They are getting taciturn. One of them hammers at the door.

The occupant comes out finally, Nikon-draped and ready to meet the day, and bows a small apology. His spoor is there to see: empty boxes and wadded foil film wrappers. It takes time to load three cameras in the dark.

How near, then, is violence. In speech. In fact.

The horses are led up ready for riders to be set upon them. The teams blow and shoulder in the harness.

Down next to the corral, Art Bentley—his unruly buckskin saddled—is into a story about a coyote hunt.

". . . could see him layin down in a patch of high weeds—just his ears, a little bit of his head." No old man's vague maunderings. Last year, it was, or the year before. His eyes glitter and he grins savagely with his own teeth.

"So I shot once, and there was five of them in there. Came out like

Art Bentley (left), telling of sod houses and coyote hunts

rabbits, every which way. Shot until my gun was empty and never did hit any of those other four."

The wagonmaster's cry sounds and the circle spins out to a line, heading away.

"That first one, he was jumping and turning. Jaw shot clean away—oh, he was an awful sight to look at."

The big buckskin snorts nervously, watching the train go.

"So I shot and killed him," Art Bentley says. "In all the years I've hunted coyotes I've never got two out of the same bunch. But that was my best chance."

He puts a foot in the stirrup and the horse shies. Tries again and the same. The third time he is nearly astride when the horse rears, eyes rolling wildly—forehooves thrashing the sky, the old man crying anger. Goes backward directly on him with a terrible sound. And that not being enough, rolls its full weight over him, the old man's breath passing out with a slow shout of rage and regret. And gains its feet and bolts off riderless to catch the wagons.

They see the horse and come back and find him sitting in the dust. Wire-rimmed glasses bent and hanging from one ear. Nose sliced cleanly in half from bridge to point, laid back on his face. One arm hanging useless from a shattered shoulder. Wrist broken, too, and three ribs.

And looking into their ashen faces the first thing he would have them know is that it wasn't the horse's fault.

"Buck just can't stand to be left behind."

So gray and still he is under a blanket in the back of the old station wagon flying floorboarded a flat ninety ahead of its chalk plume on the gravel that, for one little moment, Ruth Hefner's faith deserts her and she asks, "Is he *gone*?"

But it will take more than being wallowed on by any horse to finish the oldest of the Bentley stock.

When the wagon stops on the hospital drive he raises his bleeding face and says, "Are we there already?" And they sit him on the edge of a table and ease off the shirt, showing arms with more sinew than many half that age.

In another room, presently, the doctor—a man Art Bentley has shot ducks with—shows Ruth the X-ray against a lighted holder. The large bones of the shoulder broken and the socket shoved out of place. The cracked ribs.

"I'll sew his nose up about as pretty as it ever was," the doctor says. "But he'll need surgery for the shoulder. We'll send him over to Hays."

When last seen, he is lying flat on a wheeled stretcher, still talking—
telling the nurses that when he is mended and back on the wagon train
again there is only one horse he means to ride. The big buckskin. Says
they'll have to tie him to keep him off.

The swollen cow under the solitary tree has been dealt with, but those
who saw it in full majesty honor its memory with distance. The gentlemen
from Tokyo, in their innocence, of course elect to dine in the shade.

There has been another casualty. One of the Japanese has fallen sideways from his horse and twisted his ankle in the stirrup. He claimed his
saddle slipped. Several of his colleagues insist he toppled off asleep. He,
too, has been dispatched to town.

The others face outward from the tree trunk, empty plates beside them,
arms around flexed knees, drugged with contentment. The breeze fans
them, curling their Stetsons' brims.

They traverse the afternoon. Nothing more.

But arrive, as the others did before them, much changed. In heart, at
any rate, if not in habit. For the Japanese, as is well known, are a fastidious
people.

Showers at the evening camps are set not far outside the wagon circle.
Outhouse-sized wooden frames are covered with black plastic, and the
water flows down from metal drums on top, heated by the sun. It is a nice
touch, although most pilgrims' desire for tidiness is nullified by the formidable logistics of privacy.

The teams are unhitched and taken to water. Blue smoke drifts from the
cooking fire. The kitchen truck arrives. The bench seats have been carried
from the wagons and people are resting on them while they wait to eat.

"Lookit!" a small boy says, pointing. They all lookit.

Beyond the wagons, the gentlemen from Tokyo are occupied with their
ablutions. One is in the shower and five others have finished. They have
dealt with the privacy problem directly. Vigorously they towel, the joy of
being clean amplified by the late sun that burnishes their nakedness.

A blur crosses the circle—Ed Shedlick, the Travel Service man, in full
stride, mouth shaping a silent cry of *No!*

"Well, it's just their way," one of the wagon drivers, an ample lady of
some years, announces serenely. "They do things different from us."

The preacher having gone back to Wausau, Wisconsin, Ruth Hefner
invites one of the newcomers to say grace.

He consults his colleagues.

"You see," he tells her, "we are of another faith."

"That's all right. Do it your way."

Consults again. And finally declines, though gently, there being no precedent for conversing with the Eternal Buddha out loud, among strangers, in a public place.

But the mood of the day is secure now, past being marred by trifles.

They pass through the food line together, the folks from Ohio, Georgia, and Virginia carried along by the insistent, hastening press of these visitors from a crowded land.

And in the wrapping dark, by the fire, Barbara Hefner challenges them with her guitar and her level eyes.

This land is your land, she begins.

Having traveled far from the lights of Las Vegas to a region of the mind, they can easily follow. *This rand is my rand . . .*

The voices rising together, asking how many roads a man has to walk, asking where all the flowers have gone.

The landowner is there. And Art Bentley's son. And the families of other crew members. The accordion appears again. They dance a polka and then, arms locked—the Japanese among them—a violent round of something called The Flying Dutchman.

In all that emptiness of unfinished land their racket rises.

Ruth Hefner, seeing that against any reason or possibility it has been made to work again, slips off toward town, wrung with elation and fatigue, to do battle with the slips of paper in her pocket.

A long time the people stay, frightening the coyotes to silence, before going slowly to their wagons.

A rain cloud rolls up the sky.

The windmill clicks.

Sometime toward midnight, the fire blazes up. Dark figures have come to squat beside it. Silent and nearly motionless, they wait for the kettle to boil. The gentlemen from Tokyo are cooking noodles in the night.

7 THE PROMISE OF ELYSIAN

The ancient Greeks conceived of a realm where, after life, virtuous souls might adjourn to pass eternity in a state of unblemished contentment. They called that place Elysium.

The word has an adjectival form, *Elysian*—"sweetly blissful"—describing a condition of the spirit but also naming a place that can be visited in this life.

Pass northward up the midlands, to where the fields and tailored farms first give way to reed-rimmed lakes and the dark, mosquito-humming remnant of a once vast woodland. Just there, in southern Minnesota, is a terrain you might hope to see in tranquil dreams. The earth has been sculpted into clefts and planes and sudden rounded hills by the frozen chisel of the glacier. Warm is the sun, in season. The light is clear, the shadows sharp. Like the shadows of a mountain summer, they contain always an edge of cold recalled and soon again expected.

Through this landscape the road proceeds, then makes a bend. A water tower can be seen above the trees, and that is Elysian. Four hundred fifty-four inhabitants at the last count, but with all the constituent parts of a proper town: newspaper, bank, post office, school, churches and saloons, a street of stores, even a small museum.

Somewhere in the experience of each of us, or at least in our collective memory, there is a village. And embedded in that memory is another—of a cadence lost, of values strangely changed on the way to becoming whoever it is we are. Sometimes the sense of that comes back with an ache.

Let's stop a day, then, in this place whose name, Elysian, dares to promise a special state of being. And visit with its people, discovering how they live and to what purposes.

And then decide if what we remember was ever real, or only something afterward imagined.

I

From the vantage of the hill, for a little longer in the silent hour of early morning, all the street lamps of the village may be counted. Then a brush stroke of dusky rose appears behind the trees. A breeze quickens. And the features of the place are revealed.

A terrain of tranquil dreams

Below, and stretching away past seeing, the lake's dark shine. Along its
margin, the cabins of the summer people. Nearer, in the public park, the
baseball diamond, a holy place where boys play the game for love and
where, surprised suddenly to find themselves gotten old, they sit on the
wooden bleachers and retell all the blows they struck.

Laid out on gravel streets below the hill and mounting up it are the
houses, in which no life yet stirs. And to the left of those, the building
fronts of Main Street to which, in broad daylight now at a quarter past the
hour of five, we may quietly descend.

A truck motor whines out on the highway, and a cat goes off quick-
footed between the buildings. The street lights wink off together. A flock
of sparrows appears, pecking at something along the street, then rising
up as one and moving farther on—past Lawrence Prenzlow's hardware
store and the old Community Building, standing empty. Past the grocery
and the post office and barbershop and the small frame building of the
newspaper, the *Elysian Enterprise*. Past the bank and the old Root drug-
store building and Tiny Town sundries and on westward, pecking and
fluttering along the two-block street, until the day's first car sends them
darting off together on some other errand.

In this slow fashion it gets to be nearly seven o'clock, and a man comes
treading gingerly to try the door of Ralph's Corner Bar and find it locked.
Other men come and rattle the handle and peer inside. And, in their great
need, Ralph opens to them.

Later in the day the Corner Bar will be a place of warmth and innocence,
with meals served and families gathered. But just now Ralph's practice is
medicinal. He sets before them their prescriptions: a bottle of beer with a
tumbler of peppermint schnapps or blackberry cordial. Three of these vile
doses for each and the light comes back into their eyes and they are able to
talk with animation of the work to which they'll shortly go.

In his room at the back of the building, the little man called Schmitty
still is sleeping.

He tended bar for Ralph until a stroke four years ago, when he was
seventy, lamed him and crippled one arm. Before that he lived to fish and
hunt. As long as anyone in the village has known him those were his
devotions. Now he can do neither.

His last dog—his life's best and last dog, the weimaraner he called
Duke—is gone. He sold the guns he could no longer bring to shoulder. His
fishing rods stand unused in his room, and his outboard motor belongs to
a nephew now.

It was a fine little motor, Schmitty says. *"I gave it to him when I died."*

Schmitty, remembering great pike and his silver Duke

Later Schmitty will wake and take breakfast and perhaps go slowly, leaning on his cane, the half-block down to the barbershop for his weekly shave. Then sit again in his room or in a booth at the Corner Bar. Ralph looks out for him. They all look out for him—as people do in a village, where lives are not so soon forgotten. No one passes without a word to Schmitty. They sit with him for company. His face is young as he repeats some story of the chase.

But just now he is sleeping—dreaming, he will afterward admit, of trolling for northern pike, and of pheasant roosters rising ahead of his silver Duke.

The men empty their last beers and tumblers of schnapps and go off to the job. The banker unlocks his door. The post office opens, and after that the newspaper. Ralph drops the empty bottles down a tube into a rack in the cellar of the Corner Bar.

And the day begins.

II

On the hill above the village rears a red brick building, two stories and a turret. It used to be the school, but is the museum now. Inside sleeps all the history of the place, told in the shorthand of its artifacts.

The story moves in leaps of backward time. From the photographs and documents bearing the names of families still resident here. To the collected utensils of the first settlers. To the bird points and stone scrapers of the people whose land it was before that. And finally to the oldest relic of all.

Ten thousand springs ago, a few more or less, a giant of the antique race of bison misjudged the ice and afterward lay undisturbed in the timeless twilight of the lake's bottom, through the passing of more history than we know, until that massive skull came up tangled in the net of a fisherman seining for carp.

III

In the early 1850s there began arriving a hardy polyglot of English and Scandinavians and Germans and Irish and Bohemians to lay axes to the giant bass trees and elms and maples of the area they called the Big Woods, a southward-projecting lobe of the great primal forest that ran deep and silent up the continent to the brittle shore of the retreated ice.

Wildfires bore down upon those early, frail habitations. Sudden blizzards obscured the track and people were found in the drift, frozen with their oxen only steps from the door. Yet such was the industry of the settlers that, within twenty-five years of their first coming, the land had been for all time changed—the Big Woods substantially cleared and transformed into thrifty farms.

Margaret and Joe Clarke are sitting now with photographs and family records at a table in the house that the first Clarkes began building 118 years ago.

A great, gracious white house it is, under ancient trees, with cool porches and many rooms filled with the finest savings and finest memories of all those years. It fronts down a cleft of hills to the lake, Lake Francis or Lake Frances—a detail not yet locally agreed upon—a generous reach of whose near shore still is Clarke land.

Joe Clarke is in his middle sixties, his sister a bit older. They have made their lives together—lives of industry and substance and quiet grace, tending this house and these lands as you would keep a shrine, and rightly so. Neither ever married. There were chances, you may be sure. But that was the way of it. Thus there is no immediate heir.

The wilderness has become a land valuable almost beyond price. But years pass. And the stones in the cemetery speak unmistakably of conclusions.

"It kind of haunts you sometimes," Joe Clarke says in his shy, soft voice. "This farm has been in the Clarke name all that time. And one of these days it won't be."

Put to words, the notion smites them silent. Joe and Margaret both. They look at the table. In the coolness of the big house, a clock ticks.

Then he speaks again, with something like a smile, and still softly—though in fact it is a cry wrenched from him.

"You wouldn't really think," he says, "that anybody else would feel *at ease* here, would you?"

IV

Crimes, being so few, are remembered in detail.

Seventy years ago a farmer of the township murdered his wife but was never tried or even charged, though his misbehavior was commonly known.

In 1974, the Elysian State Bank was robbed by strangers. Gene LaFrance, the bank's president, mindful of his own and his staff's skins, was as accommodating to the robbers as a man can be while reclining trussed on his office floor. The loss was covered by insurance.

Not long after that, three boys with pistols came into Ralph's Corner Bar, and the holes in the ends of the guns, by word of the bartender, were as big around as culverts. He gave them the cash drawer. He would have given them the whole register if they'd asked.

Then a woman sitting at the bar turned and called one of the boys by name. She knew him. He was from a place just down the road.

"You know better than to do such a thing!" she said crossly to him. The boys ran out, flustered. And wrecked their car driving out of town. And were collected from the ditch and sent away for a time to improve their citizenship.

In the village, where everyone and everything are known, even a holdup man can feel the lack of privacy.

V

Morning draws on toward midday.

Bent under the raised hood of a car on the drive of his service station, Ralph Nusbaum remembers how he and the other village boys looked forward to the summer people coming to the lake cottages, their daughters with them. The sadness was always knowing the girls would go away when August ended. Now his own son is old enough to operate the station. The noon siren sounds above the fire hall. Ralph Nusbaum wipes his hands on a cloth and goes to the house for lunch.

VI

The driven nomads of the mobile society may live in correct terror of leaving their bones unvisited in alien and unfamiliar ground. But to the people of such a place as this—who have been born together and have gone to dust together, so many of them for so long—the cemetery is only a different, a later place to live.

Being as practical in the matter of death as they are in the affairs of life, the villagers often arrange for their headstones to be erected years before the actual need arises. It can be disconcerting to be driving past the graveyard and notice, near the road, a somber monument to someone you observed only twenty minutes ago marching quite lively out of the post office and up the block to deposit money in Gene LaFrance's bank.

South a block from the fire station, between Main Street and the highway, can be seen a considerable garden and in it two men working—two men who have kept the cemetery waiting and intend to do so a while longer.

Ed Schneider is ninety-three years old and Glenn Adams is eighty-eight, and their exertions in the garden, while stupendous, scarcely can be noticed taking place.

Schneider, a tiny man, lets fall the blade of his hoe to smite an intruding weed, then rests on the handle and scouts the row ahead. Adams is two full heads taller, and applies that leverage now to the tiller. He drives forward a slow step. Then waits. Then leans again. The tiller supports his leaning and, in so doing, parts the sandy ground.

Their wives have gone to the cemetery and their children have gone away, and Schneider and Adams share an apartment in the village. They will set out their produce in a box there. Other roomers will take whatever appeals and leave some change.

The two men are known by everyone in Elysian. Their names are daily spoken. People are sent to them for the answers to questions about local history. *Old-timers,* they are called—a term of affection and praise.

That is not always, or even often, the way that lives move toward their conclusion in larger and more complicated places. In the village, folks may buy their tombstones early. But they are not made to go lie under them before they're dead.

VII

He is an alcoholic who does not drink. His hair hangs full over ears and neck, though it used to reach to his shoulders, and before that came to midchest. His manner of speech is enlivened by words that should not be printed here.

He lives alone, except for two cats, in an untidy cottage around which he has gathered a bouquet of derelict trucks in varying states of ruin and reassembly—windows shot out and transmissions on the ground and engines set up on wooden blocks in the clutter of his yard. Among these rusted beauties he can be seen prowling now, in his usual dress: jeans and moccasins and a part of a shirt with no sleeves at all.

He is Timothy McCarthy, thirty-five years old. The parish priest.

Not so long ago he was a quite conventional young city cleric—black suit, black shoes, evenings at the symphony and other genteel entertainments in rich parishes where he found more bickering and hypocrisy than faith.

The parish priest, softened by service in a gentle place

It has been three years now since he was dispatched, a man disheartened and full of rage, to lodge and serve among a different people, a gentler people, than any he had ever known before. And the sweetness of this place, he freely admits, has claimed and softened him.

The problems he has found here are mostly private ones: too much drink, a kind of reticence that often makes the people, for all their decency, unable easily to share their feelings and speak their hearts. But of great sin—of malice and overweening vanity and deliberate hurt—there is little to be discovered.

His eccentricities can be explained.

The trucks, bought cheap and pirated for parts, are to carry the stones and logs for a cabin he is building in a woodland farther north. He dresses plainly because, he argues, in the village where his vocation is known to all, priestly garb would have no value except to intimidate.

And, yes, he does speak coarsely.

"In the seminary," he says, "I could with great facility discuss the noetic and ontological essence of transcendental reality. I am capable of speaking in language such as to baffle and confuse anyone in Elysian. I was trained to do it."

But so, he quickly adds, might the farmer confuse a priest in explaining the workings of his machinery. Or the banker in discussing his ledgers. Yet they have the good sense not to. They speak to be understood, as should a man whose mission is to preach the Gospel in its simplicity.

He still owns the black suit and black shoes. And even wears them sometimes, when the formality of the occasion absolutely demands. Women of the church are apt to remark, then, a trifle wistfully, how very nice he looks. And he is apt to reply, with all good humor, "Do I tell you when to wear a bra?" They cluck and turn away, but they accept him for what he is.

Before he came this was a mission parish, without a priest of its own, served by clerics visiting from other towns. And likely will be again when Tim McCarthy goes. But he does not *mean* to go—not soon, at any rate.

Where else but here might he find so easy a welcome?

VIII

They are not an unloving people, but they are a guarded people, unable often or easily to speak affection—their temperaments shaped in long silence and long cold, with only a moment's summer in between.

In the eternal emergencies of bereavement or injury or pressing need,

Marge Pribyl, unlocking mute hearts

the people draw together. But between them, in ordinary times, there is an aching silence of the heart.

Twenty-six years as the kindergarten teacher to the children of the village have made Marge Pribyl a hater of that silence. She has seen too clearly its effect. Children come to her who never have been read to, never really *talked* to. It has not occurred to them that they might have ideas worth telling and cleverness worth showing and love worth giving. Those are the lessons she tries to teach ahead of any others. For, if they are mastered, other kinds of learning—though none more important—can surely follow.

She is middle-aged now. The children of the school are the children she herself will never have, and teaching is the single passion of her life. When her classroom empties, Marge Pribyl goes home, spent from warring with the silence, along the mile of blacktop to her house, whose window looks down across a slant of bouldered hill to the Clarkes' long meadow and the dark line of woods behind.

Goes home to where she lives alone.

Goes home, of course, *to silence*.

IX

Newspapers hold up a mirror to life. And it is the duty—the privilege—of the *Elysian Enterprise* to mirror the lives of people who are not crazed by anxiety or rage, or gnawed at by the worm of despair.

A death noted. Word of villagers taking supper in other villagers' homes. A meeting announcement. Notices of a family reunion, a poetry contest, a swine seminar, and a five-day crusade by an evangelist with a puppet.

That is the run of news—the slow, sensible rendering of a week whose rhythm was much like that of the weeks preceding and all those apt to follow.

This week's top story will concern the fortunes of Elysian's Little League baseball team. The boys are playing tonight for the championship. The front page of tomorrow's edition already has been laid out, leaving space for a picture and caption from the game. The full account will have to follow a week late, but no one will mind. The news of baseball doesn't age; it only ripens.

Mary Wilcox Kennedy, the editor, is sixty-one years old, and she was born into the business of newspapering. The *Enterprise* was founded by her great-uncle in 1893. She and her husband, Harold, are the whole staff.

There was a time she might have left to make her mark in some larger place. But then she considers the small office around her. Considers all the stories of the village the generations of Wilcoxes have told. And she supposes she would choose the same life over again.

Of scandals lurid, issues raging, offenses capital, or revelations to sicken the heart there are none to report.

Someone's dog barks at night outside an open summer window, or runs through someone else's garden. The mayor receives an urgent telephone call at home. He sympathizes, but is powerless over the malfeasances of dogs. Then the beast's habits change. Sleepers sleep again and gardens flourish.

Where is any news in that?

X

On a gravel lane just north of the village, in the house overlooking the reedy pond that some folks call Swain Lake and others call Schoolhouse Lake and others call just a slough, an old man cuts with a small pair of sharp-pointed scissors from a sheet of paper, the west window lighting his work.

A long lifetime ago, when he was three years old or maybe four, Earle Swain discovered that he could see on a sheet of paper things no one had drawn there. All that was needed was to snip away the parts of the paper that didn't belong.

It might be the simplest picture—a flower growing in the woods behind the barn, or owls on a branch, awaiting winter. Some small thing he had seen. Or it might be fabulously complex. Of a boy and girl crossing a stream on stones, with the girl's bows flying and a flower in her hand, the stream running at their feet and a cattail forest behind them and smaller things growing at the margin of the water. A picture with much detail and a certain playful humor in it and, what is more, with all the animation of something really happening in life.

One like that might take several minutes to cut, the paper turning carelessly in his hands.

His mother taught him always to pick up his snips. So now, when he is eighty, the points of his scissors, quick and deft as a heron's beak, dart down to pluck a scrap from the rug. Last year the five cows who used to graze the yard were sold. So the yard has filled up—the northern jungle of vines and saplings closing dark around, with only footpaths beaten through it. Foxes have taken nearly all his chickens.

Snipped paper pictures turn crisp and yellow, then flake away. The maker of them is a country man, with a country gift. And the art is as perishable as the man. For a few years, certain people will remember his odd genius. Then no one will.

XI

There is no saying how many boys of the village were devoted to the game before him. Their numbers are long past counting. His grandfather played baseball on this field. So did the grandfather of the girl he would marry. So did both his brothers and all his friends.

He always was a worker, the people say of him. He got the paper route at nine. But what he worked at mainly was baseball.

No matter that he has come home now, a few days short of being thirty-five, his major league career likely at an end. What matters is that, of all the generations of Elysian boys who have played the game for love, only one went all the way. And Jerry Terrell is that one.

While the Little Leaguers play, he is in the stands with his wife and his father. His mother is watching from their house across the street and up the third-base line, as she did when her boys were playing. Cheerfully he writes on the objects—balls, caps, odd scraps of cardboard—the children bring him. And visits afterward with teammates from his own boyhood days—men who stayed in the village to farm or work at other jobs.

Then he and his father, Bud, cross the street to sit on the porch of the house overlooking that field where so uncountably many young men's summers have been spent, with its dugouts the two of them built as a memorial to the middle of the Terrell boys, Jimmie, the second baseman, killed in a car accident at seventeen.

Was Jerry the best ever to play the game in the town? Surely not, they agree. They speak some famous, unknown names. It is two hundred ninety feet to the fence down the right-field line. Beyond that it is another full city block to the lake. Jerry saw one of those men whose names they speak hit the ball into the lake on the fly. If such a blow had been hit in Yankee Stadium they would still be measuring—or maybe still looking for the ball. But that was a long time ago, in Elysian, from which fame does not travel far.

The years have come a long circle.

A lad named Trevor Larson has the paper route now. This night it was his hit that brought in Elysian's first two runs of a championship won by a single marker when, in the last inning, the opposing runner failed to touch home plate. Down on the field, unwilling to go sleep away their time of triumph, some of the Elysian boys in red and white are playing catch in the uncertain light.

The major leaguer watches silently a moment.

"I wish," he says finally, "that every one of them could go through what I've gone through." Says that with tenderness—and a little wonder.

"I have lived my childhood dream."

XII

In such fashion the days of summer pass gently on. The afternoon sun has warmed without punishing. Now comes the cool evening to refresh.

Across the carved and folded hills that used to be shaded by the Big Woods lies a placid geometry of twilit fields, lush with their fruiting. And in their center is this small place of gathered lives.

A party of fishermen arrives outside the white house on the rise above the lake. They look a hushed moment at Joe Clarke's great pike on the wall of the porch—the fish of all his years, creature of a lost time. Then get in their car and drive off to their cabin in a fever of hope.

By her window, in silence, Marge Pribyl looks down into the sweep of low meadow and is thinking already of September, of the children who will come to her. Wonders if their small spirits will be chilled to numbness by a silence greater than her own. And if so, wonders if once more she will find a way to warm them.

Beside another window, in the last of light, Earle Swain finishes the picture he is cutting. Cats mew at his feet. The vines and saplings of his untended yard close darker around.

Slow with age, two men put away their gardening tools and go home to their apartment. Their tomatoes are plump, their corn heavy with ears. It may be the last garden they will ever make. But for this day, at least, its rows are clean.

In his vestments of blue jeans and moccasins, the parish priest can be seen walking contemplatively among the many old trucks in the rectory's front yard. Might the transmission from the 1942 wrecker be made to fit the 1946 Chevy two-ton? An engaging speculation. Now it is full dark, though, so Tim McCarthy goes indoors and lights a cigarette and puts a religious record on his player.

In the office of the *Enterprise*, Mary and Harold Kennedy have laid the last news in the place saved for it on the front page. "Little League Baseball Champions," says the headline, which Harold set by hand.

The light in the newspaper goes out. And it is nearly the last along the street.

The quiet of the patterned fields comes to wrap the houses of the village now. The simple memories of this day are sweet. Antique memories, they seem almost to be—of a time when rage and desperation and danger were far away. It would be easy to pass a lifetime in such a place. Ask all of those who have, and would again.

The quiet comes even to the Corner Bar, where the little stroke-lamed man they call Schmitty is sitting in a booth, speaking of his silver dog, Duke, the hunting weimaraner who shared his happier times.

"It makes me cry to think of him," Schmitty says. And, saying it, does cry. Then shuffles away to his room at the back of the bar.

The establishment that was the first to open also is the last to close. Then its light, too, goes out.

And the village sleeps.

8 THE FRAGILITY OF SKEPTICISM

A Report of the Mud Camp Expedition

(Author's note: Nearly sixteen years ago, in the autumn of 1973, five of us—three journalists, a lawyer, and an insurance man—set out to investigate the accounts of strange occurrences near the town of Murphysboro in southern Illinois. We sought evidence. We pretended, in a fabulous way, to seek the beast itself, even as we disbelieved that it existed. Our expedition failed, and some reticence, some slight embarrassment, has prevented me from writing about it until now. It has taken all this time for me to understand that the point was not what we may or may not have seen and heard there in the swamp, but rather what happened in our minds.)

In past millennia the Mississippi River changed its course some fifteen miles to westward, leaving where it formerly had run a lowland wilderness of muck and water-tolerant trees and bamboo thickets. Ten miles in length, forty square miles in whole extent, it is a silent and hostile place crept over by vines, crept through by snakes and other things.

The people who eventually came to settle the area built their town atop the limestone bluff that once had defined the primal river's eastern bank, at its confluence with a lesser stream named the Big Muddy, overlooking that wilderness they called The Scatters.

In winter, when the snakes were sleeping, a few men set their traps there, or shot the ducks that used the shallow potholes of the swamp. But most counted it a place to be avoided. Anyone whose night-running hound followed game into The Scatters waited until morning to try to find the dog and fetch him out.

As it happened, I had flown across the Mississippi in the spring of 1973, outbound toward three months in Russia. It was a season of ruinous floods. Engorged by rain and by snow melt on its upper tributaries, the river had overspread the banks by miles in every direction. From the air, it seemed less a river than a vast and turbid sea. As far as one could see from the plane's window, farms and woodlots and whole hamlets had been swallowed up.

It is possible I might even have spied Murphysboro, perched dry atop its bluff, safe from the flood's harm. But I didn't know to look. And so it would not have registered in any case.

"It came just to the edge of the yard," the young woman said. "And stopped there, looking at us."

Came how? Shambling, perhaps, as a bear might move?

"No, not like that. It walked the way a person walks, arms swinging at the side."

She was seventeen years old, a leader in her high school class—pretty, a good scholar, a cheerleader. Not a girl desperate for notice. Her parents' house was in a development at the westernmost edge of Murphysboro, backed up directly to the bluff that fell away through thickets and broken ground down to The Scatters. Cheryl Ray and her friend, Randy Creath, had been sitting in the breezeway of the house, the dusk deepening, when they heard a sound of something moving in the bushes at the end of the yard.

She stepped indoors to switch on the yard lamp. When she came out again, Randy had gone near the edge of the brush and faced the thing at near quarters. Seven feet tall, they guessed it to be. Covered over with tan or dirty white hair, except the face, which was smooth. The eyes gave back the lamplight in red reflection. And the smell of it, borne to them on the warm air, was unspeakably foul.

With a boy's bravado, Randy snatched up a decorative stone from the lamp's base and flung it directly at the creature, which did not react at all but only continued to inspect them levelly—then turned in an unhurried way and walked back as it had come, back into the undergrowth and down the steep incline toward the lowland and the swamp.

"Walked," Cheryl Ray said again. "Like a man walks."

Earlier that afternoon, at another house in the outer rank of homes in that same development, a child of four years had come breathless to tell his mother about something he'd spied at the yard's edge. A big man in a furry coat, he said it was. The mother, busy in her kitchen, familiar with the extravagance of a toddler's imagination, sent him back outside to play and thought no more about it—until she read the newspaper account of what Cheryl and Randy had seen.

In a small hour of morning—at two A.M. in Riverside Park where a traveling carnival was quartered—four carnival workers heard a commotion among the ponies and, going with flashlights to investigate, found the thing standing outside the pen, watching the ponies milling in alarm. Their cries sent it off. And they did not immediately speak of what they'd seen, thinking it might frighten the paying clientele away. Only after the show had closed and they were ready to travel on to play some different town did they report the incident to the police.

Those are seven who saw. And there were two others, although these last two must remain unidentified here.

At the public boat ramp after dark, a young man and an older woman—another man's wife—were seriously occupied with whatever it was their urges commanded and the privacy of the boy's parked car allowed, when a cry from the direction of the river chilled their ardor. A cry like neither of them had ever heard: *A cross between an eagle and an elephant,* the youth would later describe it. *Starting high, and sliding down to a roar.*

Sitting up and switching on the car lights, he saw it standing thigh-deep amid the floating brush and sodden logs and other flood wrack in the swollen Big Muddy. Its eyes shone red in the sudden headlight beams. It made another horrendous hoot like the first.

Patrolman Jim Nash of the Murphysboro police department was on night duty when those two arrived at the station, their clothing still in disarray, gibbering with terror at what they'd just seen—a vision they had to report to someone, even if by doing so they might risk discovery by the lady's husband.

Patrolman Nash wrote out their statement. And with a fellow officer he went down to the boat ramp. Flashlights in hand, they made their way through thickets along the riverbank, following the splashing noises made by some large creature that kept always just outside the reach of their lights. Then came a scream. Very close, it seemed, and exactly as the boy had described—a cry altogether unknown to Nash, although he had hunted and trapped the creatures of the area for years and believed he knew all the sounds they made.

"We ran," Jim Nash would say afterward. "I don't mind saying it, we plain ran. My partner lost his revolver and had to go back the next day to find it. Now, when a policeman drops his gun and runs, you *know* he's scared."

But there was more work that night. Nash took the department's German shepherd attack dog from its pen and returned with other officers to the river. The dog made trail, and the track led first along the bottoms, then up a ravine toward higher ground in the direction of a ruined farmstead and an unused barn. At the door of the barn the dog stopped—went flat on its belly against the ground. They prodded the beast through the door, but it instantly crept out again, whimpering.

The police radioed for support. Sheriff's deputies came. The barn was surrounded while they waited for morning. Then day broke, and they went inside and nothing was there—if anything ever had been there. All they found was some evil-smelling scum that, on analysis, turned out to be from the municipal sewage lagoon, which lay on a direct line between the river and the barn. Evidently something had waded through the lagoon on the way to the abandoned farm. But what had done that?

"I wish I knew," said Tobias Berger, the Murphysboro chief of police. "And I'll bet you wish you knew, too."

That was our initial task, to hear the testimony. Nine people had seen something they were at a loss to explain or to name—nine people, most of them unknown to one another, whose accounts were consistent in every important detail. Some of them—the carnival men—no longer were anywhere about. The compromised wife, for obvious reasons, preferred not to speak. Their stories had to be gotten from the police reports.

The recitations of those who did agree to talk had a certain quality of polish. There had, after all, been telephone calls from the *New York Times*—calls from Europe, even. A tale too many times repeated begins to have a practiced sound. And yet . . .

Ross Lillard, the lawyer in our group, was and is a man of disciplined mind. By nature, by professional habit, he sifts testimony and evidence with ingrained caution. Like the others of us, he listened to the stories, asked several oblique and unexpected questions—subtracting the glibness of the replies to hear what else remained.

"They would," he said afterward, "make good witnesses in a court of law."

Then, in a borrowed Jeep and with the light of that first day failing, we clawed our way down a rutted track from the bluff on which the town stood to the beginning of The Scatters. And finally, in full darkness, entered in.

At the start, we were to have been a party of four, not five. Michael Fancher was a reporter for the *Kansas City Star,* who shortly would become the paper's city editor. Rick Solberg was an experienced *Star* photographer. I was the newspaper's editorial commentator on foreign matters. Written-out and tired after the long assignment in the Soviet Union, I had noticed the small item in the Murphysboro paper and, conspiring with Fancher, had instigated the lark. Monster hunting beats writing editorials any day.

Harlan Sorkin, a St. Louis insurance broker, agreed to join the expedition as a consultant, having previously investigated similar reports, from the state of Washington to Boggy Creek, and been interviewed on the radio and quoted in print and by that means having acquired a certain cachet as an authority in these matters.

Lillard, my lawyer friend, was an accidental addition.

Our families had had dinner together on the eve of the departure for Murphysboro, and Ross had found the notion of our venture hugely amusing. Returning home, then, he mentioned it to his mother, who was visiting from out of state.

That was indeed interesting, she said. Because his father had seen such a creature once as a boy in the woods of Tennessee. But his father had never spoken of it, said Ross, amazed. Except to her, she replied, he'd never spoken of it to anyone.

My telephone rang that night at a late hour. It was Lillard, of course, and he was no longer just amused. He was on fire to enlist.

Even in the pursuit of chimeras, one goes equipped. Or else the enterprise, whether serious or only a game, becomes hollow and without either humor or point. The job of quartermaster had earlier fallen to me.

"That has a breaking strength of two thousand pounds," the man in the marine supply store had said, fingering the braided nylon rope on the spool. "For water skiing it's way too heavy."

"It's not for skiing."

"Well, then, what do you have to tow?"

"Not tow," I said. "To tie up. We may need to tie something up."

"A boat or a plane or something?"

"An animal."

Interest quickened in his eyes. "Yeah?"

"On the order of a gorilla, but maybe bigger. A gorilla can stretch a truck tire like a rubber band."

"*Jeezus!*" the clerk said. And stripped seventy yards of the finger-thick rope from the spool.

The zoo director had not laughed. Nor had the zoo's veterinarian. The latter presented two loaded darts in a small case, and a third dart, empty, for practicing with the rifle.

"Nicotine is faster," he said. "But you have to be very specific about weight, which in this case you can't be. With nicotine there's hardly any margin for error. Too little, and there's no effect at all. Too much, and you kill the animal. What I've put in these—" He took a dart from the case and turned it carefully in his fingers. "—is more forgiving. It's a controlled substance. A hallucinogen, actually, and for veterinary use only. But I'm letting you take it because of the problem about weight. One of these will put a four hundred to six hundred pound animal down for five hours, a little more or less. But it does have one disadvantage."

And that drawback?

"Well, we generally use it only on dangerous animals that are caged. And there it makes no difference. But keep in mind, after you've gotten the dart in properly, *it will take about thirty minutes to work.*"

We thought, together, about the implications of that.

"Do you have a radio?" the zoo director asked. Our plan had not called for one. "Send one of your party out to a telephone, then," he said. "If you get something on the ground, I'll fly in a cage. You'll have it down and tied, and if it begins to come around you can always use the second dart. That gives you ten hours in all, which should be plenty. All this assumes that what you've tied up is not just some feeble-minded guy who's been roaming the woods over there in Illinois."

(*"There's this to think about,"* counselor Lillard would say later, during the long cross-state drive. *"Suppose we do find something out there. We can't know exactly what it is. And if it should turn out to be a hominid, it may very damned well have civil rights."*)

The zoo director had an afterthought.

"I'd take a fire extinguisher. We find them useful in zoo work. The hiss and sudden discharge of vapor will usually turn a charge. Beyond that, I can't think what else would be helpful. Evidently it's a primate of some sort, and primates, besides having intelligence, also are curious. So there's no point tramping around hunting for it. Just make your camp and wait. You're the bait."

I wished that he might have put it another way.

"Oh, yes," he said. "And you might try burning a can of chocolate in your fire at night. All primates are fond of chocolate."

Thus, before even arriving on the creature's own ground, the parameters of its probable weight had been considered. And the mechanics of subduing and restraining. Something of its nature was suspected. And its possible standing in law. Something known even of its dietary predilections.

Out of the thin smoke of fantasy, the chimera had suddenly begun to exhibit palpable character and shape.

Now, laboring in the Jeep's headlights, we winched aside fallen trees and maneuvered between standing ones until we came to the chosen place—unnamed on our topographic map—that would be Mud Camp.

Indian summer had ended abruptly and the weather had turned raw.

Mud Camp, near Murphysboro, Illinois

Several gasoline lanterns were hung out on branches to make a hundred-yard perimeter of light. Tents were put up and provisions stowed. Mike Fancher and Harlan Sorkin, as I remember, volunteered to take the first watch.

The others of us crawled warm inside tents and bags as a cold rain began to fall. And soon slept. And, sleeping, sank away a foot at least into the *terra infirma*. Then woke, immediately it seemed, in a sodden dawn, tents sliding away from under us, bedrolls soaked.

Mud Camp had no bottom. A forest grew there. The dropped leaves gave an appearance, a similitude, of substance and support. But that was all illusion. Trees sprang from, and leaves lay upon, the merest crust atop the deposited alluvium of the ancient river. Wet that crust and then disturb it, as we had done, and the patient bog below opened instantly to receive you.

Fancher and Sorkin, the night watchers, had waited and listened beside the smoking fire through a night that had revealed to them nothing except the outer limits of discomfort—until the fire, too, sank hopelessly and died with a hiss. They came now in their ponchos to help deal with the wreckage of the camp.

Sorkin held up his sleeping bag, a mess of mud and wetness without having yet even been slept in.

"Who *cares* what lives here?" he said. "Let's all go home." Of the five, he was the one true believer in the beast. We supposed he said it for a joke, but in his trembling misery it was impossible to be sure.

Logs were dragged and positioned side by side to make a platform on which to reerect the tents. More logs and sticks and chopped brush were laid as corduroy walkways to still another platform that supported our stores of food and equipment, chiefly contained in the Tanganyika Box—a great hinged crate that many years before had followed me home on a boat, filled with hides and heads, from the East African hunting outpost of Arusha. The Tanganyika Box held all our edibles, our lantern fuel, the portable stove, and the hallucinogenic darts, so its security was paramount.

But the mud, as I have said, was deep. Who knows how deep? The logs gradually sank away and the platforms and walkways vanished. Each several hours new materials had to be gathered and the whole operation repeated.

By these exertions, concerned mainly with various failed strategies for comfort, we managed to waste all of the second day.

Feet of a Mud Camp sleeper

I cannot remember the exact order of the second night's watches. We stood by twos, so either Lillard and Solberg or Lillard and Fancher must have been first—from dark until midnight—for one of them shook me awake and I went then with Sorkin to keep vigil at the fire. The others were in their tents.

We refilled and pumped the lanterns, brightening the lighted perimeter.

A can of chocolate syrup, forgotten until now, was dug from the Tanganyika Box and opened and put to warm and bubble in the edge of the flames, smelling chocolaty and companionable.

But the cold came seeping and the drizzle commenced again. Sorkin's boots were wet inside. His misery had grown profound. "Christ!" he said. "Why am I here?" And this time it could not be mistaken for a joke.

Far away an owl hooted. Followed by a thin, laughing call of some unknown small night animal. Sorkin peered at his watch, whose hands scarcely moved. One hour of our scheduled six had elapsed. A twig snapped, an improbable sound in that wetness. Nearer there were more rustlings. Our interest quickened. Out of the darkness came an opossum, dazzled by the lanterns, who proceeded stately across the light circle of the camp. It was an event. We returned then to working our cold toes in our boots and imagining the sensible comfort of distant beds.

Hunkered there with backs against trees, breathing the fire's smoke and praying for time to pass, we fell away into a vague state between hopelessness and dreaming. And time did pass, for it got somehow to be three o'clock in the morning.

Three o'clock exactly. The hour would afterward be fixed in all our minds.

Like an eagle's scream. It's how the sound began, but not as loud as you would expect—if you were able to expect it at all. Not at first. Then growing in volume until it seemed to fill the head. Then sliding down—what, three octaves, four?—to a rumble, vast and guttural, resonating inside some great cavity. This last seeming not just to fill the head but the world as well.

All taking place over an eternity of seconds. Enough time that we were able to turn, Sorkin and I, and each record, as in the slow moment before an automobile collision, the exact sequence of expressions that passed across the other's face: confusion, followed by denial, then crazy alarm.

There was a plan. We had refined it in the car, and rehearsed it in the wet camp the day before.

One watcher was to activate the tape recorder while the other quietly roused the sleepers. The five of us would then wait facing outward toward the perimeter of the lanterns. As the thing hove into view, Solberg, the photographer, would begin making pictures. If the flash of his strobe light did not turn it—if it still advanced—Sorkin would bring the fire extinguisher into play. Then, when it did turn, I would fire the tranquilizing dart into the creature's fleshy hindparts. Or, in case it kept coming in spite of all, Fancher and Lillard would have shotguns loaded with .oo buckshot, lethal at close range but very much a last resort. We meant to catch, not kill. And the creature, remember, might have civil rights.

That was the plan. In the instant of opportunity, it was forgotten altogether.

As the enormous sound passed to silence, Sorkin and I shouted the camp awake. Lillard afterward remembered the vexing urgency of our calls: *"Get up! Something's out here! Something's coming!"* He remembered his irritation at being disturbed so soon—only moments it seemed—after managing to achieve sleep in his wet bag and collapsing tent. His instinct was to ignore the commotion.

Then the second cry came, perhaps fifteen seconds after the first. It may have been nearer. Certainly it was louder.

Lillard's next memory is of being outside his tent, fully dressed, shotgun loaded, standing with four other thoroughly unnerved grown men in a line at the fire.

We waited, our curious array of armaments at the ready. The chocolate bubbled and stank as it burned. "At least we have the sound on tape," someone whispered. But in the first panic, I had failed to switch on the machine.

Night paled to morning. The far circle of lanterns guttered and went out. The chimera did not reveal itself. Nothing ever came. Emboldened by daylight, we prospected outward from camp in the direction of the cries. We found several impressions in the swamp floor that could, with effort of imagination, have been large footprints, but which, because of their indistinctness in the muck and leaf litter, are safer reported to have been nothing at all. The best of those we duly photographed.

But something else we found I am even now at a loss to explain.

At a distance of two hundred or so yards from the tents, we came upon a part of the lowland forest that had suffered a peculiar sort of violence. In a roughly circular area some twenty feet across, every tree had been bent, torn apart at its branchings, or entirely broken off. Not chewed off; *broken*, as you might snap a wooden pencil.

Harlan Sorkin in a misting dawn: the agony of a true believer

Living saplings, these were—some no larger than your wrist, but others as thick as a man's lower leg. Much of the bark had been stripped from them and flung about to lodge in standing trees at the edge of the circle, as if in a furious display. And the damage plainly was fresh, for the bark still was pliant and greasy-slick on its inner side. Some of the saplings had been snapped two or three feet from the ground, some a good deal higher. Can you imagine the strength required simply to lay hold of a living three-inch tree and break it off at face level?

No freak wind had done that, for the night had been uncommonly still. What might have, then? I don't pretend to know, or care to guess.

It was necessary on that third day, the last one, to make a trip to town for water. I stayed behind to keep the Tanganyika Box from sinking and, if time allowed, to explore a bit alone.

The rain had stopped. The swamp was very empty, very still.

At a crevice in the bluff, I found the entrance to a cave, but had no proper equipment for exploring it—or, to be truthful, much desire to. (Sorkin's theory had been that the creature might actually live in caves, and that, driven out by the previous spring's floods, it had made its way to higher ground where, like an opportunistic raccoon, it had discovered the delights of Murphysboro's garbage cans.)

In early afternoon, I was surprised to see at a distance through the trees the figure of another man. I called to him, but he did not hear, or in any case made no reply. Soon the Jeep could be heard bouncing and spinning along the muddy track, and the others came back—or three of them did.

Lillard, it turned out, had telephoned his law office and had learned that a friend's father had died and that the funeral was to be the next day. Still crusted with the dried goo of Mud Camp, he had gone directly to the airport.

I told of having sighted another prowler in the swamp. Yes, the others said, they'd seen him, too. While in town, they had gone to the police station to describe for Patrolman Nash the previous night's cries and compare them to the ones he'd heard. One of the witnesses had been there, the heavy-breathing young lad of the boat-ramp episode.

He had listened to their conversation with Nash. Then had asked where our camp was, and rushed out in great excitement. On the Jeep trip back in, they had met him again, afoot with a rifle. He was goddamn tired, he said, of being laughed at and called "Monster Man." He intended to look for the thing until he found it and lay it out dead on the ground. Then, he reckoned, the laughing would stop.

Lillard's gear was packed. Supper was cooked and the tin plates stowed unwashed. Two nights of lost or interrupted sleep had numbed us. The afternoon shortened. Shadows fell long across the litter of the swamp.

By some process of consensus that I do not now recall, it suddenly was decided that camp should be struck and that we should move at once fifty yards or so up a brushy incline to relocate ourselves against the face of the eastern bluff. So the rest of the equipment was packed away, all except the sleeping bags, and we accomplished this hasty transfer in the last half-hour before dark.

Some of the others remember that final night for its bitter coldness. I remember it for the sense of the imaginary become utterly real; for the intimation of some unbearable strangeness about to draw close and perhaps to manifest itself. I thought, lying in my bag, of that flindered piece of woods—of things that rage and break, and fill the solitary places with their cries.

I considered, too late, that there may be things in this world better unfound. Better not even looked for—not even in a joke.

Our backs were to the overhanging limestone cliff. To the front, between us and the lip of the declining slope, we had built a line of fires. For warmth, we told each other. Not at all for protection. Not at all to deter something that might ascend the slope toward us. Not to reveal it—face first, then torso—as it mounted the rising ground.

We tried to keep a watch. Two men at first; then one gave up to exhaustion. Then the remaining one slept, his loaded shotgun on the ground beside him pointing outward toward the edge, sparks from the fire burning a thousand pinholes in the shell of his bag.

And that was the end of it. There was no second watch.

We woke in the morning, fires burned down to cold ash. And came directly out of The Scatters and back to our various places of reason.

There is fine currency in any adventure, even a failed one.

A dry length of a sapling's trunk with the bark peeled from one side makes a weight for my papers on this desk. Rick Solberg's photographs curl and fade somewhere in a drawer. The story, though I have not written it before, has made good telling at years of cocktail parties, and around the cooking fires in several hunting camps. And Ross Lillard still gives a fine imitation of the cry, when he can be persuaded to.

But as I hear the laughter rising—and even as I join it—some part of me stands uneasily aside.

I used to do a fair amount of packing alone through big woods, carrying a blanket roll and a little food, bedding wherever darkness overtook me. I have done that since, a time or two. And may sometime again. But on that night in the swamp years ago my feeling for wilderness places forever changed. I go less comfortably, a bit less certain of what could be met in some lonely glade.

I offer no conclusions here. For where is the evidence? And without the evidence, where's the case? Some sounds in the night, some broken trees. Beyond those, nothing was found.

Something was *lost*, though. For me, it was the power ever again to surely, safely disbelieve.

III

SOWING AND REAPING

9 TRUTH AND THE CARELESS EAR

In an age of willful disinformation, the ability to unravel threads of truth from the larger tissue of deceit has become a necessary survival skill. Happily, it's a skill that, with practice and the benefit of enough hard experience, nearly anyone can master.

Thus, when a company changes hands and the new owner declares that its employees are its chief asset and no jobs will be affected, workers are alerted to the likelihood of a general bloodletting. When a public utility declares its nuclear power plant to be *as safe as human care can make it,* the prudent take that to mean "Nobody's perfect" and start looking for someplace to resettle a couple of hundred miles upwind.

Much of what passes for communication is a basically disingenuous exercise—all the more so in the city, where language is regulated by courtesy and fine discretion and empty form. The habit of plain talk is lost. So we train ourselves to listen beyond the words, hearing not so much what is *said* as what might be *meant.* And while this may armor us against the glib deceivers, it also can leave us helpless in the face of unvarnished truths directly spoken.

Of the various kinds of lies, none is worse, wrote the American philosopher William James, *"than a truth misunderstood by those who hear it."* How the blame for the misunderstanding should be apportioned between speaker and listener he doesn't say. In most cases, presumably, there's fault on both sides.

Although his grandsire was a farmer, James spent his own years tilling the field of mighty thoughts. A neurotic youth and later a frail and often sickly intellectual, the father of Pragmatism had too much wisdom ever to be attracted to the rural life. It strikes me, though, that he would have found a good deal to approve of in the manner—if not the *manners*—of people of a certain country neighborhood I know.

Men there speak bluntly, and with a ferocious determination not to be misunderstood.

That area is a reach of gullied country at the northern edge of the Ozarks, just where the productive region of slow midland rivers and fertile prairie mounts into a harder terrain of steep ravines, broken stones, and broken hopes. Farms fail, and fences fall. Fields grow up in sprouts.

The country is astir with landless, planless folk, shunted by bad luck or incapacity from one tenant house to the next.

I'm an outsider, a city man, although I've owned land and farmed in that neighborhood for more than twenty years, now. That's long enough to be known by nearly all my neighbors and fellow landholders, and to have had dealings with quite a few of them; long enough to be welcome at a chair in the country cafe at morning coffee time. Not nearly long enough, however, for me to have mastered the art of pure, straightforward country speech—either the use of it or the hearing of it.

An example . . .

I am standing with a neighbor outside his machine shed, discussing the matter of a calf of mine that has crept through or under his fence, when a truck pulls in the drive and a man gets out, looking as hard-used as the truck, to ask about renting a house on another farm the neighbor owns.

My neighbor does not immediately reply.

First, he passes his eyes slowly, searchingly, from the crown of the applicant's ill-barbered head, past the faded jacket and the knobby wrists that hang redly from its cuffs, down to the very soles of the work-worn shoes. The fellow needs a roof, no doubt of that. Then the eyes swing to the truck, behind whose windshield a wife and two youngsters sit crowded together on the seat, hope feebly warring with their expectation of another rebuff. Finally, the stare locks again on the man, holding him as rigidly, as impersonally, as a headgate grips a caught steer.

The first question absolutely takes the breath.

"Is your wife *clean?*"

The other's face goes momentarily blank, as if from a blow.

"What say?"

"Look here, I've put a deal of money in that house, fixing it up. I'll not stand for trash and filth. So if she isn't a clean woman, there's no use us even talking."

I back off a step, not wanting to be in the way when the fight begins. But the man just answers flatly, "She's clean," registering neither anger nor hurt.

"Maybe." The eyes still grip him. "The other thing I won't tolerate is stealing."

The man looks back, unblinking.

"You can cut stove wood, but that's it. Not one nail or board of mine is yours. If you ever take it in your mind to steal, you just as well head straight for the road. Because I've got eyes in the back of my head, and there's nothing I hate worse'n a thief."

The man nods.

The eyes take a final inventory: the man, the truck, the huddled family peering out through the glass.

"I guess I might take a chance on you for a month, and we'll see how it goes. The rent's cash. In advance." The neighbor turns back to me. "Now," he says, "about that calf of yours . . ."

The new tenant, thus dismissed, strides back toward the truck with a light step. In this forthright exchange, no deliberate insult has been intended and, as nearly as can be told, none perceived. What was sought—what has been established—is a basis for a relationship whose rules are perfectly known, unthreatened by any creeping rot of ambiguity.

It's the way business is done in that country, by the few men successful in the management of their property and their affairs. I'm not one of them.

On my lands, too, there are tenant houses that must be kept occupied. The problem lies with the owner, and a lifetime's habit of delicate circumlocution. Repeatedly, to the eventual bitter regret of all concerned, he has shown himself incapable of speaking in a manner to be clearly understood.

"About the place here," he generally begins, face flushed with embarrassment, his manner suggesting an awful, secret shame. "I know there are some problems. In fact, as you can see, it's pretty much *a mess.*"

What has happened, actually, is that the immediate past tenants have, through determined and imaginative abuse, reduced the house to a ruin. Doors have been torn from hinges. Panes of the custom-built windows have been broken, and cardboard nailed over the holes. A leaking refrigerator has rotted out the kitchen floor. Live coals spilling from the Franklin stove have burned holes in the rug.

The yard outside, rutted shin-deep by cars and trucks wandering freely across it, is a wonder of abandoned washing-machine carcasses, treadless tires, bent pieces of roofing tin, tangles of rope and wire. A glittering surf of bottles and aluminum cans washes up against the side of the storage shed. As far as one can see, more bottles sparkle in the grass.

He was witness to this catastrophe as it happened, of course. A couple of times, in inarticulate despair, he even appeared unannounced and rushed around the yard in a mute, panting frenzy, clawing at that infinity of junk, flinging it in heaps, while the tenants watched baffled from the house. But some reticence—tact, the dread of unpleasantness, whatever— prevented his ever speaking of it directly. And in time he'd given up.

Now his words rush out in a torrent of mortification.

"Obviously you wouldn't think of living here the way it is. There'll have to be some money spent. But whatever it takes to make the place comfortable for you, I'll do. To tell the truth," he says, "I'll consider myself real lucky if you decide to take it."

They say nothing. A profound suspicion fills them. They are trying to puzzle out his hidden agenda.

"I don't want this to be temporary, either," he tells them. "I'm tired of having people move in and out. I want this to really be your home. What I'm looking for is a permanent relationship."

A *permanent relationship*? What kind of nut is this, they are wondering. They came to rent a house, not to marry him.

"As a show of good faith," he says, "I'd like to start you off with two months free rent while you're getting settled in."

Their eyes, narrowing, lock on him coolly, impersonally, as a headgate grips a caught steer.

"Make it *three* months," he says.

He leaves a blood trail wider than an Interstate highway, this city fellow. The one thing they're sure of is that anyone who talks like that is not to be trusted. He has something up his sleeve, so the only thing to do is to keep your guard up and hope to nail him before he nails you.

But they need somewhere to live, so against their better judgment they take it.

His heart expands with gratitude.

"Anything you see around here that you can use, feel free," he gushes. "That tank out by the drive is where I keep my tractor gas. There's no lock on it, but what's the need of a padlock between people of good will?"

"We'll treat the place like it was our own," they tell him.

That's precisely what the last tenants told him—and they meant it. Now, as then, his mind nimbly translates it to mean, *They'll take care of it the way I would.* But that isn't what they said at all! They told him the absolute, literal truth. He just refused to hear it.

Another time, on another farm, I happened to be present when a young man came to ask for a common hand's job, which in that neighborhood paid the minimum wage.

"I hear there's a position open," he said.

"Nope," the farmer told him. "There isn't but one *position* around here, and I've got it. The rest is just work."

"O.K.," the flustered lad stammered. "Work, then. I'll give you your three thirty-five an hour's worth."

"Yeah," said the farmer sadly. "That's what I'm afraid of."

The process may seem harsh, but my country neighbors clarify their meanings with a scrupulousness even the philosopher James could not fault. It is the outsider's problem if, disabled by habit, he declines to hear what they say.

10   THE BROKEN TWIG

Every stranger is a book begun in the middle. Often the start of the story isn't learned, if it ever is, until somewhere very near the end.

We were tramping, he and I, on a February afternoon through snow halfway to our knees, following first one then another of the old logging trails that lay like a maze across the hills. I can't recall what errand took us to the woods. We may just have been prowling for the pleasure of it.

The winter sky was low; the sun threw no shadows. We were temporarily lost. As we stood looking across folds of timbered land that should have been familiar, he chose that moment, for no explainable reason, to speak of his life's first chapter. He told it as information I might use. And maybe *ought* to use, or else count myself, not him, responsible for anything that followed.

Three years before I'd have been glad indeed to know it—and all the rest as well. By now, though, the stranger had become a friend. And so, as he correctly guessed, the information was of no help at all.

His passage through the world, I expect, had been by a series of such careful calculations.

Forty cows to care for, a field of hay to make, fences to keep. In return for that, a house, a truck, his meat at butchering time, a small wage. Autumn just coming on.

She, stylish in a pantsuit she had sewn, her yellow hair beehived and so incredibly *bouffant* as to prompt our daughter, who was seven then and meant it for a compliment, to whisper, "I like your wig." (That was her glory, he'd say another day—the yellow hair she'd never cut.)

And the impression of him? Of health and huge strength. He looked years younger than his fifty-two—a bulking presence of a man, more than six feet and two hundred pounds, fit as an athlete. Bullet head shorn to a bristle. A well-made face with humor in it, from which the eyes looked straight out with a disarming frankness. Confidence flowed from him, but without conceit; the sense of an immense vitality easily, gracefully contained.

I spelled it out again, carefully: *house, truck, small wage.* What was offered wasn't much, but it was what there was. And the question had to be asked: how would that attract, or how hold, a man like him?

He revealed, then, as much of himself as he wanted known, or was able to confront.

As a boy, he said, he'd grown up on a farm. Then he'd taken to the sea for a while—and he loosened his sleeve to display a mere detail of what would later prove a larger tapestry of rich tattoos. After the sea he'd done a lot of different work. He'd hostled cattle at a stockyard. He'd put in crops and fed fattening calves for a man in Iowa, until that man went bankrupt speculating in pork bellies. And after that he'd worked for a farmer in Kansas.

But raising children—and they'd raised two daughters—called for more money than a farmhand's wage. So he'd taken up construction. His last work had been on bridges and buildings, high work. He'd seen men killed at it—had fallen once himself—and though the pay was good, he woke up every morning a little bit afraid to go out again and walk the high steel. Until one day, his girls grown and married, he had said to himself he didn't have to do that any more.

And then he had read my advertisement in the newspaper. It was what he'd been dreaming of—a place in the country again. They would get by. They could do with less. "What's a life," he said, "if you don't smell the roses?"

A cliché that, but who could argue with it? Who *cared* to argue—with autumn marching on toward winter, and cows to be fed, and the last keeper of them already gone off to a city job, and a house wanting to be lived in?

Humility requires references. Arrogance is sure of knowing any man sufficiently by his look and manner, by peering into the window of his eyes. So it was done, and we clasped hands to seal it. They would come the next week. They drove away, and we were left, my wife and I, to our relief and self-congratulation. Only the smallest voice of caution whispered.

What brings a man to that age—a man like him—owning nothing but his strength and his pride, glad to have half a job at half a salary? How is it that some men happen to own the land, while other men, and sometimes abler ones, must trade their lives for hire? *Bad luck*, we answered. *That, and a world of injustice.*

Yet the answer did not entirely satisfy.

"No," my wife said finally. "There's something more—something he hasn't told us yet."

But what? Prison, maybe. But if that, surely for some offense long behind him. Or a problem of the commoner kind—drink perhaps? Except that he had turned down the can of beer I'd offered, saying he never used it. He'd seen too much of what drink did to other men. Plainly his health was sound. Dishonesty? Every instinct ruled it out.

"It's something," my wife said. "He has a secret."

Someday we might know it, we told ourselves. And we would deal with it then. For now, at least, the cows would be tended, the house lived in. A great need is caution's soporific.

But the strength of him was real.

In two weeks, a month at most, the farm had submitted to a new and happy discipline. Sagging fences were drawn tight, and without even my suggestion, a partly built one had been finished. My small herd of half-wild cattle grew gentle to his constant presence among them.

Broken things were mended, machines oiled, scattered tools collected and safely stored, a leaning shed winched straight and made into his workshop, the grounds mown slick and scoured for cast-off cans and rubbish, which he hauled to the dump. All evidence of disorder or neglect was swept away as by the quick gesture of a giant's hand—his hand. And then he turned his attention to the house itself.

Termites were found in the wood of the downstairs flooring. He tore out the floors down to the exposed earth, and treated that with chemical, then, supporting the house with jacks and blocks, replaced the weakened joists. Would I mind, he asked, if he made the small living room and an adjoining bedroom into a single more spacious place for sitting? I didn't mind, of course. So he simply picked up a chain saw and cut out the intervening wall. While another man might have brought the house down by doing that, for him the result was splendid. Another assault with the saw opened a different wall of that room for French doors leading out to the porch. Ceilings were lowered and new carpets laid. Storm windows? If I would buy them, he would put them up.

His plans were as boundless as his energy. In hardly more than a season, the old house was transformed. All this cost money, to be sure. A good deal of money—several thousand dollars.

"But why don't we do it *right*?" he'd always say. "And only have to do it once."

That, I decided, must be the defect in him. *Improvidence.* He had a hundred skills, yet no notion at all of thrift.

Winter gave way to spring. One of the heifers might have died in hard calving. But he thrust his arms into her and expertly (or, if not expertly, at least successfully) turned the calf and saved them both, without the veterinarian even having to be called.

"Where will you make your garden?" I asked him one day, as the ground warmed, for every provident country household had its garden.

"It's a waste of time, gardening," he said, as if it were something anyone should know.

They went in the truck to town to shop for food—she a beehived golden vision, he paying for what she chose: tinned ham, sliced cheese and lunch meat in plastic packages, potato chips and pretzels, flaccid supermarket bread and frozen TV dinners, oceans of bottled Coke and 7-Up. All of it more expensive by the pound than sirloin steak.

At night, sunk in a chair in the L-shaped living room of the house he had wholly remade, he was a man content. She neither baked nor put up produce in jars. What they ate came out of cans or on foil trays. He loved her for other things than country skills. And always indoors he went in stocking feet. So did anyone else who came in his house. Farm life for a woman, he said, ought to be more than cleaning up what men brought in on their boots.

Then it was hot, and haying time.

The old machinery hummed faultlessly. His daughters' husbands came to help. They admired him—loved him, you would almost have said—and he liked their company. Stripped to the waist and sweating fiercely, his torso a writhing gallery of red and blue tattoos, he stacked the bales his sons-in-law threw up from the wagon. He swore at the heat and swore at the dust with the transparent joy of a man who can think of nothing he would rather be doing. The barn filled to the rafters with sweet new bales.

Never had the haying gone so quickly or so well.

"You know what we need?" he cried down from the stack. "We need a place to run a few hogs. Let me have some sows to work with and I'll make us both some money."

I cannot remember any time when the land gave me such happiness.

That country is uncommonly lovely in certain seasons. We spent many hours afoot together in the woods, and he was a fine companion in those times—his regard for nature great, his eye for detail keen. "When there's something to think about, I go to the timber," he'd say. "I'm like an Indian. I'm a part of the woods."

He discovered springs that, in a decade's ownership of the farm, I'd never known about. He knew where a badger denned; where, in season, the mushrooms were likeliest to be found. Together, on a limestone ledge beside a favorite fern-choked valley, we often would sit to smoke, both of us considering our luck.

On one such walk he seemed withdrawn, however. Almost hostile. I wondered if I had given some unmeant offense and waited for him to speak.

"We can't make it on what we get," he blurted suddenly. There was something like anger in his voice—a hint of accusation.

Startled, I turned the numbers in my mind. His worth to me and, in some larger way, his human worth, which was inestimable. And also my own possibilities, which were finite, the farm having until then been always more a burden than a boon. But, yes, there was a margin, a slight one, to work with.

I mentioned a certain number of dollars. The sum was not large. It was sufficient, though. His defect of improvidence could not be changed, but neither, I was relieved to find, was it insatiable.

Immediately he brightened. The anger passed from his mind as quickly as from a child's. He stood to walk again, and his lunging stride pulled me along panting behind. "I'm a part of the woods," he cried happily. It was as if the moment never had occurred.

Frost crisped the oaks and the afternoons shortened. His sons-in-law came to hunt deer, and one had an easy chance, but missed. Sock-footed they sat before the Franklin stove and joked about that failure.

"If you're such a damn Indian," the son-in-law replied, pretending resentment, "why don't *you* shoot one?"

"Bring me another Coke," he told his wife. It was his style—a mix of tenderness and blunt command. Worshipfully she filled his glass. They all worshiped him.

"Because," he answered the question in his own good time, "who'd want to kill a deer?"

Then the oak leaves rode off on a wind and the winter closed down. When the weather shut the roads, I kept in touch often by telephone. In past years, with the farm in other hands, I had sometimes dreaded calling. The problems had been endless, and all unsolvable. But that winter, as I had the one before, I dialed the number with a light heart.

"Fine!" he would cry into the instrument, with which he was never quite at ease. "Everything's fine!"

And fine things always were. Invariably.

That winter, the newspaper I worked for, and in which we'd managed to accumulate a bit of stock, was sold. Thus we found ourselves burdened with an unexpected, and as it turned out a quite brief, prosperity. A sudden sum of money had to be dealt with.

Writers, as a class, know little about the more complicated kinds of investment. But farming—the abiding value of the land—I flattered myself to imagine I understood. I thought of the changes his strong and capable hands had wrought in a single year, and the solution came clear. Who could doubt that in his stewardship more land would soon pay for itself? And more than that, would make possible a wage fitting so remarkable a man—a wage that would hold him and compensate him for life's past unfairnesses. He was a resource who must be kept, in order that his returns and mine might multiply together. What's more, he was now a friend.

Several tracts in the neighborhood were for sale, and we inspected them together.

By the time the spring was green we had made our choice: six hundred eighty acres, much of it woodland pasture but also with some fine meadows and stream-bottom farming fields; a good house; rough barn; machine shed; a fenced lot and small farrowing house where he could raise the hogs he said we needed. The papers were signed, and the money was paid down—nearly all the money, saving back enough for the additional cattle I would have to buy, the new fences that needed to be built, hog feeders and waterers, and other immediate requirements.

My holdings now amounted to nearly eleven hundred acres in all. A vast and vain number. We discussed, he and I, what sort of salary would suit his responsibilities as manager—not employee, mind you, but *manager*—of such a farm. He seemed strangely indifferent to this discussion of dollars. Whatever I decided would be fine, he said. The sum I settled on, I afterward discovered, was elegant indeed by the standard of the neighborhood. And it was an amount I could not really afford.

But never mind. The whole future of the farm, of my investment, was in those capable hands. In time, the returns would come.

Twenty-five cows we bought at a fixed amount from a man in another county, and twenty more at auction from a neighbor who was selling down his herd. All had the last fall's husky calves still at their sides. The price paid at the sale turned out to have been a fair one. Still, I was glad not to have known at the time what he told me later, as if it had been a huge joke on us both: unable to make a particle of sense of the auctioneer's barking, he just kept bidding until everyone else had stopped.

Within days, two of the new cows were dead. One stepped into a broken gate as she was unloaded from the truck, dislocated a hip, and was ground for hamburger. The other swelled up at the side with a tumor and had to be destroyed. So far, in our twenty months together, those were the first reverses. I received the news calmly. Farming, I told him—for reassurance, and to prove my reasonableness—was not without its risks and disappointments.

As if I knew the meaning of those words. As if I knew anything at all.

Hay time again. And the start of the unraveling.

He wanted to remain in the house he had remade, on the farm we now called the Home Place. One daughter and her family took up residence in the new house, three miles away. Her husband had work in town, but could do small things around the farm to pay the rent. On weekends, he and the other son-in-law, now unemployed, would come to the Home Place to help with the haying.

But the haying did not proceed.

The grass matured and began to coarsen and drop its seed. On cloudless days there were reports of rain—and, true, who could guess the weather two hours by car from where the caller sat? The old machines that a year before hummed perfectly seemed now to have become vexatious and nearly useless.

June passed into July. The barn did not fill up.

I took a walk with the resident son-in-law one afternoon and told him my concern. Something seemed suddenly and terribly wrong. The wonderful vitality was gone. Did he know, or could he guess, any reason for the change?

"I can't hardly talk about it," the son-in-law said. "I love that man like a father. He may"—hesitating—"he may be getting restless. In all the time I've known him, this is the longest he ever stayed in one place."

Loyalty stopped him there. Questions were useless.

"That's all I'll say. He may just be restless."

I began to hate the telephone again, in the way I had nearly forgotten. Cattle must eat, though, and hay must be made. Almost nightly I called the farm.

"Fine," his answer would come to me over the wire. But without the old elation. A little sullenly, even. "Everything's fine now."

Then, driving there to see the progress and to have my worry relieved, I would find that, of the eighty acres of hay ground, perhaps three or four acres had been mowed down and left unbaled, to dry to straw and then rot in the field.

Sunk in his chair in the L-shaped room, with another day of perfect haying weather far gone, he gave me a sheet of lined loose-leaf notebook paper. What he'd written in pencil on it, for his grandson, was poetry—

classic proletarian poetry of the kind that unlettered English coal miners and factory workers used to write about inequity and exploitation.

Doggerel, scrawled in a cramped hand and full of outlandish misspellings, it nevertheless had a power of anger and of ideas.

He said, "We can't make it any more on what we get." Eyes narrowed to a squint, voice surly, he clearly meant it as a challenge. Which I answered the best way I knew.

"Let's finish up the haying"—*Finish! Christ, it had scarcely begun!*—"and then we'll talk about it."

But he seemed already uninterested. "Bring us some Coke and ice," he called to her. Again he had forgotten, quickly as a child might.

Her voice across a hundred miles was a garbled shriek of hysteria and bottomless despair.

"Oh . . . oh! He's gone."

"Who's gone?"

"He's gone. He's drinking terrible and he's gone clear off. And, oh, I don't know what to do!"

So that was his secret after all. A sordid and common kind of secret—and somehow, because of that, both a relief and more depressing. I drove to the farm. The roadside passed in a rush to where more hay lay rotted and where they waited, freed now to speak truth.

"I seen it coming," the son-in-law said. "He's been sober five years, but I could see the change. And then I begun finding empty bottles hid around the place."

He'd been sighted, they said. Twice in the last week they'd glimpsed him in the timber, and even found where he'd bedded there. Drunk and crazy in the leaves and summer grass like a wounded wolf. And clever as one. One night it rained, and they knew he had slept on the porch of an unused house on a neighboring farm. But he wouldn't let them come near him. He hid.

"He left this for you," she said, "on the porch of that house."

Another pencil-scrawled note, with my name at the top. Meaning what? Read in one light, it seemed freighted with sinister promise. In another, it was only a cry of mystical desolation.

Look for me in the hills. You won't see me, but I'll be there. Watching. Watching you from the woods.

I turned the odd piece of paper in my hand. An idea came.

"Leave a note for him. Put it on the door of that old house. Say you've told me everything, and that we have to talk."

That night he scrawled an answer. The next day I raced down the road again. The son-in-law had gone back to his town job. She was there alone. "Does he have a gun?" I asked her. She thought he didn't.

So, putting one foot ahead of the other like a soldier marching to a war he didn't make, I crossed the fence and set off down a slanting meadow toward the house with the woods behind. From a distance I could make him out, a solitary presence and, in that moment, menacing.

Then, nearer, it was plain that the violence, if there'd been any, had gone out of him. He raised his face from behind his hands, and the transformation of a week was astonishing. He seemed physically to have grown smaller by a third—to have been deflated and painted a sickly gray—so that his great, looming, bullish presence was replaced by a shrunken concavity that filthy, slack-hanging clothes could not conceal.

"Fire me," he said, pronouncing it *fahr.* "You can see what I am." His voice a pathetic croak. "Useless to anybody. A rummy. A rotten drunk."

He stank. And he had begun soundlessly to cry.

"That's not what you are," I said. "Hell, man, it's been five years." And he looked at me in a way that said I'd never know—that no one would ever know—how long five years could be.

I don't remember what else I said. Maybe an hour went by, maybe more. Somehow, then, we were progressing together slowly up the meadow to the house, then into it. Then to the L-shaped room where he fell cramping on the sofa, which creaked as the tremors wracked him.

"I'm no good," he said again. "You'd just as well *fahr* me."

A man came to the house—a substantial farmer of the neighborhood, a stranger, but well acquainted with that hell from having occupied it himself. There was no need my staying, he said. There was nothing I could do to help.

And then, to the frail thing quaking on the couch: "You'll make it. I'll sit right here until it's done."

"But damn," the thin voice croaked. "It's so *hard.*"

Two mornings later, or it may have been three, she called again. No hysteria was left in her, only numb hurt and bafflement. How much could anyone stand? How many forgivings could be asked? Maybe now—her voice broke—maybe now she would finally give him up.

That time, when he left, he took the truck.

A wild career it must have been, for this time the news was not of momentary sightings in the adjoining woods, but of acts of purposeful self-destruction in the saloons of various nearby towns. He would appear at some tavern door at opening and sit there wordlessly the whole day, drinking a quart. When the place closed, he would carry out another quart to the truck and drink it until he slept, and sleep until he waked, then drive to a different town to wait—a ruined apparition—outside some other tavern door.

Bourbon kills selectively, but trucks are less discriminate. I imagined the bodies of some family strewn in the wreckage across a highway. The truck was mine. The liability might be mine, and also some part of the guilt. I telephoned the sheriff and the highway patrol. I wouldn't prosecute, I said, but I meant to have him stopped. Then I called her to make clear what I had done.

"Leave him notes," I said. "As many as you have to. Tell him to park the truck and leave it. Otherwise he's going to be picked up and probably jailed."

One of those notes he evidently saw, because her next call was to say that he and the truck were found. Somehow he had contrived to get himself to the state hospital and commit himself for drying out. The son-in-law would go to take him clothes and bring back the truck. Her voice was bright and cheerful as she spoke of these plans. Yesterday's horror seemed to be quite forgotten. They all could hardly wait, she said, until he was out of there and home.

August was paling to September before he and I walked again across a pasture of the Home Place. Rains had freshened the grass. The cattle were sleek. Hay for winter somehow would be found—at a price. His gray dog was at his heels, plainly glad to have him back.

I marveled, silently, at the ability of flesh to heal. In little more than a month he had returned to his accustomed size. The bulk was there again, the sense of power and wonderful potential. And nearly all the pride.

"They wanted to *hahr* me at the hospital," he declared, a spring in his lunging stride. "But I told them I already had a job. I guess I still do."

Hadn't we doubled the herd, I said, and more than doubled the land? Weren't the first sixteen gilts almost of an age for breeding in the hog lot at the new farm? Wasn't the future all ahead for both of us? *Of course* he had a job.

Anyway, I knew his secret now. And against the known, one is fairly armed.

"But it'll be no good," he said, "if every time something goes wrong you think, 'I wonder if he's drinking again?' If I decide to take another drink, by God I'll tell you."

That autumn we replaced the old truck with a finer, heavier one, with four-wheel drive for feeding cattle in the snow. That was the last of my brief prosperity; part of the money for the truck had to be borrowed. When I delivered the machine, the farm's name already was lettered on its side. And also his name, as manager, to certify that the healing was complete.

The vocation of farming consists, in the main, of timely labors faithfully performed. But sometimes it asks more.

How to describe—how begin to suggest—the labor of building in every sort of weather, in blistering heat and brutal cold, and most of the time alone, an infinity of barbed wire fence? Several miles of it. If you have ever attempted such a thing the memory will be forever fresh. If you haven't, it is useless to explain. Suffice to say that the task is of mythic scale, like the carving of Rushmore.

In autumn the bulldozers came and cleared a thirty-foot strip along the new farm's outer boundary. The land lay oddly, in parcels assembled over the years, so that its perimeter amounted to five miles in all. And not neat, straight miles, for it mounted and descended sharp-ledged hills, crossed four streams and numberless ravines, and made fourteen separate cornerings, the farthest of those three miles by tractor from the road.

The bulldozers left. He set out along the line with posts and wire on the wagon. And for most of a year that would be his life. Rod by rod, quarter-mile by hard-won quarter, the fence crept forward. Tools wore out or broke against the stones; the man endured.

Soon, during the worst winter in the memory of that neighborhood, cattle had to be fed. Snow mounted to the knees. The temperature fell to twenty below. The price of hay went higher by the week. One terrible morning when I had driven the hundred miles to help with feeding, he steered the truck bucking and plunging through the drifts while I threw down bales from the back. Afterward we found two heifers dead where they had frozen leaning against a shed.

Finally, in a sudden wash of green, another spring arrived. Progress on the fence resumed. The gilts showed heavy with pigs.

He moved into the house on the new farm, vacated by the son-in-law, whose own family was well started now and who wanted a place of his own, not caring to be forever a renter in the world. And the move was logical, for it put him nearer the hogs and the fencing. But the house at the Home Place still needed to be lived in.

Of several applicants, his preference—and he was the one the decision needed to suit—was a boy in his twenties out of the shoeless poverty of a wretched Ozark hollow some miles away. The boy had rotted teeth, a sweet, listless wife, and two children, one defective. Theirs would be the house with the L-shaped room, and a steady wage that may have been their first.

Why he chose that boy I later understood. For the lad was spirit-broken, able to understand and follow orders but unlikely to show initiative, to have an independent thought, or to present a threat or challenge of any sort. And in the first weeks, as they labored together out on the fence line—the one commanding, the other hurrying to obey—the work went smoothly and well.

The pigs came in good numbers, a hundred fifteen of them from the sixteen gilts. Then a hard rain sent sheets of water running off the hillside by the house and through the hog lot, and some of those were caught and drowned in their hutches. Just how many drowned I was never able to learn.

"Pigs everywhere," he said, his voice a growl over the phone. "Dead ones and live ones. Goddamn it, what's done's done. I'll count later. There's fence to build."

No. Count them now. That's what I should have said—but I didn't. And control began to pass.

The winter's bills were paid.

The grass of another summer rippled lush in the hayfield. I dreaded what June would bring, and I dreaded it with reason.

"The mower's junk!" he cried one afternoon as I drove through the gate into the field. His face was florid—either with rage or from his bending to make some adjustment on the machine. He flung down the wrench in futility.

"You can get me a decent mower to cut with," he said. "Or, by God, you can *hahr* it mowed." And he stormed away on foot toward the house.

The mower, though it had always worked before, *was* old, and temperamental as old things are. So I paid a neighbor to cut the field—an unforeseen expense. The whole of the year's hay lay curing in the swath. The baler was pulled to the field's edge in readiness. And then I had to make a trip on business.

A fortnight later I called from halfway across the country. Called repeatedly, one day and all the next, and listened to the telephone ring unanswered. Then I dialed the number of the Home Place.

"They're gone," the boy said.

I was dizzy to hear it. But not, I suppose, surprised.

"Him and her both. He left the next day after you were here, and I ain't

seen him no more. All that hay was mowed down and rained on twice, so
I finally just rolled it up before it spoilt."

"Baled it, you mean?"

"Yeah. And put it in the barn—most of it."

"By yourself?"

"Yeah. There was forty-some hundred bales." The boy sounded
astonished by his own feat. He had found in himself a capacity that neither he nor anyone else had ever suspected. The irony was that the dili-
gence that earned my thanks—and double pay for the month—turned out
to be the very thing another man could not forgive him. Ever.

Some days afterward, back from where I'd been, I drove to the farm
and, seeing the truck in the drive, went directly to the fence. Two men
were working at a distance. The larger figure detached himself and came
stamping, rigid with fury, along the quarter-mile of line.

"The hay's put up," he said.

"I know." I nodded down the line. "He put it up."

The face was ashen, the jaw corded, the tattoos alive as he clenched and
opened his hands.

"You called to check up on me," he said. "You called that son of a bitch.
And now I know what you're thinking."

"What's that?"

"You think I'm back in the bottle. But I said I'd tell you first, didn't I?
And have I told you?"

"No, you haven't."

"Then I *ain't!*" he cried.

And for a while again after that, until sometime in the fall when the last
corner was joined and the fence complete at last, it is possible that he
wasn't.

Calves had to be sold small for cash to settle some bills. The surviving
pigs fattened, but the market broke and receipts amounted to less than
their feed. Of the regular and recurring expenses, the monthly statement
for fuel was the most punishing.

I told him my concern.

"The damned truck eats gas," he said. "It needs tuning—or maybe
there's a leak." So the truck was tuned, and no leak was found. The
mechanic was paid. And the next week the gas supplier delivered two
hundred fifty gallons to the tank on the drive outside the house. In not
quite a month the tank was empty again.

I spread out the year's gas bills on the table for him to see. We'd had this

conversation before, too many times, and his face colored with irritation—
or something else. Assuming the truck ran no farther than eight miles on
a gallon, I said, working it out on paper while he watched, two hundred
fifty gallons amounted to *two thousand* miles in a month.

"It takes what it takes," he answered.

I did the further division. That came to nearly seventy miles of travel
every day. He looked at the paper and pushed it away with distaste.

"Don't ask me where the gas is going," he said hotly. Then he named
the boy, his helper—spoke the name with a hiss of hatred. "Ask him about
it, why don't you?"

But wasn't the tank kept locked? The boy had no key.

"Are you saying I've stole the damn gas?"

"I'm saying we're using too much," I told him. Because that was all I
wanted to believe. "We're going to have to cut way back."

He called for a Coke and ice. His good humor returned.

"What's happened," he said cheerfully, "is that he's found some way to
siphon it out with the tank locked. What you ought to do is just get rid of
the son of a bitch."

For the moment, then, the subject was closed. But the bills from the
supplier continued to arrive with undiminished frequency.

You may reasonably ask how, through these crises and disappointments, I could continue to count him as more than an employee; how he
could remain also a friend. And really it is hard to explain, though I will
try. You have to remember, now, what the farm had been before him. And
how that clutter had given way so miraculously to order. You must understand again, if possible, the heroism represented by those miles of new
fence. And then imagine him striding huge among the cattle in the mornings and late afternoons—the cows so perfectly easy to have him near, his
gray dog a worshipful shadow at his heel. His way with animals was
amazing to see.

All of the finest possibilities were in him, more plainly to be seen than
any of the rest and also, surely, more important. I was able to believe that
until the very last.

The end comes back now in a foreshortened rush of images. An autumn
wind has felled a tree across the fence, the new fence, and we are mending it together. I notice, then, that the gray dog has not followed us into the
woods, which is odd, because the dog is with him always. I mention that.

"Killed," he says, without looking up from his work.

It's sad to hear. I ask him how it happened.

"I shot him," he says flatly. And a ghastly shadow comes across the day. Then another and worse moment.

My car has turned into the drive. He comes stamping up from the hog lot to meet it, his fists gathered, walking in that rigid way whose meaning I have come to recognize. It is shortly before Christmas.

"Get rid of him," he says without any preface—by *him* meaning, of course, the helper in the house at the Home Place. "Or else I quit. Right now, today." It is a bluff, or so I calculate. In the next breath his rage may pass. But just then, by dismal chance, the boy himself appears with his family in their wreck of an ancient car. They are headed to the store, but seeing us standing in the drive, they have drawn to a stop.

"Him or me!" A livid scream.

My head is racing now. The boy is limited in a hundred ways. But wasn't he the one who saved the hay? Yes, that. Could he operate the farm, though? Can that even be imagined? And if not, am I then powerless over what is about to happen?

Again: *"Him or me!"*

The boy climbs from the car, his face a dull puzzlement. And I am trying to buy time. "We need to discuss—"

"Discuss, hell! Yer *fahred!*" The bitterness of the summer's shame spat out at last, as he bends victorious into the face of the startled boy. "*Fahred,* goddamn it. And you know why!"

Maybe it could not have been deflected. We all are trapped. But the boy is the victim, and I am swept over by the feeling of having failed him and failed myself. By a sense that somehow, through a long succession of fatal errors, I have failed us all.

Still there is worse.

It is the first of March, a day on the dividing line between winter and spring. My two small daughters and I have driven down to begin some project at our cabin on the Home Place. The errand has nothing to do with farming, so I have not bothered to announce our coming in advance.

I remember, as I drive, that one of the tools we will need is in the machine shed at the new farm, so we go directly there. Approaching on the road, I am glad to notice him there outside the house. I turn in and stop. The rest of what I see registers as in a sequence of time-slowed photographic frames. The truck is in the shed. On the drive is the late-model car he has bought from his saved wages. The hose from the gasoline storage tank is in his hand, and its nozzle is in the tank of the car.

The pictures stop, frozen at that frame. We look at one another through the glass with unspeakable regret.

Finally I must get out of my car and walk toward and past him to the shed to get the needed tool. Rage I am expecting, and would prefer. Rage, and his excuses, however implausible. Instead, he is stumbling after me, whining frantic words of ingratiation. Fawning. All the bulk and force are gone from him. He smells sourly of what he has drunk.

And as I find the tool and turn, I look into a slack face emptied of everything but horror and pleading. What I want is to be away from there. What I want, more than that, is never to have come—just to erase the day and be deceived a little longer, at whatever cost. But it can't be done. I walk back to the car where my daughters are waiting, having noticed none of this.

The last view—the last ever—is of him standing on the drive, helpless as a beaten child abandoned to his pain.

That night I wrote a letter, and the next day posted it from the city. A fool's gesture, you might think, but I meant it at the time. *Nothing,* I wrote, *was so broken that it could not be fixed. No calamity had to be final. If he would agree to take himself to the hospital again—if he was able to do just that—then maybe we could put things back together as before.*

I suppose that could not have happened. And he knew it, if I didn't. He had lost too much.

When I drove down the following weekend to have his answer, he was no place to be found. He had hidden somewhere. The son-in-law was there instead, to speak for him: "He won't go to the hospital this time. He says it's too hard. He means just to give in to it."

Furiously the end came then, and with threats of violence.

A breeding boar was sold out of the hog lot—sold for cash and the money kept and spent. In a confusion of fear and obligation, they passed on by telephone the alarming communiqués.

"He's acting crazy," the son-in-law reported. "He says he'll kill anyone who calls him a thief. He went out with his gun and talked about shooting the cattle. He said he had half a mind to cut all the wires in the fence."

He didn't cut the fence, and wouldn't, I knew. The fence was his monument.

The house was emptied, their belongings loaded into the back of the son-in-law's pickup truck and in several trips carried away to somewhere. A new man came to feed the hogs and tend the cattle and live in the house. Several weeks later, the phone rang at a late hour of night and her voice came thinly, tentatively over the wire.

"He wants to come back," she said.

But there was, I told her, nothing to come back to. By then I knew it was the truth.

Shortly after that, the carcass of our registered herd bull was found in a shallow draw, logs rolled up beside it and the remains covered with brush, decomposed beyond our knowing surely how it had died. What I felt was less anger than sick regret. When I stayed nights at the cabin that spring, I left my daughters at home and went alone. Any pleasure in the farm was gone. At night, with the stillness of the woods around, I slept with a loaded shotgun on a chair beside my bed.

I hoped never to have to use it. I never really expected he would come.

Still, not a month before the episode at the gas tank, there was that one fine February afternoon I mentioned at the start, when the new snow lay clean and unbroken ahead of us. And when he had spoken at last of the larger secret he carried—worse than his weakness for drink or anything else about him I already knew or would afterward learn.

The thing that explained him, and would defeat us both.

He was nine years old, he said, when his parents told him to go. Times were hard. There were too many children in the family, they told him. There wasn't money enough, or even food enough. Someone had to leave, and they had decided he was the one. No promise that a relative would take him in. No hint of where he was supposed to go or what he was to do when he got there. Just the command, uttered without emotion as he recalled: *Leave.*

"When?" he seemed to think he'd asked.

"Now," they'd answered.

So, wearing his worn clothes and carrying nothing, he had walked out to the road. One way led toward town, the other away from it. That was all he knew. He took the second direction, toward open country.

Later that day an old German man and his wife stopped in a wagon and asked where he was going. When he said he didn't know, they took him home with them. They worked him hard, those two old Germans did. Chores before daylight and long after dark, and never a dime's pay, but they clothed him and fed him. And through all of that he never remembered being once afraid.

What he felt then, and what he mainly still felt—confessing this forty-five years afterward, as we stood briefly lost together in the woods—was unbearable guilt.

He wondered what could have been so wrong with him that his parents had just sent him away, as you'd rid yourself of a cur dog. He'd never heard of anyone doing that. But there must have been a reason, he always thought. Some badness particular to him. The rest of his life he'd spent looking for some place in the world where he might be fit to live. Even in the best of times, he could not help thinking of the road—of the suddenness with which you might be sent out to walk it.

The Germans didn't run him off, though. He just grew big for his age. And they, being old, died. And after that he never stayed anywhere very long.

11 BRINGING IN THE SHEAVES

A Harvest Journal

Agriculture, the art of making the land more productive, is practiced throughout the world—in some areas by methods not far removed from the conditions of several centuries ago . . .

—Encyclopaedia Britannica

God did not will that the way of cultivation should be easy.

—Virgil

My wheat field is a longish forty, 44.83 acres by exact measure on the aerial photograph. But leaving out the pond corner, Homer's sweet corn and melon patch, the fence borders, three grass waterways, and the untilled ditchy end, the planted acreage is only thirty-six.

Last year I depended on another man to cut my wheat. He is a prudent and successful farmer. Which means, of course, that he combined his own wheat first. And after that planted soybeans in the stubble. And finished putting up his hay. And only later, a good deal later, found time for me. But July turned wet. Weeds took the crop, part of which could not be harvested at all. The wheat averaged thirty-two bushels to the acre and was of poor quality. And I promised myself never to be in such a fix again.

So this year I have bought a small combine of the antique sort that is pulled behind a tractor. Though old, it is in fine condition, always having been shedded, never rained on. The last owner used it to harvest grass seed, and said that on a good day he could get over fifteen acres. In wheat we will have to run slower. With luck we might cut nine acres a day, and thus would need four days to get the harvest in.

To be safe, we've allowed a week for the job.

Saturday, July 2

Homer is sixty-four years old and emphatically retired from any kind of regular work. Slight of stature, shy and gentle of nature, he is a great slayer of squirrels and occasionally, when they visit the pond in autumn, of ducks as well. He and Waneta now are the tenants in my house. They are not only loyal but unfailingly dependable—virtues that I have learned, from the earlier catastrophes, to prize above any other. Homer also is an accepting and profoundly patient man, patient with me and with my venerable machines. Or maybe it is something even deeper than patience: an Ozark fatalism learned through generations of acquaintance with disappointment and mischance.

The combine, according to the manual, has seventy-four grease fittings. Working without the manual Homer has found all but seven of them; after attending to those seven, we pull our machine from barn to field.

Never have I seen a prettier stand of ripe wheat—even if it *is* mine. Perfectly clean of weeds, it ripples like brushed fur across the slight undulation of the land. Our goal this first afternoon is only to cut a test load in the pickup truck, then fetch home from the elevator in the town of Lowry City the grain wagon whose loan was arranged a month ago.

The old combine works perfectly. Grain spills in a heavy stream from the auger spout. Astonishingly, we cannot make quite one pass the short way across the field's end before the eighteen-bushel bin is full. The smallness of the cut, just five feet, causes the unharvested acreage to seem suddenly vast.

Two bins and part of a third put our battered pickup far down on its springs, and we set out for Lowry City to tow the wagon back. The man there is apologetic. Somehow he has forgotten my need. But he knows a farmer who should be nearly finished combining grass seed and might have a heavy truck to rent. I call that farmer's number and get his wife. *Yes,* she says, *they've about finished the grass. They'll be starting tomorrow on wheat.* No help there.

The elevator man is surprised. He didn't think those folks had wheat this year. It's a bad situation, he agrees—and turns away to help another customer.

We take our few bushels back to the farm. And I strike out, then, in my car over gravel roads, stopping at strangers' gates. My plaintive spiel becomes slick with practice, but every truck and wagon in the county is in use. I see in the listeners' faces pure amazement that any man would be so foolish as to have a field of ripe wheat and no way to haul it. By nightfall I have driven nearly a hundred convoluted and intersecting miles without result.

Sitting at Homer's table, I punch the numbers into a pocket calculator: the distance in feet not quite across the end of a forty-acre field . . . multiplied by five feet, the combine's swath . . . the product of that divided in

turn into the square footage of an acre, which is forty-three thousand five
hundred sixty . . . and, finally, that quotient multiplied by the eighteen-
bushel capacity of the harvester's bin. The calculator displays its answer. I
erase it and go through the process again. The number is the same.

One hundred two bushels to the acre.

"That's a good many trips in a pickup truck," Homer says. Eighty round
trips, to be exact about it, each taking a full hour. In total, two full weeks of
waiting for the truck to go and come—not even counting the actual harvest
time.

The field of wheat looms bigger than we knew.

Sunday, July 3

We try a different town. At Charley Heiman's elevator in Rockville, our
wheat, forty-seven bushels of it, tests dry, weight fifty-eight pounds, the
price three dollars a bushel.

"But we've got a problem," I tell Charley. "Our pickup is all we have to
haul in." He eyes it, parked there on his scale.

"How much wheat you got?"

Thirty-six acres, I tell him. Good wheat, dead ripe.

"You got a problem," Charley agrees. All his grain buggies, too, are
promised out. He puts his mind to it, though, and telephones a man in
Appleton City, several miles to the north. "Hey, you know that old
wooden wagon of yours," he shouts into the phone. "I just rented it."

No prize, that wagon. It won't track good with a load on, the owner
warns. Can't be pulled much over twenty miles an hour. And if you turn
too sharp the frame will run up on a front tire and maybe blow it out.
Also, the bed has some holes that might need to be patched over with
cardboard or feed sacks. But never mind those trifling defects. The inten-
sity of my gratitude must strike him as pathetic. We fly to get the wagon,
and by middle afternoon we have cut a load.

The road between the farm and the Rockville elevator has three hills,
two medium and one extra bad. Making the first loaded run, the full
wagon whipping crazily behind the truck, Homer proceeds with some
care. And on the first hill, the extra bad one, he stalls out just below the
crest. The truck will not go forward. The wagon cannot be backed.

He waits there until, by luck, a man comes along with a four-wheel-
drive and a tow chain and helps him over the top. Always after that,
Homer just opens the throttle on the downslope before that hill, the load
careening from shoulder to shoulder behind, and puts himself in the
hands of whatever Providence oversees such inescapable risk-takings.

One hundred twenty-eight bushels, that load makes. Before dark, with the elevator closed and storm clouds mounting up, we have filled the wagon again and pulled it to the shelter of the barn.

Monday, July 4

Rain drips steadily from the cabin eaves at dawn. The farmhouse is silent at this hour, Homer and Waneta still sleeping. Leaving a note on their kitchen table, I drive the ninety-five miles back to the city to attend a July Fourth party I had expected to miss. The weather clears in midafternoon and the evening is fine. The party is outdoors, and a lady at my table—owner of some business or other—holds forth noisily about the shiftlessness of ordinary folks, folks not like herself.

"It's a disgrace," she keeps saying. "You just can't get anyone to work anymore. Even for the minimum wage."

Murmurs of feeble disagreement are heard, but with the help of her husband she shouts them down, manning the battlements against spongers and layabouts and welfare cheats. They are splendidly turned-out, those two. But what has their cleverness gotten them, if even on Independence Day they are beset at every hand by fecklessness and deceit?

My own thoughts are elsewhere. I am thinking of the field that lies before us. And of Homer, at sixty-four, uncomplaining beside me under the punishing sun. And of him careening up that hill, his life at risk for a wagon load of wheat.

And I wonder what country those handsome people live in.

Tuesday, July 5

Another race southward, with breakfast on the road. Homer already has taken last night's wheat to town. By noon, he guesses, we can cut again. We should make a new test, but don't—and pay for that mistake. The moisture is up, the test weight down, the discount fifty-six dollars on a hundred-bushel load. The next wagon is discounted, too, but only half as much. By evening we have laid off a new land in the standing wheat and made a noticeable start on its perimeter. The last load is pulled to the barn.

And now, after scraping off the grease and grain dust, I have come with Homer and Waneta to another, different kind of party—not in a sculpted garden, this one, but on the grass behind a plain farmhouse on the next road west.

The people of that house are having a hog roast for the neighborhood. Lights shine softly from wires strung across the yard. Beer is drawn from kegs into paper cups. Ladies have brought covered dishes—beans and slaw—to embellish the hog. And with the country food there is country music, played by people who came with their guitars and fiddles and who sit on folding chairs under the electric bulbs.

Men dance with their wives and their small daughters. Women dance together, the soft lights throwing shadows from all the hound-lean figures moving gracefully on the open square of grass. Hardship is no stranger to this quarter of the country, and times now are harder than many can remember. Jobs have disappeared. Farms have gone back to the bank. The drought has deepened, speeding ruin. But just for this night, in good, weathered, tired country faces, the worry is a bit less easily seen.

The man who runs the locker plant across from Charley Heiman's elevator confesses to have begun writing a novel about his experiences in an almost-forgotten war. Other men stand aside and speak quietly of bird dogs or treeing dogs, or of tomorrow's work in the wheat or the hay.

"Say, how's your wheat making?" one of them asks, more to be friendly than really to know.

"Well," I tell him, "the first cut—I hardly believe it, but the first cut made a hundred bushels." Immediately I wish I hadn't published such a claim, because it is clear from his expression, despite courtesy's strivings, that he shares my disbelief.

"The best part," I blurt out, to fill the silence, "is that all our old machines are running good."

Thus committing two sins of arrogance in a single breath.

Between Wednesday, July 6, and Thursday, July 7
Insomnia is not generally thought of as a rural affliction, but I can tell you that the sales of sleeping potions in country places must be very great.

The above sentence will be read, if it is read at all, at a sensible hour. But it is being written at five minutes past four o'clock in the morning. Shortly before midnight, the window of the house across the road went dark. Two hours after that, the dogs of a neighbor on the hill a half-mile east struck up a desultory yapping that continued, more or less unbroken, until the whippoorwills began thirty minutes or so ago. Each of those events, and lesser ones between, I can fix in time with lamentable exactitude.

And why has sleep refused to come? Let me tell you about the day just past.

With dew still on, while Homer took the previous evening's wagon load to town, I serviced the machines. Then he returned and, starting up the tractor, I pulled ahead. From the front of the engine there came a sudden *chunk*-ing sound, followed by a quick glint of flying metal. And our harvest subsided in a hiss of steam and geysers of rusty water. A fan blade had come loose and demolished the tractor's radiator.

We removed the ruined parts—the fan and radiator—which is something neither of us had ever done before, and I set about looking for replacements. The pieces were located by telephone in a tractor salvage yard the better part of fifty miles away. They were old but, of course, being needed, they commanded a fancy price. I drove there in a wild careen and left my money and carried back the parts.

They didn't fit. Or, rather, the fan didn't. More telephone calls produced a fan in a different town, and that was another thirty miles and most of another hour's delay. The afternoon drew on.

The second fan fit exactly. So we put the radiator on, and attached the hoses and belts and whatnot, and started up the tractor. The radiator had more holes than a *No Hunting* sign in deer season. A friend stopped by and found us in our frenzy. He knew of a salvage yard in yet another town. He didn't know the telephone number, but if we hurried we might get there before dark.

What was another fifty miles more or less? Again we set forth—this time through blue evening. The junkyard in that town turned out to be for ruined bulldozers, not ruined tractors. No one was there anyway. But a man in a nearby auto-repair shop knew the telephone number of a fellow who might know still *another* fellow who had once owned a tractor as old as ours. And if he still had it, he might sell the radiator.

Thus, from highway to back lane, from village to village and one pay phone to the next, we plunged along the cooling trail that finally ended in full darkness in some dismal hamlet before the house of a man whose name we didn't even reliably know and who wasn't, in any case, at home.

Defeated, we found our way back to the nearer neighborhood. Orderly folk were going to their beds. But we stopped to share our troubles with Homer's son-in-law. And the son-in-law knew of still one more salvage yard. So I telephoned and woke those people up. And, yes, there was a chance, they said—a *good* chance, although, mind you, nothing ever is sure—that the part we sought might be somewhere out there in their acres of derelict machines.

They couldn't know until morning, though. And on that fragile hope I have awaited the dawn. Which, I notice, has just now begun to break.

The whippoorwills are singing crazily. The bed is a tangle from sleepless turning. The wheat is ripe in the field. Somewhere, most probably, a storm is gathering to blow flat the crop upon which certain of my own and

my creditors' plans depend. Country despairs may be of a simple kind,
but they run deep. In that new promised land of junk I have an appoint-
ment now to keep. And miles to go before I reap.
And miles to go before I reap.

That is how yesterday was lost.

At today's junkyard, dogs prowl the beaten grounds of a house located
directly amid the inventory—big dogs, growling and bristling, two of
them loose, a third chained to a tractor wheel. Inside the house a radio is
playing. But no one appears. The owner, I afterward discover, is away at a
convention for the blind. His wife has gone on an early-morning errand.
Nearly an hour passes before the son comes out shirtless to call off the
dogs and free the customer from his car.

The selection of radiators does not make the heart leap up. Rusty ones,
many times patched, can be had for a hundred dollars; better-looking
ones for a hundred fifty. All of them of unknown soundness. This is no
time for parsimony, so I take one of the better kind, and have the sense to
spend another three dollars to have it tested. Mercifully, it holds water.

We install the radiator and are running again before the sun is high,
managing to make three loads before evening. Good news! The price for
wheat at the elevator, instead of weakening as the harvest proceeds, is
edging up. We have cut a thousand dollars' worth of grain in a day—not so
bad for two old men with two old machines under a hundred-degree sun.

Two more loads cut and hauled to town. There would be a third, except
that on a round in late afternoon the combine gives a sudden lurch to the
side and Homer, springing forward from his place beside the wagon, sig-
nals me to halt. The tractor's drawbar has come loose, broken at a weld,
the welded piece lost somewhere in the stubble.

Who ever heard of that happening before? But never mind, a drawbar is
a common part and surely not so costly. In early morning I will make
another visit to the junkyard, and by tomorrow forenoon we'll be fixed.
An inconsequential delay, this one.

A fool is ever sanguine.

The wife is gone again. The son still lies abed. But the blind junk man is
back from his convention and, calling off the yard wolves, feels in a

shed among boxes of miscellaneous parts. The shed is unlighted. What does he care about light?

He has the drawbar. Racing to the farm—having driven sixty miles before breakfast—I go with Homer to the field to make this perfunctory repair. The piece will not fit. In generations of past ownership, the hangers on the underside of the tractor, from which the bar must be suspended, have been so cobbled up and modified that they no longer will accept the standard part.

In despair and disbelief, I leap back in the car and go to Appleton City, where I remember there is a welder's shop.

It is a marvelous craft, welding. Really it is nearer art than craft, and it is good to know you still can find it practiced in the old way, with fine attention to detail. But art is not quickly done. Art demands its own time. I lack a critical measurement, and must go back to the field to get it—thirty more wasted miles. Then holes have to be bored, with graduated bits, from smaller to larger. Alignments must be made and checked. The mask drops. The tongue of blue fire licks the steel to orange. Noon comes and passes. Somewhere other men are sitting to their meals. But I wait, hungry, fidgeting, watching the bar take form.

Sixty-five dollars it will cost, and will fit exactly when we slide it into place. But that will not be until four o'clock. And then, after running possibly five minutes, the tractor will sputter, choke down, and die with a cough.

Homer grinds the battery down to dead, then speaks of a mechanic he knows. We drive there and the mechanic is at home. In look and speech and manner, his likeness to Humphrey Bogart is astonishing. But he has a splitting headache and, anyway, all his tools have been stolen out of the back of his truck. We might try his son, he says. The son lives just five miles up that road and if he hasn't gone fishing might come to look at the tractor.

A quarter-mile from the son's house my right-rear car tire goes flat. The jack is in the compartment with the spare, but there is no lug wrench and no handle for the jack. I plod through the fire of afternoon to the son's place. He comes with his tools and plugs the hole in the tire while it still is on the car, inflates the tire from a compressed air bottle, then follows us to the farm where he divines the trouble to be in the tractor's timing. He adjusts that and pulls the tractor with his truck to start it. The engine purrs; the battery charges up.

I have to set out immediately on the hundred-and-ninety-mile round trip to the city, leaving Homer alone to salvage what he can of the day.

Tonight there is another gathering of fancy folk, which my wife has pronounced obligatory. Friends are giving the party for their son and the girl he will shortly wed. They have practiced living together, so we are celebrating not so much the children's devotion as the parents' huge relief.

There must be two hundred guests at tables on the lawn. There are liveried servers and champagne toasts. The father has prepared an emotional speech. It is dark, and I keep my greasy nails below the table except when bringing food to my mouth. The evening draws on. The wine stops being poured. People begin to leave.

"It's good to see you—as long as it's not professionally," a tall, sepulchral man tells the doctor at our table. The doctor is a plastic surgeon, specializing in the reconstruction of shattered faces.

"Same to you, I'm sure," the surgeon says. The first man is a mortician.

The jeweler, sitting between, is pleased to see them both. Their wives are decorated with his goods.

Sunday, July 10

I stop to visit a country friend on another matter. The friend has finished cutting his wheat—as who has not by now? The roadside, beyond the fences, bristles with the stubble fields of all those abler and more provident men.

Would we find his truck to be of any use? the friend asks, purely as an afterthought. *It's old but reliable. And now that his wheat is in, it will only sit unused in the shed until fall.*

I wring his hand and fly lightly over the roads to report this happy news. Our luck, it seems, has turned. The tractor runs perfectly. By suppertime we have filled both the wagon and the larger truck. The elevator is not open today, the harvest being all but finished. But we will take those loads first thing tomorrow and add the tickets to our growing stack.

Monday, July 11

I drive the big truck and Homer, following behind, negotiates the hills with the wagon. But after one hill he does not reappear in the rearview mirror, so I pull to the side and stop, and presently he comes racing in the pickup without any wagon attached.

"A wheel come off," he reports.

I get out and walk around the pickup, looking at the tires.

"Not the truck," he says. "A wheel come off the *wagon*." Homer chews tobacco and wears false teeth, and whenever he is distraught or baffled or vexed by something he increases the rate of his spitting and flashes his lower plate by levering it upward and forward with his tongue. These activities are a substitute for cursing, and help him to compose his thoughts.

He has found the wheel where it rolled away into the woods. But the lug bolts are broken off and, as the wagon is ancient, the wheels are of an archaic kind. I go on with the big truck to Rockville and unload, then try the hardware store. But no such bolts can be found. The auto-supply dealer in Appleton City has bolts that, though different, might be made to work.

I am surprised, when I get back, to find our wagon and its problem the center of attention of a considerable gang of rough-looking men. It turns out the men have jacked up a house and intend to move it along that road, but can't until we have cleared the way. The house movers help. The odd bolts do work. Immediately we pull the wagon to Appleton City to return it to its owner. Henceforth we will cut only into the big truck.

The field grows smaller. What remains now? Eight acres, or ten at most.

But again the tractor stalls, exactly as it did before. And I have to go once more for the son of Bogart. And this time, instead of going flat, the car tire blows out. Still, of course, I am without tire tool or jack handle, so must walk to a farmhouse to borrow those.

Suddenly, also, something is wrong with my car's transmission. It will not shift into the driving range. But I proceed in low gear to the mechanic's house and, never minding the car, it's the tractor I speak to him about. He says he will come presently to look at it. So with the car's engine whining at fifty miles an hour in low gear, I race back to be there before him.

The temperature in middle afternoon is one hundred four degrees. The tractor is broken. The car is broken. I am nearly broken. I imagine that my wife and one daughter have gone to the swimming pool to escape the punishment of such a day. The other daughter, I remember, is canoeing in Canada—being caressed by mild breezes as she paddles with her camp friends across some sylvan lake.

"Oh, dear ones! I love you all so!" I scream aloud into the scalding wind, this ordeal having been transformed in my mind into a ceremony of devotion that will help finance their amusements. Even to my own ear, it is the shout of someone crazed. My grip is failing.

The tractor is out of time again. The mechanic speculates that the gears inside the distributor may be stripped, and dismantling the apparatus finds that to be so. Finds also that the distributor itself is off an altogether different and even older make of tractor, for which parts may be un-available. He shims the worn gears with three large washers so that what remains of their teeth will mesh, and supposes that will last until we finish our wheat.

Barn swallows dart low over the cut portion of the field, hunting insects in the stubble. From the neighboring meadow, quail whistle in the gathering dusk.

"We'll get it yet," Homer says, hope reborn powerfully in him.

But on the radio at night, the late-week forecast is for rain.

Tuesday, July 12

The heads of wheat hang low. The straws have begun slightly to bend. It is another day above one hundred degrees, and the cut grain falls from the sickle onto the canvases of the combine with a rattle like tin. In all this country there is no other unharvested field.

Homer is gone a long time with the first load, having had to take a far way around to town. Now it's the house movers who have lost a wheel. Their rig slewed sideways across the main road. One corner of the house is in the ditch. When last he saw them, Homer says, they were trying to decide whether to dismantle it or just burn it where it stood.

We are well into the day's second load, and Homer has spelled me on the tractor seat. At the far end of the round, the combine plugs full and he shuts off the engine and climbs down to clear it. Again he starts the tractor; again stops it and climbs down. I am concerned about him in the heat, and cross the field to see if I can help.

We discover that the straw rack is not moving, and because of that the innards of the machine have become compacted with unexpelled trash. Looking further, we notice that a piece is gone from the backside of the combine—several pieces, actually: the slip clutch and spring and pulley by which the straw rack is powered. My instinct is to rush away in a frenzy to a junkyard, but I have no car to rush away in. It is in Appleton City, having its transmission repaired at great cost.

Homer, in the Ozark habit of poverty and thrift, sets off hunting in the stubble. Miraculously, he does find the pieces. But even after they are put on again the straw rack refuses to work. Maybe if we put a big washer atop the spring and screwed the nut down tight the pulley would turn, Homer speculates. I am sick to death of speculations; sick of fixing machines with wire and washers and other oddments. What I need now are certainties, and I remember seeing on one of my cross-country careens a combine of the same kind as mine rusting in the weeds behind someone's barn. So I drive there in the pickup and get the man from his lunch and go with him to the weeds.

I explain my problem in a voice reedy with defeat. We look at his machine.

"What you need's a big washer," the man says. "Then put on the nut and screw it down real tight. It ought to turn."

Homer has the wisdom not to crow. No, it's decency that keeps him from it, for there is no malice in him. The remedy is complete, and by late afternoon we take our second load to town. The road is clear. By whatever device, the stranded house has disappeared.

"I hear you got hundred-bushel wheat out there," Charley Heiman says. "Man, that's the best wheat I ever heard of." His face is empty of detectable expression.

Word of two-headed calves and other unnatural wonders travels wide.

Wednesday, July 13

Hardly have we started when a fearful clicking is heard from the combine's sickle bar and Homer rushes out from the slight shade of the truck, waving for me to stop. At its power end, the sickle runs in a cast-metal guide, and that part hangs loose, broken at a bolt hole.

By a little after noon a replacement guide has been found, bought, and bolted on. We start up the machine and it clicks as before, but less. So we run the combine up to cutting speed and pull forward and instantly the new part breaks.

Evidently something has been out of adjustment for years, because, inspecting the original guide, we see where it has worn to make a fit. But where is that maladjustment? Yet another guide is bought, and we take the sickle out of the machine one more time. Twice more. Three times. My sense of grief and impotence expands, and so does Homer's. He is flashing his lower plate and spitting almost continuously—spitting on his shoes and trousers and sometimes even on his hands as he hunts for a wrench in the grass.

We go forth in the truck into the countryside, looking at other men's machines. Those other men are finished in their fields. They welcome visitors, and Homer, too, is gregarious. I stand first on one foot and then on the other as the conversations meander like slow rivers, refusing to be hurried. That cadence is born of the awful loneliness of men who do not talk enough. And then too much.

The heat moderates. The light changes toward evening. By logic we have clarified the fault. Returning to the field, we use a hacksaw and hammer to alter the sickle, and it works exactly as it should, without a click. Homer drives the tractor and combine over the crest of the field and out of view. The sound of threshing fades to silence. Quail whistle. Homer does not come back.

I follow after in the truck and find him stopped there, spitting and flashing. The engine has again slipped time.

Over the telephone, the son of Bogart gives me part numbers for the gears inside the distributor. I write those down, and also the names of implement dealers in several distant towns where there is a chance they might be found. If they can be found at all.

Thursday, July 14

Going, I left the pickup in Appleton City and took the car, whose transmission was mended. (*"Drive easy,"* the repairman said, *"and trade quick."*) Coming, a hundred fifty miles later, I left the car—more work still needed doing—and took the truck. The two different gears for the distributor had to be gotten at dealers an hour apart.

We are sitting now in Homer's yard, watching the road, also watching nasty-looking clouds collect in the west and south. The mechanic has said he would come directly, but noon passes. Then one o'clock. A blue truck approaches on the road and I leap up to meet it at the gate. The truck goes on by our lane, though. "That wasn't him," Homer says, unnecessarily. More time passes. Another blue truck appears, and this one turns. Bogart and son both are in it.

The parts fit. The tractor growls to life again, and Homer sets off on a test run.

"Anyone ever tell you you looked just like Humphrey Bogart?" I ask the father.

"Yeah," he says, and smiles a crooked smile. I would give a lot just once to hear him say *"Play it again, Sam."* But at that moment, fifty yards away, the tractor sputters and dies again. It's a problem with the fuel, they agree, and clean the line. The engine runs again.

"Mighta been the fuel line the whole time," Bogie says as they drive away.

We cut a round, two rounds, then that bank of clouds moves in and the rain comes. It is just a sprinkle as we drive our half-load to the barn, but it soon becomes a downpour—a half-inch in a quarter of an hour. Homer takes me to Appleton City to get the car, now fully restored. And I aim it, still spareless, jackless, toward the city.

Friday, July 15

At home.

Saturday, July 16

Starting just before noon, we cut a short truckload—two hundred bush-els—and put that in the bin for next year's seed, and are back in the field by two o'clock. A single cloud appears behind the trees. Light and fleecy that cloud. Then it turns dark and drops a skirt of rain and races in *against* the wind to stand directly over our field.

The drops are huge and cold. I can see Homer flashing wetly beside the truck.

Three acres left, or maybe four.

Sunday, July 17

At home. Homer reports by telephone the field is muddy. And also that the wheat is beginning to go down—not bad yet, but beginning to. We might cut again by Tuesday.

Monday, July 18

At home. Sun and hot dry wind.

Tuesday, July 19

Homer is sitting in the yard, not flashing or spitting or anything. Looking perfectly beatific.

"Finished up yesterday evening," he says. "Hauled in a load, and there's part of another in the barn. That's all. It's done."

Were it not apt to be misunderstood in that country I would smother him with kisses. As it is, I grip his hand with solemn fervency and try not to burst into tears or otherwise dishonor myself.

Finished. My God, there's magic in that word!

We take those last few bushels in to Charley Heiman, whose book-keeper totals up our tickets on her machine. Counting our seed wheat in the bin, we have made two thousand five hundred twenty-five bushels—an average of seventy and a fraction to the acre.

"That's not a hundred, but it's still damn good wheat," Charley says, rebuke and compliment at once.

Counting my own time as valueless, I have spent $1,526.16 in fuel, wages, and repairs to my old machines. The road miles I have driven are the exact equivalent of a trip from New York City to Dallas, Texas. Charley writes out a check, and I hand him back a smaller one to clear my overdue account.

Wednesday, July 20

I am a stranger in my own office. My suntan is as rich as the ones some men bring back from cruises in the Caribbean. But, unlike theirs, mine ends at collar and sleeve line.

On the desk are stacked notations from the switchboard of calls to be returned.

A fellow in another city wants to consult with me about my family's financial future.

"I've been trying to get you for two weeks," he says, sounding a little peevish on the line.

"Well, most of the time I was at the farm."

"Oh?" His voice brightens. "Gentleman farmer, are you?"

"Right," I tell him. There'd be no use trying to explain.

"Smart way to go," he says. I know from his tone that if we were in the same room he would nudge me and wink. "Great tax shelter, farms."

IV

COMING TO TERMS

12 THE EGG

It is reported in the Guinness Book of World Records *that on February 18, 1977, one Peter Dowdeswell in Corby, England, ate fourteen hard-boiled eggs in fifty-eight seconds. And that on the 26th day of the next year he ate thirteen raw eggs, less their shells, in 2.2 seconds. And that on April 8 of the ensuing spring he swallowed no fewer than thirty-two soft-boiled eggs, though it took him seventy-eight seconds to do it, thus collecting all the fame for himself.*

The book doesn't say whether the rage has come over him since. But if you lived in Corby, England, and kept poultry, Master Dowdeswell is nobody you'd want loose in your henhouse.

She was a fine, slight woman, my grandmother Sue—small even when I was small, and becoming even tinier as the years passed and I grew larger, though never by very much. Sometimes I think the luck of having been loved by her was a principal part of the capital I have carried against the later misfortunes of a life.

On a farmlet past the edge of the city she kept hens. Flowers and hens. My grandfather had a small field that he plowed and planted to potatoes, and another of alfalfa. The fields, the tool shed, and the chair before the fireplace were his. His name was Guy Cyrus Middleton. The hens and the flowers and the kitchen were hers.

Possibly there were ten acres in all. I can't remember. During the part of one year I lived with them, the more distant of those acres—anything much beyond the yard—remained an unmapped rumor. Six or seven years old, I must have been. Now I understand that they only played at farming. His job at an office in the city gave them their living. The fields and the alfalfa fragrant after cutting gave them something more.

Guy Cyrus Middleton was to my mind the arch-enemy of rabbits. He had an air rifle for chasing them away from the flowers and off the lawn at evening. It was not one of those you could pump up to lethal power—those were just coming in. It gave a puny *whoosh* of wind and flung the BB out on a slow parabola, at most to startle, not to hurt. But I thought of him as a layer-waste of rabbits. One day in the potatoes, as I rode behind him on the seat, his plow turned up a whole burrow of them and I thought he would be glad. The young still were blind and not yet furred. They were too many and too small to be saved. He shut off the machine and, sick at the violence of the plow, went straight to the house and sat unspeaking in his chair in front of the fireplace in which no fire burned.

Not long after that, by accident, I broke his air rifle, and lied about the breaking. As far as I know he never replaced it, but whether that was because of sadness about the lie or sadness about rabbits I can't say.

The largest of all known eggs, larger even than the dinosaurs', was laid by the extinct Elephant Bird of Madagascar. Its dimensions were thirteen inches by nine and one-half inches, and its fluid capacity was two gallons. The hummingbird egg, by contrast, is about the size of a pea. A mature bullfrog is said to produce as many as twenty-five thousand eggs in a season, an ocean sunfish twenty-eight million. A woman during her lifetime will release an average of four hundred eighty eggs susceptible to fertilization. All this can be learned in a couple of hours in the reference department of any decent library.

Every egg, from whatever source, is a single cell with nucleus and surrounding parts, the largest cell that occurs in Nature. Inside it is the code that determines— or half-determines—the shape that protoplasm will finally assume and, apart from shape, its further possibilities. And each egg, regardless of its source, represents the possibility of a life. So the code, obviously, is everything, the whole difference. Except for that, the world would belong to the ocean sunfish.

The hens frightened me, though in a boy's pride I never said so. And I marveled at the matter-of-fact courage with which, twice daily, she went in among them. Small as she was, large as hens are, she would just march directly inside the coop and after a tempest of resentful cackling would march out again, with eight or ten eggs—occasionally a whole dozen—in her bowl. They were of different sorts: pale beige, deeper tan with freckles, rarely white.

When she decided I'd watched enough times to be responsible, she sent me out alone. The hook of the gate on the outer pen was hard to work. Once inside the wire, there was nastiness to be avoided underfoot. But the worst was the dark interior of the chicken house itself—its floor limed with droppings, the line of boxes against the far wall occupied by killer birds whose prospective broods I proposed to snatch out from under them.

"Keep your face away from the one in the third box," she would say. "That one pecks."

A useless warning if, being short of arm, you had no choice but to push up close in terror with your face exactly at the level of *all* the boxes. What else was there to do except skip that one and just report it empty? As with the lie about the broken gun, it was an innocent deceit, told in trembling and shame, and utterly transparent. It takes years of practice to learn to lie convincingly and for gain.

Or she might say: "Don't take the eggs from the hen in the corner box. She's setting."

The eggs of all the others would go into omelets or into cakes. Whereas the eggs of that one, no different in any way, would by the simple luck of remaining undisturbed become hens and roosters, tasting cracked corn, pecking gravel in the pen, escaping into the yard to chase grasshoppers— creatures alive, dreaming chicken dreams, lusting and rutting in their turn. The caprice of that stunned me, for I think I knew then that I was learning how most of the important matters of the universe would be decided.

So, there in the shadow, among all those sharp beaks and quick gray-lidded eyes, I would insinuate a sweating hand beneath the feathered underparts and feel there—only feel, never look—for the prize. Despite the warnings I never was pecked. The hens grumbled some, but in the end gave up their hope of immortality without a fight.

Afterward, when I was out of there and giddy with relief, I would look at the eggs in the bowl and think that, except for me, each one of them would almost surely have been a chicken. For all my fear and smallness, then, I was the ultimate prophylaxis.

Smooth, still warm as life, an egg was immensely satisfying in the hand. But taken in to the basket on a shelf of the glass-windowed porch, they all quickly cooled.

On a March day in 1979, in Central Park, New York, again according to Guinness, *William Cole and Jonathan Heller set a record for throwing a hen's egg and catching it unbroken. The measured distance was three hundred fifty feet, and it was achieved, the book says, on the fifty-eighth try.*

In Central Park, life is cheap.

Her courage was the real kind, having to do with more than hens. I remember that she had just stepped inside to check the nests, me safely behind, when she stopped and gave a cry not so much of alarm as of outrage. I bolted back out into the pen, and she came marching out, too, face set, and went to the tool shed and returned with a hoe.

"Do you see him?" she said indignantly—the snake being *him*. No snake was ever *her*, though in logic some must be.

The creature was draped like a shiny black cable between two of the

Sue Middleton, her hens, and her friends

nest boxes, having finished in one and started over to the other. The egg he had swallowed unbroken had progressed several inches along him, and the bulge of it could be plainly seen, its shape still perfectly distinct. Now, it was one thing to put an egg in a cake. Or even clumsily to stumble and drop a whole bowl of them. Such things are normal. The entitlement is written in our code.

This business with the snake was different, though. Moments ago the egg had contained the possibility of animate life. Then this horrifying slick malignity had unhinged its jaw and, with a slight rippling motion, swallowed it up. Never to that moment had I witnessed anything so disgusting, so preternaturally nasty. But then it would still be years before anyone would hear of Peter Dowdeswell in Corby, England.

"We'll wait until he comes down," she said, her fine, blue-veined hands opening and closing around the handle of the hoe.

And finally, once more from the book of important facts, it was on April 7 of 1982, only thirty-seven months after the Cole-to-Heller throw in the park (or Heller-to-Cole, because in this case it makes a difference), Siegfried Berndt in Leicester, England, completed his construction of the world's largest chocolate Easter egg.

It stood ten feet tall and weighed seven thousand five hundred sixty-one pounds, thirteen and one-half ounces, and contained enough sugar to send half the population of Leicester into a diabetic seizure. Otherwise, there was no potential in it, no code at all, no promise of becoming. I suppose the author of that curiosity was extremely proud and had his picture taken with it.

I wonder if anyone ever told him that alongside, say, a bullfrog's, his egg was a simpleton's work.

They left the farmlet for the imagined security of town, although there's no real safety anywhere. Sickness crippled him and fixed him in his chair. And she, her smallness refined down to elements of the purest, most unyielding kind, bore his weight on ten thousand—a hundred thousand— halting steps from chair and window down a hall to bed, and then to window again. He watched the rabbits that came brazenly to feed, and I don't know what he thought.

I suppose he thought of his losses. I would have.

When that ended, she was in her eighties and I was grown and supposed to be recording for history the urgent matters of the day—traffic-court proceedings and the noon soirees of various clubs named after animals. But I chose some days instead to go sit several hours with her. The smelting hadn't scarred or hardened her, only made her finer, more beautiful.

While I spent those times remembering, she always looked ahead.

All of which is only to explain a peculiar feeling I sometimes have when I take an unbroken egg in hand. It used to happen when our daughters were small and the year turned to spring and, with cups of dye arranged on newspapers, we colored eggs for hiding in the night. It has even happened in the gray of morning when I have opened the refrigerator with nothing more reflective than breakfast on my mind.

I take one or two out of the carton. The shape is evocative to hold. For just an instant she and I are together in the doorway of the coop. All the eggs are still under the hens, still warm, with their promise still in them. I am small, and full of fears I foolishly think will pass. A lot of things have not yet happened.

That was a long time ago, before it occurred to anyone that the snake might win.

13   THE LEAVE-TAKING

One daughter has gone away to college in a different, a distant state. Her sister will follow—not to there, perhaps, but to somewhere—in a year. Then a phase of their lives will be finished, and also of ours.

Haste, more than anything, characterized her leaving. A job occupied many of her summer days. Weekends and evenings there were friends to see. Then things had to be packed in boxes and carted to the shipping company. And that was it. One sudden morning we drove early to the plane, and in a rush she was gone.

I'd have given a lot for just a day in some still place—one day of slow words with easy silences between, in which to reflect on what's been learned, if anything has, from our time of living together. But there wasn't any space for talking. When times of change overtake us, words always are crowded aside.

"Don't let the work get ahead of you," I said instead. "Keep up with things."

"I will," she promised.

"Be careful about friends you choose, and whose car you ride in."

"You're preaching."

"No, I'm not. These all are sensible things. Oh, yes, and don't borrow or lend money. That only leads to trouble."

"You *are too!*"

"What?"

"Preaching."

Her mother was doing the same. It's what passed for conversation in the last days: a kind of emergency kit of random, desperate notions, flung all together in the hope that one or two might somehow later prove of use.

Don't go anywhere without bus fare. Always have a quarter for the phone. Breakfast is the most important meal of the day. Balance your checkbook. Be careful at night alone. Be careful of New York. Get your rest. Change your sheets and your typewriter ribbon regularly. Call home collect.

As if the displaced heart could be defended by a few small artifices. As if all life's hazards were only matters of logistics. As if *any of that,* in the time of things changing forever, were what anyone really meant to say.

Beside me on the desk, now, is a book by a man to whom I owe an unpayable debt—not so much for anything learned about writing, since his grace of language is wholly original and resists imitation, but for a certain oblique manner of examining experience to look for the meaning in common things.

In the book is an essay he wrote about a sparrow hawk he once caught, and afterward released, while on a scientific expedition in a dry, windy meadow somewhere in the high mountains. The piece compares machines, and all their dazzling but bloodless virtuosity, to living creatures—the mouse, the bird—which are capable of passions and devotions no machine can ever feel.

I have sent a copy of that essay to my daughter. And in doing so, am carried back to a night more than twenty winters ago, to a rough cottage on the edge of the city, when I read it aloud to a few friends whom my wife-to-be and I had gathered to announce our intention, against all the modern odds, of spending the rest of our lives together.

The cottage was on a marvelous old estate. There was the great house, horse barns, another medium-sized house in which dear friends lived, and our small one of three rooms, which must once have been the groundskeeper's lodging. The buildings were arranged beside a small, still pond, with lily pads and a boat house. Over these placid grounds, reached by a gravel lane off the highway at the start of open country, towered the dark crowns of splendid long-needled pines.

Strong light of spring and summer mornings filled our little house. Several times I went out while mist still was on the pond and fished a part of an hour before going to the office. I liked to imagine I was *providing*— catching breakfast for our camp. The fish in the pond were too small for eating, but they came eagerly to a fly, making sudden circles as they rose. The early mornings were wonderful, before the hum of truck tires had begun out on the highway, with a wife just waking in the cottage and the two beagles hunting over the wet grass of the fenced yard and a white cat watching through the screen of the porch.

We never told the children much about that place, where we found so much easy happiness in our earliest months together, and where a sudden telephone call also brought the news of the first of the bitter griefs. In the carelessness of years getting away, it's the kind of thing parents forget—or haven't time—to talk about. But for us, and therefore in a very practical sense for our daughters, too, that was the beginning.

In the city, in a house with more rooms, we made a nursery. The week we brought the first baby from the hospital to her crib at home, a cemetery salesman—tipped off by a newspaper birth announcement—knocked at the door to ask if we might now be interested in burial plots. I ran the unctuous rascal off my property. We were young. Our family was just begun. And here came this fellow, impatient to get us underground. The worm starts working early.

Soon the nursery had two cribs, slatted cages from which the sisters as quickly as possible escaped. They crept into their grandmother's room, into her bed, and those three wrapped up in blankets together and ate soda crackers at strange hours. It was the last innocent time.

Because in that house, our second but the first one they remember, the grandmother died. The white cat died. Then there was yet another house. And soon afterward the remaining grandparents died. Then both the beagles. There's no ranking losses at that age. All of them are insupportable.

Being older by a year, and therefore comprehending more, the first one may have been worse affected. She refused to play in the yard unless the house door was left open. And when the time came for starting school, the terror of separation grew. She was inconsolable, the teacher reported. Each day, I suppose, she was wondering what else would be subtracted in her absence. When so much has been swept carelessly away, how, if you are small and powerless, can you believe that anything will last? We tried to explain that loss goes with loving, and that the alternative—having nothing and no one to lose—is immeasurably worse.

We must have convinced her, because the tears ended, she stayed in school. She was armed, though, with a useful if terrible piece of knowledge. That, contrary to rumors, the universe is not benign. It is, if not cruel, at best indifferent. Everyone learns that eventually. The only hurt is learning it so young.

"Jump," I told her. "Jump across, and I'll catch your hand."

It was winter in the oak woods. A dry snow had fallen, whitening the crisp leaf litter underfoot, and we had left the warmth of cabin and stove to adventure an hour together. She was, I think, about three years old, her sister still a bit too small for hiking.

We were headed back, and had come to the little stream branch that empties down a shallow draw into the lake. I stepped easily across, at a place where the rivulet slowed to make a small pool, perhaps three feet wide and as many deep. Then I turned to where she was waiting on the other side.

"Jump," I said. "And I'll catch your hand." She smiled, gathering her small legs under her.

I can't explain how it happened. I only recall her expression as the amber, leaf-stained water closed coldly over her and she sank away, her smile changing not to fright but to a look of astonished betrayal. She still remembers, too—how strange the day looked from that perspective, the dark shape of my outstretched arm receding above, the light of the sky falling down softly through a filter of suspended leaf matter.

It was an accident. She understands, and insists she has forgiven. But she *does* remember. So much for blind faith, even in people supposed to be most dependable.

The years took on a comfortable pattern, insofar as our respective tyrannies of work and learning admit of any comfort at all.

In March, there was for several years a sojourn on a southern shore, where Gulf currents threw in upon the sand their freight of broken and collected wonders—empty seashells, the blown-glass floats from the nets of Japanese fishermen, spiral egg cases of the whelk and jellyfish sadly drying.

In early summer there were the Colorado mountains, hard climbs to high places, the sharp wind carrying words and breath away, lunches eaten huddled close beside a sheltering rock. And at summer's end—just before school began and the feeling of being prisoners reclaimed us all— there was a short excursion to the Minnesota lake country. For personal reasons, I believe the northern trip always mattered most to me. As a boy, I went there many times with my own parents. So the sense of my daughters being young there, *and myself being young there*, tends to get confused in my mind.

An uncle, who was the mythic storehouse of outdoor wisdom in my boyhood, survived—grayer but even wiser—to be a guide for them. They went out in the fog before dawn, as I had. They heard the great fish leaping, dreamed to the lap of waves against the side of the boat, and watched the sun flame low over drowned willow forests in reed-rimmed bays that to them seemed impossibly remote and wild. They guided home at night, as I had, by the speck of lighted cabin window on the opposite shore.

Through all our years, theirs and mine, the cabin remained. The lake and bend of the cove were unchanged in the quiet hours. The heron stalked the edge as always. Only the people went. All of them went, until there were only the shadows of them moving in the mind.

One cool morning, on the last of one of those northern summer trips, I stood at the dock and watched a hen mallard herding her late clutch of ducklings among the weeds. Short weeks ago they had been fluffballs. Now they were nearly fledged, and soon would be testing their wings down the long highway of the continent. I thought of my own young, still asleep in the cabin, hurrying toward their own time of flight.

"How sudden it is!" I gasped aloud, into the unlistening morning.

One minute, everything is beginning. A careless, unexamined moment later, everything is moving toward conclusions. I realized, then, that while I was surprised by that, I wasn't frightened by it.

All right, I thought, silently this time. *The players keep changing but the shadows stay, and the story goes on and on, and that's the important thing, isn't it?*

It's another common lesson, and they'll learn it. Everyone has to.

The purpose of a clique is to exclude, to hurt. There isn't any other.

Hardly anyone, I suppose, manages to get through a whole life without sometime being wounded in that way. In the adult years, cliques and in-groups of one sort or other may be based on shared interests, or on wealth and class, or on various criteria of actual achievement. But with the cliques of childhood, the only common denominator is shared viciousness.

Being small, shy, without flair, not noticeably gifted, I found myself more often than not on the outside of some group, looking in. The agony of that, when you are young, is that your experience is so limited. You easily can be misled into imagining that the mean-spirited little world you happen to be caught in is representative of the world everywhere. But time is a great leveler. And life is fairer, in the long run, than it sometimes seems.

For me, the watershed was going away to college where I knew no one, had no history except a transcript, and therefore was free to reinvent myself from scratch, with the possibilities limited only by my own imag-ination. For the first time, I realized that all of the power over myself and what I might be was in my own hands. I still remember the elation of that.

For my daughters, I think the great change came during a year we spent living in Paris. Their schoolmates there were from fifty-three countries—the children, mostly, of foreign-service or international-business families. And many of them had been bounced around the world enough to know the value of friendship—even, or perhaps especially, of the hasty kind.

It was a school without cliques. There simply wasn't time to waste in pettiness. Flung together for a short while, wrapped round by a city that was at once splendid and alien to them all, friends simply found one another in an urgent yet easy way. In that place, all of them were out-siders. And so none was.

Coming home, then, my daughters discovered a fine and amazing thing. The world of their earlier childhood was only one of many worlds—and one of the lesser ones, at that. Never again could any clique hold their happiness hostage. Because the truth is that a clique is the prisoner of itself.

Some years ago, I went to a high school reunion—the twenty-fifth, I think it may have been. You cannot help noticing, at such events, how many of the one-time creepers at the edges have made satisfying lives or even great successes, and how many of the charmed ones have wound up traveling a less happy road. It's nothing to admit feeling glad about. One oughtn't to take pleasure from someone else's disappointment, even someone of the cruel and haughty kind.

But there is a lesson in it. ("You're preaching," she would say.) All youth is only preparation. The score is added up later, and one has to set one's pace for the longer game. I cannot imagine anything sadder than a lifetime spent trying to recapture the recollected triumphs of one's fifteenth year.

The album pages turn faster now.

There was the time I came suddenly upon one of them in her gown, at an early hour of morning in an upstairs hall, and was amazed for a moment to find this lovely stranger in my house—then recognized her, and realized with a start that, practically unnoticed, they both had grown to be young women.

"That's how it happens," their mother said. "You don't see the seasons changing. But one day it's cooler, the days are shorter. One day the wrinkles come. That's how it is with growing up."

They began to have strong opinions of their own, and to argue for ideas they'd come by independently. We delivered them to planes and to chilly train stations in other cities, and they went off alone to see things we'd never seen and maybe never would, to begin collecting experiences uniquely theirs.

We lived a summer in Africa. They came home from there before me, and I remember how one day the young leper who begged outside the bakery intercepted me, not to plead for alms but to ask, "Where are the *mademoiselles*?" He was someone they had come to know—a friend. They had managed to see beyond the disease itself to the eyes from which the perfectly undisfigured spirit of a boy about their age looked out. And I was unbearably proud.

She played tennis, the older one. Size was against her, as it was against me in my dreams of a football life. But she ran for every ball, was modest in winning and graceful when she didn't. And either way, when the match ended, stayed to the very last to cheer her teammates on. Wimbledon is not in her future. She will never, I'm relieved to know, have to look across the net at the corded jaw and knotty forearms of a Navratilova. There will be other tests, though. For nearly all of us, whatever we do, there's always someone seeded higher in the draw. But all the honor isn't found on center court. You still can make a pretty reasonable life, winning a few more than you lose, by running down every ball.

And in the end, what's known of anyone is only the shadow that's left. Who was the number-one tennis player in the world during those two years that a little girl named Anne Frank was hiding with her family in the upper room of an Amsterdam warehouse and writing in her diary? Probably you could find it in some book. But where has the fame gone? Which shadow has lasted?

Preaching! Preaching! It's a compulsion that comes over you when the time for sensible teaching has run out.

"Would you like to see where your mother and I lived first?"

It was the last afternoon, and we'd made the final trip to the shipping company together. I remember when all that area was woodland and pasture. Now the manufactured sprawl of subdivisions and commercial buildings ran away to the horizon far beyond. We turned off the Interstate and down the gravel lane.

"Our little house is—"

We negotiated the lane's last bend.

"Where?" she said.

The last time I'd gone there, alone, ten years or so ago, the whole estate already was untenanted and sunk in neglect. Hoboes or vandals had bedded on the mattress in our cottage and written crazy, vile inscriptions on the walls. But even deteriorated as it was then, the place remained more or less intact. You still could tell what a marvel it had been.

"Where you see those pickup trucks," I said. "Our cottage was there." It had become a parking lot for some nearby manufacturing plant.

"That's sad," she said.

"It was a good place," I told her, still under control, being cool about it. "We were happy here."

I took her hand, and we walked through a tangle of vines and fallen branches where there used to be a gate leading to the rest of the grounds. The great pine trees were mostly dead or dying, broken at their tops.

"The walk here was shady," I told her. "It was covered with soft pine needles. And all along the walks there were resting places, with benches made of cement by real artists, so cleverly that you would swear they were made of wood, with knots and bark."

She must have thought I was hallucinating. All that could be seen anywhere was a bristling riot of rank undergrowth, and beyond that a suggestion of more elaborate ruin.

"Here was the house where our friends lived." It was blasted, as if by an explosion—part of the stone walls toppled outward, and the roof fallen to ground level. "We were all young, then. I guess we talked a hundred nights away, up there on the second floor. We all had big plans."

Plunging on through deadfall and itching weeds, I led her to the edge of the pond, which alone had not much changed. The boat house survived. The circles of small fish rising still dappled the polished surface. Crickets sang.

"On hot days that summer, we'd come home from work and swim. The pond was cool. The world just kind of went away." Faster, my control slipping, I pulled her after me toward the principal wreckage—the immense heap of charred logs and tumbled masonry that once had been the center of that enclosed, halcyon world.

"This was the great house," I told her. "The logs were brought in by truck all the way from the Pacific Northwest. There was a stone fireplace so big that, on the second floor, the chimney divided and a walkway passed through. Wooden floors and polished log walls that glowed in lamplight. I believe it was the grandest house I ever saw. It was a wonder," I said. "Nothing like this place will ever exist in the world again."

She looked around her, trying to reconstruct the whole vanished complex in her mind.

"But *why?*" she said.

"Why what?"

"Why couldn't it have been left? Why did it have to be ruined?"

"Because the land became valuable. The city came this way. There was a great deal of money to be gotten."

"But there's nothing else here. I don't understand."

"It's what certain people do," I told her. "If a dollar could be made by tearing down the Cathedral of Chartres for its stones, you can be sure some man would do it." Memories were shaking me.

It wasn't just that place. I was thinking, at the same time, of mountains ripped apart for coal, or their flanks scarred by the switchback roads of the developers; of streams foaming with effluent. And bottles glinting in the tarry goo of oil-blackened beaches. And of silent northern lakes churned endlessly by power boats. And of redwood forests flattened to make patio decks.

"Then how can anything be safe?" she asked.

"The only way, maybe, is to buy the land as far as you can see, so you never have to look at *that*—" I gestured out toward the highway, toward the prefabricated dung of progress.

"And build a fence all around it. *And inside your fence keep a tiger.*" I could hear my own voice, tinny and distraught, with that urgent, confidential craziness of people to whom visions are revealed. "He'd be your friend, the tiger. He'd roll over for you to scratch his stomach, like a cat. But—" This last part I whispered. *"But when anyone else came . . ."*

"Your eyes are shining in a funny way," she said.

The anger was subsiding, then. We stood another quiet minute in that ruined place.

"Anyway, this is where we began." I took her hand, and we started back toward the car. "Now everything's beginning new for you, and it's a wonderful time," I told her. "Just keep up with your work. And be serious about life. And steer clear of boys who wear earrings."

And the next morning, armed with these last garbled and demented instructions, she was driven to the airport and sent on her way in the world.

For as long as I have been acquainted there, more than half my life now, people of my country neighborhood have nurtured their idea of the panther.

No one I've ever known has actually seen the creature. But nearly everyone has a relative or friend who knows a man—nameless, perhaps, but not to be disbelieved—who only last week met the thing in the lights of his pickup truck on some night lane as it bounded across between two fingers of the woods. Or who found its pug marks pressed deep into the sand of the stream bank at the bottom of his calf pasture—prints that, when others came to look at them, had been washed away by rain.

On a certain rise of ground where two lanes meet there stands what must once have been a fine stone house, or even a grand and rather pretentious house, far gone now in neglect. The crossroad is at the geographic center of the county, and the story told locally, with whatever truth, is that the house's builder imagined it would one day be the courthouse. But his gamble failed. The town grew up on the river instead, seven miles distant. Some years later the man left and the house was abandoned. Cornices crumbled and plaster fell. Time and weeds took that road corner, though the square outline of the house still can be spied through an enclosing jungle of trees. For a time it was rumored that the panther denned in its cellar.

I went there once with a flashlight and crept cautiously down the stone stairway into the mouth of the dark, a nightmare of cobwebs like gauze across my face. Empty kerosene cans, broken dishes, a rusted stove-pipe oven, and heaps of faded ledger sheets were all I found. It was a cramped, wet cellar. And except for the persimmon-seeded scat of a raccoon, and mice scuttling quickly among the stones at the edge of the light's beam, there was no evidence of any other animals using the place.

I decided then, and have believed since, that there is no panther anywhere about—that it is a creature only imagined, although the invention is undeliberate and the myth may, in its way, actually be *necessary*.

Suppose that you had lived so long in a place, had failed so long there, that nothing was left undiscovered. Everything about the locality was known, and the sum of everything known was disappointment. It would still be necessary to believe in something more. You would make a myth, if nothing else were possible. You would put in the too-well-known woods some wild thing—something strange, anyway, capable of mystery and surprise. And its presence at the edge of the mind would somehow comfort you by its suggestion of other possibilities still unexhausted—about that place, or even about yourself.

The panther of that neighborhood lives not in any earthen den or stone cellar, but in the aching need of beaten spirits. And it is real enough that when people speak of it I do not argue any more or ask for proof.

That reach of country, seen from the window of a car passing quickly through, has what the eye records as a kind of ragged beauty.

Rust orange meadows of broomsedge, rippling in the wind, undulate away black-speckled with colonizing cedars to wash up against the bristling wall of darker woods. In the land's sudden folds are steep, stony places where, in the wet of springtime or for several hours after a beating rain, short-lived little streamlets rush sparkling and muttering down.

Wooden barns, like foundered ships, lean against the sky, their spines broken, tin roofs curling open to weather, unpainted plank sides a fine shade of polished silver. Somewhere near each barn would be the smaller stone rectangle of a house foundation, a house burned. And in the woods behind, a network of stone walls laid up by the first man who cleared the meadow.

The walls do not lie straight, but bend and wander by now-inscrutable caprice. The man is long gone to earth somewhere nearabouts, and unable to explain the purpose of all that labor, if he ever really knew. Other people followed him and built frailer fences, whose split posts burned in the April wildfires and hung awhile in the wire, then fell. Those people left, too. And sprouts and weeds and rot and the deliberate or accidental fires of the unwitnessed seasons claimed everything.

Just *undid it all* and took back the land with a kind of heartless ease. So that from the car window, as you pass now, there is only faint and rather charming evidence of anyone having been there at all. You might even call it lovely in its way. But it's a landscape of exhaustion and defeat. And if I'd known in time what I know about it now, I would have had nothing to do with that country. I'd have run from there as fast as legs or wheels could carry me.

I didn't, though. I stopped, and stayed, and let the ruin and the failure draw me in. And my purpose now is only to describe—for whatever use the warning may be to someone else—the terrible, sweet way in which it happened.

Breastworks of a battle lost: some forgotten man's stone fence

Forty scrub-timbered acres at a road corner not far from the Osage River, a rough one-room shack of native oak boards sawed somewhere in the hills nearby and nailed up green, a pond that was hardly more than a mudhole. That scrap of weekend country land was the single capricious big investment of their whole lives—lives pinched to caution, as so many were, by memory of the Great Depression.

I was a young man then, two years past twenty, away serving in the army, and my parents, whose names were Hugh and Dorothy, would have been only a few years older than I am now. They told me in a letter what they'd done. Fifteen hundred dollars they'd paid for the place, and their extravagance must have frightened them a little.

The man they bought it from had built the shack himself—hastily, while the unseasoned oak still would accept a nail. He'd covered over the outside with a patchwork of many-colored asphalt shingles scavenged from roofing jobs in town, and then entertained himself by lying on his cot inside, drinking whisky from the bottle and loosing pistol shots at mice—real ones, or creatures of his tremens—that dodged among the roof planks. The inner ceiling was pocked by his fusillades. Outside, the endless bottles he had emptied glittered where he had flung them among the weeds.

Hugh and Dorothy gathered up the junk and paid someone to haul it off. They found a man with a bulldozer, and hired him to spend a half-day raising the earthen dam so that the mudhole became a real if smallish lake, which they stocked with fingerling game fish. They planted redbud and dogwood trees beside the cabin. By repeated journeys over it with a mower, Hugh beat the weedy clearing down into something near a lawn. As a rite of ownership, on trees along the road they tacked up signs forbidding trespass.

All this their happy letters told.

One day, they wrote, they were having a picnic on the freshly mown lawn and noticed a gaunt old man squatting on his haunches at the gate out by the gravel lane. Hugh went down to ask what he wanted. The fellow wore ragged clothes and a mean look. He was there, he said, about those trespass signs. He didn't like them. He'd freely used that land, had swum his horses in the pond when it pleased him to, for a good deal longer than they had owned it. He didn't like being told where he could go and where he couldn't.

Fires burned across the country regularly, he declared, and spat. *Neighbors helped neighbors. But any man forbidden entry would gladly let a cabin burn.*

The old man wasn't a neighbor at all, Hugh discovered later. He was only the malicious patriarch of an evil-spirited clan—a whole tribe of truants who, between intermittent floodings, camped in the doorless houses, shared the houses with sharp-backed hogs, in a derelict hamlet beside the river several miles away. Passing afoot on some errand of likely mischief, he had seen the signs. And they had fanned the coals of his everlasting hatred of men unlike himself, with their concept of property.

The next year I came home from soldiering, took a newspaper job. And the summer after that helped build a screened porch onto the front of the country place. We spent most of a week at that, Hugh and I, swearing sometimes at each other but mostly at our shared ineptitude with tools. And in the end were immoderately pleased with our work, however botched and out-of-square it might have been.

Years passed. The cabin was broken into twice by thieves, but never set afire. The minnows in the pond grew to be serious fish. The dogwoods and redbuds reached their age for flowering.

In one of those years—because I had read the writers of the generation before mine and supposed it was a young man's obligation to do it—I left newspapering to spend several months sleeping in the orchards, olive groves, and threadbare pensions of France and Spain. I came home from that adventure all but penniless, no job and autumn turning, and had to borrow the cabin for a winter's living; it wasn't used in that season anyhow.

A glorious if lonely winter it was, as I remember it now across these nearly thirty years. The unhurried days fell neatly into segments—one part for cutting stove wood, one part for hunting squirrels and rabbits for the pot, another part spent at the typewriter trying to learn better how to put one word after another. Just as the weather hardened, two little hound pups came to me, strays out of the frozen woods, and after that we hunted together. They were my best company and my friends.

Between the days' obligations there remained a lot of time for daydreaming and aimless rambling. Exploring out, I must have walked, in that winter, several hundred miles in all across unfenced saffron fields, through empty woods, past deserted houses staring blankly from glassless window sockets, sinking slowly to ground alongside those leaning silver barns.

Saw that same sad scene in scores of repetitions—*and learned nothing from it.*

Actually, of all that land I saw, the part that I cared for most—except for the cabin acreage itself—was a small, steep valley that adjoined it immediately to the north. Second-growth white oak trees, well spaced and straight, grew on the valley's sides and gave home to plentiful squirrels, each squirrel a supper. An intermittent stream running down out of a wild pasture above tumbled over the polished lip of a limestone ledge, fell a dozen feet to carve a pool, then meandered on between mossy banks and, in season, a knee-high jungle of mixed ferns.

If a man ever had some money, I told myself, he'd be a fool not to try to buy a place like that. I found out who the owners were—city people—and even wrote them a letter saying that. They wrote back, brusquely I thought, that their valley wasn't for sale. In any case, it was part of a larger tract of four hundred acres which, if ever sold, they'd not want to divide. Evidently, though, they saved my letter.

Skip a few more years.

I'd gone back, finally, to the newspaper. I'd met and loved a woman. On a raw March weekend, with city friends helping, we planted several thousand pine seedlings in the cabin woods. And after the friends left, the two of us together, hands aching with cold, set out two hundred young dogwoods along the road frontage. The next month, in April, we were married.

That spring's wildfires took half the pine trees. In summer, the rural electric cooperative sprayed its right-of-way, and the wind-drift of herbicide killed all the dogwoods but three. And the spring after that the letter came. Those people would sell the place after all—but not the valley separately. The whole of it, four hundred acres or nothing.

And so it happened that on a pretty afternoon I sat with my wife of a year on a boulder in the cool shadow of the valley of ferns, with water rushing cheerfully over stones and around bends, and asked her leave to do an illogical and awful thing. The price was reasonable. That is, it was possible at least to imagine that someday the place might be paid for. The people whose land it was had had dreams of their own, but dreams and their health failed them. *Time had run out,* they said—a concept not easily understood until it happens—and they had to let it go.

A sale contract was signed. In the week between then and the closing, timber thieves with saws and trucks savaged the woods, felling every tree of size, leaving a litter of raw stumps and wilting crowns. Or maybe they weren't thieves. Maybe the owners had arranged that treachery. I never could find out. They're dead, and it doesn't matter now.

The worst of the people in that country are animated by a feckless

Derelict barn, waiting for the fire

wickedness that can take the breath. They will steal without conscience, fight for exercise, kill out of grudge, swerve their battered cars to squash a small animal on the pavement for sport, cruise the back roads with cans of gasoline and set a thousand acres of woodland afire for no better reason than that they are bored and would like to watch it burn.

Those are the worst kind, and, although blessedly few, their numbers over the years have remained fairly constant.

The *best* of the people in those hills, on the other hand, are so kind, so unfailingly gentle, so generous with their loyalty, their affection, and their few material goods that it seems simply inconceivable that they all sprang from the same stock and were shaped by the same experiences, though plainly enough it's true.

Like all the other untenanted farms, mine once had been home to someone. The Ginter Place it continued to be called, though any Ginters had decades before departed. Some time past the barn had burned, but the house remained, or what had been the house—porch fallen, roof open to animals and sky, camped in freely by passers-by on foot. Only by a miracle was anything left at all.

The man and woman who came to live there, who made the house tight from weather and, having saved it, filled it with their lives, were of the second and wonderful kind. We fenced some fields, that man and a neighbor and I, to rent for pasturage. Then someone set a fire out by the road and the just-greening pasture burned to a desert of sifting ash. We bought a machine to pull behind our ancient tractor and harvest grass seed. First the machine broke. Then the tractor broke. The price for a pound of grass seed fell to less than a nickel—and *do you know* how much fine seed it takes to make a pound?

It wasn't enough just to let the land lie idle as it had lain for a generation. Hugh, my father, was country born. He had lived nearly his whole life in the city, but kept somehow a farmer's passion for the fruitful destiny of land. It wasn't right, he argued, for anyone to own a parcel of the earth and not cause it to produce. To produce *something*. And not meaning to blame him now—I did it gladly and of my own volition—I bought from a neighbor six heifer calves and, not yet knowing it, further committed myself to my own destruction.

Hugh and Dorothy died, leaving pictures of themselves in joyful times on the cabin wall and the still-animate shadows of themselves upon every foot of the path between the cabin and the little lake on that corner of ground where their dreams had been so richly accomplished. After that I sat more often at the table of my friends in the farmhouse. I loved them dearly as one could love a brother and sister, neither of which I ever had. But that man died, too. And his wife, wounded by all the memories that pressed upon her (even if they were good ones), left to live in a town nearby.

New people came, and for a while it was wonderful again. My herd increased. The old farmhouse was made finer, redone from roof down at a cost of more thousands than we've ever spent improving any house in which we ourselves have lived. My wages hesitated only briefly in the checking account before passing through and on to make some further, never final, contribution to rural elegance.

But I have already recorded here the catastrophe that came to . . . how this hired man—no, this friend, this *collaborator*—turned from a wonder of power and energy into a pathetic, mewling husk that stumbled crazed through the woods, cradling his bottle and, like some shot animal, bedding in the leaves wherever he happened to fall.

The spring before, down the path behind the cabin, I'd built a tree house for my two small daughters—a stilt house, actually, up among the trees—on the hillside looking down upon the lake. I liked to think of the pleasure they would have sleeping there, which they did do at least once and possibly twice.

But for a long time after that man left, for the greater part of a year, I went to the farm alone, never with my family. My two little hounds were dead under stone cairns next to a rabbit trail. The paths in my woods were unwalked. The fish in the lake swam unmolested. I wore out two automobiles driving the ninety-five miles of highway from the city to that corner, but it wasn't ever a trip made in happy expectation. Only multiplying problems brought me now.

The young man who sat with his wife beside a stream in a valley of ferns all those years ago could not have been me. Nor could he, in his fatuous hunger for it, have been talking about any piece of land I know.

Other men and boys have come to work for me, either for hire or for their rent—some of them cruelly disabled by their pasts, others dim-witted and treacherous to boot. The first act of one of them, upon moving in, was to collect up his own unwanted refuse and any trash the others had left behind, load it all on a cart, and, instead of using the pit provided for disposal, dump the whole mess for his greater convenience into my one clear spring. Controlling myself, I then hired him to clean it out, which he did, cheating me on the hours.

If I sound hard about this, experience with some people—with certain kinds of people—will *make* you hard.

One boy of the neighborhood (I'd known him initially as a boy, then after a while he grew physically to resemble a man) had asked repeatedly for a chance, only a *chance*, to live in the house and work the farm. At some critical moment or other, without alternatives, I had to turn to him. We needed a grain bin, he insisted. So I borrowed to buy one and have it built, and he used it to store a crop grown on someone else's land. We had to have a machine to grind the feed. I bought it. He broke it.

In many ways he was able enough. The trouble was that his appetite for work, his will to do anything on anyone's behalf, even his own—at no time very great—failed him utterly when the seasons came round for hunting deer and wild turkey. One May morning, in pigging time, the telephone rang on my office desk and his wife was on the line. "We're having some real nice litters," she announced, promisingly enough. "But A-----'s gone off to the turkey woods and the sows are eating the pigs about as fast as they're born. I just thought you'd want to know."

No! I didn't want to know. I was ninety-five miles and two hours by car away, and the grisly brunch would no doubt be polished off long before I could do anything about it.

Oddly, though of course he's gone from the place and though I wonder how I ever could have put anything of mine in his charge, I hold no malice toward that man-child as he drifts on through the years of his arrested boyhood. In a way, I even envy him. His great, round cherubic face is perfectly uncreased by any earthly care. And he is fine company, especially in the woods. I sat beside him once, the two of us leaning against the same tree, and watched him call a wild turkey gobbler to within ten steps. The bird sensed no trouble until it was already doomed.

That was wonderful to see. That kind of virtuosity with a turkey call comes only with application and endless practice—while the sows eat the other man's pigs.

Somewhere in all this the government took an interest in my impoverishment. Only the mind of the bureaucrat would suspect that a taxpayer of modest means had, deliberately and for some hidden reason, contrived his own near-total ruin.

The audit lasted three months, required hundreds of hours of solitary work sorting and matching ledger entries, invoices, and canceled checks. There were several trips to the Internal Revenue Service offices carrying cardboard boxes of these assembled sortings. The auditor assigned to my case was a sweet and patient woman, a city woman, who as far as I could tell had never set foot on a farm and did not know a horse from a Hereford. Numbers were her province, not woe. She just tapped into her adding machine figures from the boxes of papers I brought, then asked new questions, waiting for me to bring more boxes.

In the end, all the columns of numbers matched. It was demonstrated that I had not ruined myself for gain. But there remained, in the mind of the IRS, the possibility that the farm was a hobby and an amusement—in other words, that I had ruined myself for *pleasure*. To lay this last suspicion to rest, I was invited to submit an informal statement amounting to a kind of recapitulation or chronology of my involvement on the land.

I sat down to begin.

Broken machinery. Broken men. Pig-eating sows. Bulls gone lame while breeding. Money-eating tenant houses. Fields of mown and rotting hay. Flash floods. Fires. Barren cows. Four-cent-a-pound grass seed. Rust in the wheat. Morning glories in the soybeans. Droughts that opened fissures underfoot. Threatened violence. Deceit and betrayal and disappointment without end.

I put it all on paper, as I have done here, although in even richer detail and burdened throughout with numbers. It is a queer experience to write a summary of the last more than twenty years of your life and to watch as it unfolds into a fool's story. The story of Job pales alongside the compendium of tribulations I set down, all of them perfectly true. When it was finished, we howled with laughter, my wife and I—the laughter of hysteria and heartbreak.

The brief statement I'd been asked to prepare ran to more than fifteen typewritten pages, single-spaced. And after they had read it, with what must have been pity and amazement, the auditors closed the book on my defeats.

Since Homer and Waneta came to live in the farmhouse, the place has been inhabited once more by people of the gentle and decent kind. And they are people of that neighborhood, with children and other kinfolk broadcast all across its hills.

As a young man, Homer went off to soldier in the European war, was wounded, came home again, worked at jobs of different sorts, observed the growing up of sons and daughters, and finally, through the small stipends owed him for his services to Flag and Mammon, was able in his sixties to more or less retire. Idleness doesn't suit him, though. And so we came to an arrangement that has satisfied us both.

Homer lives in the house and grows a vast, productive garden just beside it. Intermittently, between the predations of coyotes, foxes, and stray dogs, Waneta keeps ducks and hens. Homer, for a share of the calves, tends the herd, sold down again to but twenty-five cows and one bull—calls the veterinarian from time to time when one of them is sick; in winter, feeds them the hay I have paid some other man to make. Some years we plant a crop in one of the fields. Other years, through failure of spirit or of the weather, we don't.

Homer's expectations are not Homeric, but neither, any more, are mine. In fact, we are a perfect fit, he and I—men who have given most of what they had to give, realists now, at ease with the limited possibilities. I have the sense of everything sliding slowly backward. Trees fall and lie on fences. The bull exhibits a yawning uninterest in his duties. Our few calves are born late, and go later and lighter to market than they should. The hog lot is empty and grown up in weeds. Metal gates hang at crazy angles from the gateposts and cannot be opened. The first woody sprouts, the forest's outriders, have begun crossing the fences into my fields.

I rage at these things, because I am supposed to. But at some deeper level I am at peace, serene. However late it comes, the sure knowledge that you are beaten is at least a victory of reason.

Over the years, I used to communicate endlessly by telephone with the farm, somehow imagining that problems would yield to conversation. Now even that has ended. Homer's various relatives came almost daily to use his phone, others called him collect, and in his sweetness he hadn't the heart to prevent it. In no time, they ran up such a storm of charges to his account that there was not a dream of ever paying it, and the phone company disconnected him for all time.

Now, if there is some emergency, he rings me from the telephone I had put in our cabin on the corner. The cabin is locked, and he and I have the only keys. He calls, in the normal run of things, every couple of months or so, and Homer is not much for writing letters. So if there's any other news I want, I drive the ninety-five miles of highway and country road and sit at his table to get it.

That's what I had done, one afternoon of the spring just past—gone to the farm to discuss some plans for the season ahead and also to make a start, at least, at setting down these remembrances and thoughts about the land.

The day began prettily for April. Then, as I drove, the sky went slaty and an unseasonably bitter snap blew in. I arrived later than I'd meant to, after dark, and went directly to the cabin, deciding to leave the talk until morning and begin the writing instead.

Before anything, though, I had to purge the cabin of about a million wasps. Evidently they'd multiplied in the attic, warmed with the day, found entry through a crack somewhere, and swarmed in by their utterly inestimable numbers—then been smitten by the sudden cold. Dead or stunned, they lay like black fur over every square inch of carpet.

Shuddering, I swept up that awful mess with broom and dust pan, filled buckets with them and emptied the buckets at the edge of the woods. Then I built a small fire in the stove, worked awhile, put out the light, and wrapped myself in a blanket and went to sleep. It's easy to overlook one wasp among a million. He was in the folds of the blanket somewhere and woke to my warmth and stung me.

Then it was morning and I went up to the farmhouse to talk with Homer, whose stove also was going.

"Did you ever see such a nasty mess as those wasps?" he said. "I went down there to be sure the water was hooked up all right. But when I looked inside I just shut the door and locked the place up and came back home. I never seen anything like it."

"It was bad, all right," I said.

Waneta brought us cups of coffee, as she always does. In her kitchen the pot is always going, and you don't have to ask for it. In fact, sitting at that table and drinking Waneta's coffee is about the last pleasure left in farming. The north window view from the table is past a row of old cedars and across a field corner, down into a grassy swale where there used to be another old farmhouse, bought several years ago by an outsider like myself. He spent a good deal of money on it, I heard—all new windows and doors, metal siding, a new roof. Not long after he'd moved his things into it, the house burned.

In spite of the cold spell, I could see through the window how the brush of another spring had begun to lay a pale wash of green across the countryside.

"The front pasture sure needs a little fertilizer," Homer was saying.

"I know," I told him.

"And it's not too soon to start thinking about how we're going to get our hay put up."

"I know."

"There's a fella I think maybe I could get to do it for about eight dollars a bale, big bales. Same as we paid last year. We fed just over a hundred bales this winter and we got off light. It was an easy winter."

I shuffled the numbers in my head and could feel the familiar hopelessness start to rise, so I tried to keep at least part of my thoughts on the faint greenness outside the window.

"Even if we don't put on any fertilizer we still ought to have pasture enough."

"Pasture," Homer said. "But nothing saved back then for hay ground. Man's got to fertilize to make any hay."

"Well, suppose we did. That's about seven hundred dollars I don't have right now. Then we pay someone eight dollars a bale to roll it up. That's another eight hundred dollars I don't have. There'd be fifteen hundred in it, and we'd just be trading dollars, wouldn't we. Because there ought to be lots of hay around this fall that can be bought for fifteen dollars a bale. Or maybe less."

Homer thought about it. "I guess so. But you'd just think that with all this ground . . ."

"Unless we could maybe find someone who wanted to put up hay on shares."

"I doubt it," he said, and he would know. We turned, then, from his agenda to mine.

"How many calves will we have to sell?"

"Eighteen," Homer said. "Not counting the one born blind and with its tongue hanging out its mouth."

"*Eighteen!*" I'd remembered it as more. I always remembered things not quite as they really were. "But we've got twenty-five cows. Twenty-five cows and only eighteen calves. You'd think we'd come out better than that."

"I don't know," Homer said—calf numbers being like any of the other ungovernable mysteries of the world. "I done the best I could." I could tell he was a little hurt by my outburst.

"Of course you did. I *know* you did. That's not the point. All I'm saying is that we've somehow got to get the number up. How do we stand now on the rent?"

"Not too good," he said.

One of Homer's daughters and her new baby lived in the other farmhouse, the one on the newer place, and the rent had been slow and irregular in coming. How can you ask a man to play flinty-eyed landlord to his own child?

"Well, calves and the rent are where the hay money's coming from, and I want it paid."

"I talked to them."

"I know, but I want it *paid*." I didn't like the hardness I heard in my own

A casualty, like its owner, of the brutal power of the land

voice. But time and circumstances can do that to you. "Paid up by the tenth of next month, or they'll have to find another place."

Waneta came with the pot from the kitchen and refilled our cups. Homer was looking out the window, too, at the season as it tried fitfully to turn.

"You know my brother over at Rockville?" he said finally. "A man he knows, I forget his name, saw a panther on the road the other night. Somewhere between here and there. Said it crossed right in the headlights of his car."

I am left with what I began with: the little acreage on the road corner; the cabin, a bit improved and enlarged over the years; and down the path behind it the small lake, wrapped round by woods and bordered by the few of all those thousands of pine seedlings that managed to survive and grow to be trees.

And I love that place still—even if I must go there mostly alone now; even if my daughters have become young women, and nights spent curled on the hard bunks of a tree house no longer figure very large in their plans; even with the place so haunted by hound-shadows and peo-ple-shadows and the strangely mocking memories of a younger and less complicated time.

But for all the rest, I feel nothing. *Nothing.* When I walk over it on some unavoidable errand, it's only with a strangely detached sensation, as if I already were a trespasser on the *next man's* land. And I would be rid of it in a minute—to an oil sheik or a German businessman, to anyone—if there were any buyers, which nowadays there aren't.

I used to marvel at how people could put their whole lives in a piece of the earth and show so little for it. Now I find I've almost done that. Another year's payment has just been made to the bank. Next year there will be another. And after that another—and so on, for more years than I am apt to have. And if by some miracle I should get it paid for, what difference will that have made?

You hear men speak of *taming* the land. But that land of stones and bristling oaks and orange grasses is fearfully powerful. It broke me as surely as it has defeated and broken all those people who, for longer than I have known it, have tried to scratch their livings there.

It is powerful, and it is fast-forgetting. Houses bleach and lean and are gone. One night this spring I heard there were more than ninety wildfires burning in the county, most of them deliberately set. Some year, one of those will come sweeping unresisted to obliterate every trace of anything I've touched. Fire only does time's work, but does it faster.

15 RETREAT

Dorothy caught a great fish from the pond. Hugh retired. One evening he stood holding his small granddaughter under the weight of near stars and told her—he who never rode an airplane—that there were men walking on the moon. Another afternoon he raked up leaves in a pile for the girls to jump in. The next day he died; Dorothy the next year. And now the girls are grown and gone, or going.

That's the standard chronology of families, isn't it. Ordinary losses, in the usual order.

Now, through the long dark of every year, the cabin mostly is untenanted. For a weekend in November, several friends and I use it as a base for scouting out legendary breakfasts in country cafes while speaking in the abstract of hunting deer. Then I snap the padlock shut, we drive out the gate, the iron stove creaks away to cold, and winter closes down.

But during the frozen months, when I am a prisoner of ambition and city walls, my mind goes often to that little woods cabin. And foolish as the notion is, I wonder sometimes if a floor can miss footsteps, if old boards can miss the sounds of being lived between.

Not that the desertion is quite complete. The survivor mice still harbor there, safe from gunfire. They materialize with the frost, coming from somewhere—from under leaves, from out of their tunnels in the bent grass—to find a surer shelter. And their seeking is irresistible. Somewhere between the foundation stones they find a crevice. Or where two boards do not perfectly join, a crack is enlarged by an eternity of patient gnawing. In waves they come, and nothing I know of will turn them.

Oh, there are means of killing once they're in: poisons, traps, newfangled death rays. But what's the reason? The actual damage mice do always has seemed to me exaggerated. A part of a page of newspaper—not enough to start a stove fire, and bearing only antique news about the world, if any news at all—may be shredded to make a provident nest. Tinned and bottled food is safe enough. It's true a bar of soap may be eaten. But, heaven knows, if hunger comes to *that* they're welcome to it. Then, in spring, after the ice has left the pond but before the birdfoot violets or the first peeping of frogs, the mice are gone again.

Recently I made the two-hour drive to open the cabin for another year,

The pond, late winter

as I have done—or helped to do—for all but one of the last thirty Aprils. This time I went alone. The stove, my old iron friend, came willingly alight to chase the last memory of chill. The coffee water warmed. There was no sense at all of any interruption. I was struck, as I always am, by how easily and naturally life returns to a house so long neglected and how soon the abandonment is forgotten. More than that, I could not help marveling at the power of so humble and small a place to guard such a store of private history, keeping all of it safe, unchanged, through the seasons and the years.

As I sat with the hot cup, I could see at the room's far end a ceiling panel pieced clumsily together, where Hugh cut it in error. And I could hear again, alive as anything, his cry of dismay on discovering he'd measured wrong. Outside, the redbuds were showing color, as they have every spring since I was young. Beside the porch was the quince a friend and I transplanted from beside the ruin of a fallen settler house. A few steps beyond was the flowering crab, a gift one year to my mother. She would have loved to see how splendid it has become. The pine trees at the edge of our clearing that a girl and I planted together—set them out as switches on a bitter day a month before we married—have lengthened into solid presences against the sky.

Spring sunlight through the window struck to life the pictures on the walls. Some of them were photographs of people dead, of friends lost, smiling in beautiful indifference to rushing time. Others were drawings done in a childish hand by daughters who have gotten on with the adventures of their own lives. But there was no sadness in any of that. The cabin is like a time capsule. Much of what I have cared most about in the world is contained there—changeless. No matter how the years careen ahead, and no matter how long I am away, I can turn the key in the lock, step through the door, and it all resumes again. And that is reassuring, because the heart is prodigal. Eventually, unless you're careful, so much just gets away.

A single wasp, the last waker, circled against the ceiling, dinged once against the metal light shade, then hummed benignly past my head and through the door into the brilliance of the gentler season. The wasps, the mice, and me and all of mine, I was thinking then, are carried on the same quick flow. But what luck it is to have one place in the world where you know, whatever overtakes you, if only you can make it there once more, you have it all.

Waiting for the sound of footsteps